PTH2 3010

P9-CSF-143

Pres

The Story of Lester Young

Pres

The Story of Lester Young

Luc Delannoy

Translated by Elena B. Odio

The University of Arkansas Press · Fayetteville · 1993

Originally published as *Lester Young: Profesion Président,* copyright © 1987
Editions Denoël
English translation copyright 1993 by the Board of Trustees of the University
of Arkansas

All rights reserved
Manufactured in the United States of America

97 96 95 94 93   5 4 3 2 1

Designed by Ellen Beeler

The paper used in this publication meets the minimum requirements of the
American National Standard for Permanence of Paper for Printed Library
Materials Z39.48-1984. ∞

Library of Congress Cataloging-in-Publication Data

Delannoy, Luc.
   [Lester Young. English]
   Pres: the story of Lester Young / Luc Delannoy, author; Elena B. Odio,
   translator.
      p. cm.
   Translation of: Lester Young.
   Discography:
   Includes bibliographical references and index.
   ISBN 1-55728-263-3 (c: alk. paper). —ISBN 1-55728-264-1 (p: alk.
   paper)
   1. Young, Lester, 1909–1959. 2. Jazz musicians—United States—
   Biography. I. Title.
ML419.Y7D413   1993
788.7'165'092—dc20   92-22003
[B]   CIP
                                          MN

For my daughter, Julie

I've known for a long time, since the beginning
—I had some sort of advance warning—
that art cannot, must not produce
personal gain. . . . it is a tragic enterprise.

Gombrowicz, *Diary* (1967)

Acknowledgments

I would like to express my utmost thanks to Gunther H.; to Dan Morgenstern and the Institute of Jazz Studies at Rutgers University; to Wendell Gault for his understanding; to Gérard Bourgadier and Jean-Louis Houdebine for their assistance; to all—musicians or not—who contributed to the completion of this work, most notably Jimmy Gourley, Henri Renaud, and René Urtregger for their reminiscences. Thanks to Chang, also, who made this trip possible.

L.D.

A Note to the Reader of the American Edition:

Every effort has been made to locate or recreate the original English quotations throughout the book. We are especially grateful for the help of Don Luck of the Institute of Jazz Studies at Rutgers University. Any discrepancies between the original English sources and back-translations from the French are the fault of the editors.

Contents

Introduction *xiii*

Prologue: Manhattan *1*

Part One: Lester Leaps In

    1. " . . . My Father" *7*

    2. "A Hot Little Number. . . . " *10*

    3. Sunrise *13*

    4. Trumbauer Was My Idol *19*

    5. Salina, Kansas *25*

    6. The Blue Devil *30*

    7. Kansas City, All the Difference *40*

    8. Henderson and Heartbreak *51*

    9. Basie *60*

  10. The Confirmation *68*

  11. Perfect Harmony *76*

  12. Reproaches *83*

  13. Source and Spirit *94*

  14. The Rift *103*

Part Two: Lester Leaps Again

  15. It's Sad but True *115*

  16. Sidelined *124*

17. Guardhouse Barracks Blues   *134*

18. Watch Your Step   *149*

19. Bebop, Cool, and Swing, Too   *157*

20. You Stupid Sonovabitch   *176*

21. Critical Reviews   *192*

22. Paris, La Louisiane   *201*

Notes   *211*

Bibliography   *223*

Discography   *225*

Index   *243*

Introduction

Introduction in the form of a letter to Gunther H.
Leticia, Colombia

Dear Gunther,

. . . We crossed an open expanse; beneath us, caressing the old wooden hull, the Amazon stretched, slowly, powerfully.

I sat thinking of the reason that had convinced you sixteen years ago to establish yourself in this South American outpost. It was your profession: geology. Strange!

What an odd meeting, and what an astonishing figure you cut. I'll say nothing else about you, but please allow me to describe the ritual.

In your adoptive city, there is an unpretentious cafe called El Rincón. They serve *comida criolla* there, along with some insipid bottled drinks. And from 6:00 to 8:30 every evening now, for the last three years, you have been there. Your apéritif is usually one brandy and a few words exchanged with the other patrons, who call out to you, "Guillermo! *el alemán*! . . ."

You have never missed that appointment. Over the last three years you have arrived at precisely 6:00 P.M. with an armload of cassettes that you hand to the owner, who in turn immediately slips them into an old tape player. Then, for more than two hours, the room is filled with music. Conversations are at a minimum. People listen to the music you love. In the beginning you explain vaguely, "Now let's listen to some jazz."

A polite silence: you were taken for a fool. But little by little, interest in jazz grew, and the entire city ended up patronizing El

Rincón. Whatever questions are directed at you are answered with a grumble. For you, jazz is simply to be listened to.

You brought together the most incredible group of jazz lovers I have ever met. In remote regions of Colombia, Peru, or Brazil, sweltering in the heat, subject to power failures, jazz lives an exciting life and penetrates the local customs.

You were someone I had to talk to.

One night, I took advantage of an opportunity to drop the name of Lester Young.

With that, we were friends. I remember your words to me:

> As with any adventure, jazz is primarily an affair for explorers. Many musicians easily take on mythical or heroic proportions, or both, depending on the affection you have for them. And as you read about them, scarce though their biographies may be, you have a tendency to give preference to those points that confirm the image first formed in your mind by certain recordings or magazine articles.
>
> Inherent in the task of a biographer is the risk of shattering those images. But the biographer can just as easily be swept along by them, and try to enlarge them and to present them in a still more favorable light. Either way, someone will say, "Your work is not objective." In your effort to avoid all subjectivity, you will haunt libraries and bury yourself in books. Precise details, veracity, and your concern about them will transform you into a punctilious bureaucrat. Your work will be impartial, encyclopedic, collegiate; in short, it will be serious and inspire trust. You will have a true reference work in hand. But what becomes of your hero?
>
> A sad case. For Lester Young was the only explorer on his particular island, though scarcely heroic in the eyes of society. Look instead for something in the magisterial, serious vein. . . .

I was very close to sharing this opinion of yours, close to searching out the nearest library, that is. But in a sudden about-face, you took me down by the river to visit a Brazilian village that you have a special affection for, Benjamin Constant. I quickly realized that contact between you and your universe had been lost. You were traveling back in time, reviewing the course of your life.

It all began with an anecdote that made both of us smile. It happened back in October of 1956, in Frankfurt, the city where you were born; you were twenty-one. Lester had just taken part in a jam session with several of your musician friends. He was already suffering from malnutrition then. That evening no restaurant could be found willing to prepare him a light meal. You persuaded him somehow to come to your apartment. You offered him a bottle of Scotch, and Lester agreed to eat a little of what you prepared for him: some fish baked in aluminum foil!

We never reached that Brazilian village, at least I don't remember doing so. All I remember is you telling me about the Pres.

Lester's self-effacement down through the years, his reclusiveness makes any attempt at biography difficult. Little noted, if not completely ignored, by his contemporaries, the major part of Young's life is a puzzle punctuated by mysteries and dead silences which you have rendered passionately. Most of the accounts I might have had access to were about the final part of his life, when he had invented an eccentric personality for himself that was popularized by the media.

You recalled the rest of his life, making it unnecessary for me to depend upon the less reliable memories of others. You assured me that "of those who lived in Pres's time, few have left any memoirs; and often, when the time comes to revive old memories, discreet forgetfulness is the sole response."

The next day you showed me your library: a few newspaper clippings, some books, and a series of cassette recordings carefully laid out in a closet under a sixty-watt bulb that is never turned off, a precaution against the humidity. . . . The more precise your recollections became, the more I abandoned the idea of a magnum opus as you had recommended the night before. Forty-eight hours later, I had made my decision: Lester Young's story would be spun around what you graciously conveyed to me through your reminiscences.

The journey which you reinfused with life reminded me of Lester. But there was a moment when I sensed your doubts; you were afraid of your memories. A few of them, deliberately suppressed, might have resurfaced and destroyed those which you prized, the best ones, those that sustain your dreams today. A fear of traveling similar to Lester's; a fear of finding the world opposed to one's own convictions. A fear of fighting for them. For often, Pres would end his journeys before they even began. When he took off for Paris in February of 1959, he had already riddled his life with false hopes: those of a career in the States. The reality no longer mattered. The trip to France was uneventful, but it brought those close to Lester the beginning of the memory.

The pages that follow are doubtlessly incomplete, just as the deeds and responses of Lester Young were. The intention was only to open a door, to conjure up—or put to flight—a few dreams and demons. While I never doubted your remembrances—which so possessed you—I did take the liberty of reviving a few others, which, it should be noted, never contradicted your memory, to which I dedicate this work.

Prologue: Manhattan

Manhattan, March 14, 1959

That day he showed up pale and slump-shouldered, barely holding onto his saxophone case. Elaine Swaine, his last and closest companion, had to coax and nearly had to carry him off the plane. He said nothing about the plane, the trip, his return from Paris, his affliction, the final flight, not a word. He entered his room at the Alvin Hotel, Fifty-second Street, New York. What time was it? What difference did it make? For him, time had ceased to exist long ago.

The room looked the same as when he had left it a few weeks before: the bed, the table, the chairs, the easy chair next to the window overlooking Birdland, the nightstand with photos of relatives, the record player, the stack of records: Dick Haymes, Lady Day, Ella, Sarah, Al Hibbler, Frank Sinatra. There was also the gin stashed away, and the bourbon in the clock. He had returned to his universe. He took possession of it, marked it. His first move was to unpack his instrument. He rested the sax on the table, next to the crumpled black hat.

He sat down. From the chair, he watched the street. He drank gin, bourbon. He poured again and again. He smoked, and he drank some more. How could he hold that cigarette with fingers so weak and transparent? The smoke rose. The spirals glided to the ceiling, sliced intermittently by the fan blades. He gazed at Birdland. What did he see? Ghosts? A void? Maybe nothing; maybe there was nothing in the gaze itself by that time. Maybe the world itself was gone by that particular moment. He remained in this collapsed state, in the silence of the room, in the din of the street. Then he stretched out. Elaine held his hand, spoke to him, told him some New York jazz gossip, what had happened in the city while he had been gone. He was listening to his favorite tune by Frank Sinatra.

His lips moved as he blew into an imaginary mouthpiece. He was accompanying Frankie. He'd have given anything to cut a record with him.

Here was I, a gypsy for a world to romance
Now the world is in my arms . . .

The notes faded out; his lips ceased to move. The twitch of a smile, his last, and he faded away. Elaine hurried to the phone for medical help. But when the doctor arrived, there was nothing left for him to do but confirm the death of Lester Willis Young, March 15, 1959, at 3:00 A.M in New York City. Cause of death: cardiac arrest due to malnutrition and cirrhosis of the liver.

Then the police arrived. In that hotel room, what was left of Lester Young? A saxophone, the Pres's, the one he called "Baby," stuffed in a postal sack, along with five hundred dollars in travelers' checks, a ring, a wallet, and one unpaid bill for seventy-five dollars. That was all the police found. That was all that remained of Lester Young. That was it. The end of the journey.

Manhattan, March 19, 1959

Nearly three hundred people assembled in front of the Universal Funeral Chapel at the corner of Fifty-second Street and Lexington Avenue, six blocks from the Alvin Hotel where Lester had lived. After the eulogy was delivered by his friend the Reverend O. D. Dempsey, Count Basie's wife read from her husband's telegram: "If I were going to compliment anyone, I'd certainly do it for a guy like Pres Young. As a jazzman, he was tops."

Al Hibbler sang. Everyone there wanted to participate. A few pictures were taken—the uninvited were quickly sidelined. Billie

Holiday, raw from alcohol and tears, left supported by Paul Quinichette and Budd Johnson. Elaine Swaine was taken home by Ira Gitler.

Others stayed around, hiding their pain behind a mask of dignity. The family thanked everybody, and little by little the crowd broke up. Jimmy Rushing, Jo Jones, Dizzy, Henry "Red" Allen, Tyree Gleen, Illinois Jacquet, Dickie Wells, Gene Cedric, Billy Taylor, Toni Scott, Sonny Greer, Milt Hinton, Buddy Tate, Ed Lewis, Rudi Blesh, John Hammond, Norman Granz, Leonard Feather, Alan Morrison, Gunther H., Dan Morgenstern, and others.

A small cortege of close friends was formed. It reached Evergreen Cemetery, Queens, an hour later.

From that moment on, all that remained was one man's musical legacy and a few memories . . .

PART ONE

Lester Leaps In

Chapter 1

" ... My Father"

Lester Willis Young was born on August 27, 1909, in Woodville, a rural community in Mississippi, roughly a hundred miles from the Louisiana state line. His family was relatively comfortable financially. Lester's mother, Lizetta, was a Creole born in Louisiana who taught for a living, and to earn additional income, she took in sewing. Her husband, Willis Handy—son of an evangelist and a blacksmith who together ran a general store at Natalbany, Louisiana—applied his talents as an instrumentalist in traveling minstrel and variety shows.[1]

Willis Handy's profession put a strain on the couple's relationship. He was away from Woodville most of the year and spent only the winter with the family. To feel less isolated and be closer to her relatives, Lizetta convinced her husband to move. She settled near Hammond on a farm north of Lake Pontchartrain where her family lived. When Lester was four, she took him to Algiers, a suburb of New Orleans on the other side of the Mississippi.

Nearly two hundred years after being founded by Jean-Baptiste Le Moyne, New Orleans—this city where jazz grew up—was seething with activity and crawling with people of all kinds in search of better jobs.

Among the black musicians of that time, some could boast of belonging to the privileged artisan and skilled-labor caste. This was true of Lester's grandfather, a blacksmith, as it was for Sidney Bechet, a tailor, and for Barney Bigard, a cigar maker. But most jazz musicians belonged to another, less privileged, class, that of unskilled workers. Last of all, there was the most impoverished group, that for which jobs and decent housing were completely out of reach; it included the male and female blues singers. They were generally looked down upon by the urban musicians because of the lack of status that kept them on the road.

The hope of many a road musician was to become a recording artist to escape from anonymity and, at the same time, to acquire some freedom. The aim of many, therefore, was to be hired by a road show, a ballroom orchestra, or a street band. Two dance halls on Iberville Street, in Storyville, were symbols of hope for these musicians: the Tuxedo and Ranch 101. Dance bands fought to land engagements there in 1910. This went on until one unfortunate day in 1913 when an exchange of gunfire at the Tuxedo bar brought about not only the deaths of both hall proprietors, but also the closing of most other establishments of that type all over the district.

It was in this milieu where everyone was out to get ahead that Lester Young discovered his first musical universe. No sooner did he turn five than he was crossing the bridge across the river to slip into the city that was already applauding Louis Armstrong, Sidney Bechet, King Oliver, and Jelly Roll Morton. After spending the early hours in school, he shined shoes, delivered newspapers, and did odd jobs for the merchants. He followed the trucks on which musicians assembled to drive around town announcing upcoming concerts, dances, and parties; he distributed their fliers, followed parades and funerals, and came home exhausted every night to

Algiers. And while Willis Handy toured the South, simultaneously playing and giving lessons on cornet, trumpet, soprano sax, drums, piano, and even in singing,[2] his wife gave birth to a baby girl, Irma, who was followed in 1917 by another son, Leonidas Raymond, called Lee.

The war that had been raging in Europe since 1914, America's participation in it, and the resulting economic and social changes that followed all played a part in the radical transformation of the musical landscape. A migration of workers to the industrial North, where factories were operating at full capacity, reached its peak in 1917. About this time the nightclubs, bars, dance halls, gambling casinos and other houses of ill repute in Storyville were forced to close as a result of constant pressure by the Department of the Navy.

The immediate result was that many musicians stopped playing and went back to their former occupations as skilled and unskilled laborers, seeking employment both in the North and the South. Others signed up with road shows that took over the itineraries of the old minstrel shows. Still others headed for Chicago where Prohibition and the era of Al Capone would prove favorable to them. For practical reasons, those who emigrated from the Delta in search of better jobs and adventure preferred to head upriver, and some stopped and settled along the way. Many did so in Kansas City, which was fast becoming an important business center under the direction of its future mayor, Tom Pendergast.

Lester quit school in 1919. His father returned to Algiers at that time, and a few weeks later his parents were divorced. For Lester, it was an opportunity to get to know his father. "I didn't know my father before I was ten; I didn't even know I had one." Not long after the divorce, Willis Handy remarried. His second wife was a young woman named Sarah. Accompanied by Lester, Irma, and Lee, the couple spent several months in Memphis before heading on to Minneapolis.

Chapter 2

"A Hot Little Number...."

In 1920, Minneapolis was the largest city in the upper Midwest, and its more than 380,000 inhabitants made it the seventeenth largest in the country. The presence of twelve private schools, eighty-two public schools, and one university also attested to an enduring concern for excellence in the field of education. Thanks to its granaries, Minneapolis was at that time able to feed a broad section of the United States; simultaneously, it was focusing industrial activity in the areas of lumber and flour milling and on the production of agricultural machinery as well. A large portion of the required energy came from the electric plant constructed alongside St. Anthony's Falls, on the Mississippi; the work force was provided by a large population of both Scandinavian and German immigrants that likewise contributed to the city's cultural development.

It was in the Swedish section, where the wealthy came to look for household help, that the Young family settled. After enrolling his children in school, Willis Handy put his mind to finding work again and decided to form a family orchestra. When he was not taking them to concerts, he was giving Sarah saxophone lessons and Lester lessons in violin, trumpet, and percussion instruments; Irma and Lee, for their part, were each taking singing lessons and learning to play the saxophone.

At the age of eleven, Lester opted for the drums.

At the same time, at Red Bank, New Jersey, William Basey, who was five years older than Lester, abandoned the drums he had been practicing for three years and switched to the piano.

Encouraged by his stepmother, Lester applied for the position of drummer in his father's orchestra. Willis signed him up and promptly took the family on the road, at times tagging along with minstrel shows, and at others with carnivals. The group toured Minnesota, Kansas, Nebraska, North Dakota, and South Dakota, moving gradually toward the southern states as it went.

One minstrel show the Youngs worked with was serious about its business: it performed only one week in each town, had a large tent housing several hundred spectators, and featured a show lasting nearly three hours, with a dozen or so different acts, as well as an intermission long enough to permit the sale of programs and souvenir photos of the most popular numbers. All the comedians and musicians who performed with the minstrel shows were black.

The carnival shows were more modest by contrast. They were a tighter-knit unit, with far fewer numbers, and the show rarely exceeded forty minutes in length. It all depended on the public, really. If the audience was large, it benefited from several performances in a row; naturally, these would be shortened versions— twenty minutes or so at most. But if the audience was small, the performance would be lengthened so as not to disappoint those few. The carnival shows were mostly geared to whites, and the Youngs were the only black family in their show.[3]

Beyond playing the drums, Lester's specialties were dancing and singing. He did well enough for spectators to throw money on stage. Whatever he happened to be doing, Lester would calmly stop and walk over to pick up the money. The public was amused, and more coins would fall at Lester's feet.

. . . He held it [the drumstick] between his forefinger and his middle finger. He didn't play anything with the thumb at all, and that's the way he held his drumsticks. But he held the left hand conventional—forefinger and the thumb. But the other, he held it between his forefinger and his middle finger . . . I have never seen anyone, you know, as long as I played drums after that, I never did see anyone ever do that. And if he had continued to do percussion, he would still be the one and only one to play that way. He knew he was not holding the sticks correctly, but that was his way of playing, and he played perfectly well! (Lee Young)[4]

Despite the joys experienced by Lester, Irma, and Lee on discovering immortals like dancer Bill "Bojangles" Robinson, touring turned out to be tiring, and after the show Lester was always the last to collect his things. As he would confirm in several interviews given later, he quickly lost interest and decided to give up the instrument.

No sooner would I find myself in friendly surroundings and sight a hot little number—you know what I mean?—than the girl's mother would show up: "Come on, Mary, let's get out of here." Damn! Here I am trying to tear down this set of drums and stuff because that's the chick I want, if you know what I mean, and she would call the girl once, and then again, while I was struggling to pack up that shit. Finally, I just said to myself, "Who needs this?" I have had it with percussion instruments. To hell with the drums and all the other guys with their clarinet, trombone, and trumpet cases—while I'm left looking like a fool with the other shit. . . . What a pile of junk![5]

Chapter 3

Sunrise

In 1922 Lester gave up the drums for the saxophone; his father had bought him an alto at a pawnshop. Having quit the TOBA circuit, the family returned to Minneapolis. Willis Handy decided to form another band and invited two cousins who played the sax, Isiah "Sport" and Austin "Boots" Young, to join it. He was now directing an entire saxophone orchestra. Lee became the vocalist, but only toured with them when his schooling permitted.

Dancing was the rage then, and orchestras were flourishing all over the country. This was the heyday of the "ballrooms." While Fletcher Henderson and Bix Beiderbecke were creating more sophisticated music up north and back east, the southwestern and central states drew their repertoire straight from the blues and gospel singing of the South, and they played for white as well as black audiences.

Bands of this sort based themselves in a specific section of the country and, whenever possible, confined their engagements to that area, never aspiring to a national reputation. Most of the time it was local musicians who made up their ranks, but traveling musicians were occasionally invited to supplement their numbers for certain concerts. Jealous of their territory, they resented the presence of orchestras from other parts of the country. They would compete with these outsiders at every available opportunity to show the public, once and for all, their undeniable superiority.

Among the more popular bands of the period, one could list the George Morrison Orchestra of Denver, Art Bronson of Salina, the Dixie Ramblers and Lloyd Hunter's Serenaders in Omaha, the Blue Devils of Oklahoma City, Clarence Love and the Southern Serenaders at Tulsa, Troy Floyd in San Antonio, the Happy Black Aces in Amarillo, the Deluxe Melody Boys of Austin, the Blue Syncopaters in El Paso, Alphonso Trent and Terence T. Holder and his Clouds of Joy in Dallas, the Missourians with Cab Calloway, Charlie Creath in St. Louis, and Bennie Moten and George Lee in Kansas City.

The Young family was not, properly speaking, a regional band, since its travels took it from north to south across most of the country. For several months, the band had its base in Albuquerque, New Mexico—a city where there were neither blacks nor black bands. Orchestras from the surrounding states were willing to accept the group as long as it did not overstep its provisional territorial boundaries. Yet the Young orchestra never benefitted from the kind of prestige won by some of its competitors.

Nothing was easy down South; Lester learned the saxophone, but he also learned about racism. One morning he attended a religious service with his sister, Irma, and heard the pastor say that sin was as black as hell. To be saved you needed to join the order of penitents, which was reserved for whites. These words wounded him deeply and left a lifelong mark. Lester never again set foot in a church.

In fact, from then on he was wary of whites, whom he referred to with contempt as "the gray boys." He would say little on the subject of racism during his lifetime, and those who knew him always avoided the subject, knowing that it was painful to him.

Not long before he died, in an interview with François Postif in Paris, Lester indicated that nothing had changed:

> I'd have left here the other night if I had had five hundred dollars. I can't stand this crap, you know? It's all a bunch of crap, and they want every black to be an Uncle Tom, an Uncle Remus, or an Uncle Sam, and that's something I can neither tolerate nor become.
>
> *Postif:* Not here, you know, not in France.
>
> *Young:* Shit! Sheeit! Are you kidding? I've been here for two weeks and have already felt it. I'm only telling you what I know. Seeing is believing; just hearing people talk about it is shit—a lot of huffing and puffing. Right here, in Gay Paree. Mack, this sort of thing couldn't happen to you, don't you get it? You are not colored like I am, understand? It's me they are going to take advantage of. All I can do, though, is tell you that it happened. But I'm not going to go on telling you that part of the story. It just happened. And it was at the hands of someone that you wouldn't care to believe it about, a truly "gray" individual. In the end, you know, it's the same story everywhere. You fight for your life, and that's all. Until death separates us all.[6]

While touring at the beginning of the summer of 1924 and participating in the Lackman and Carson Show with his family in Mobile, Alabama, Lester met a young trumpeter two years his junior called Cootie Williams. Williams, who had just witnessed a performance by the Handy/Young saxophone ensemble, persuaded his father to introduce him to the band. As the introductions were being made, Cootie pulled out his trumpet and began playing in front of Willis and Lester. Willis Handy immediately offered to hire him. Cootie's father explained that his son was underage and that if he really wanted a Williams on the team, an older brother was available. Willis negotiated, and finally both Cootie and his brother got to spend the summer with the Youngs, the brother as agent, and Cootie as trumpeter.[7]

Everywhere the band performed, it was Lester—in short pants like most of the other band members—who got the most applause. The strength and determination that emanated from him and his music fascinated so many musicians that Lester received frequent invitations to join all-white bands. Of course, none of the invitations panned out; Willis Handy was looking out for the family.

> He was a stylist, [Cootie Williams said years later]. Yeah, I learned something from him. . . . In the beat, in different syncopations that he had. . . . he was nice. But during that time, I couldn't hang out with him. And I would be with Lee and Irma. . . . The father never did give me no money. He was supposed to send my father the money. . . . Sometimes he'd give me 50 cents. Sometimes. . . . But he'd feed me. We'd go to dinner.[8]

Something else was to upset Lester at that time besides racism: his father kicked him out of the band because he couldn't read sheet music. Unlike his sister and brother, Lester played by ear, placing little importance on technique or on reading the score.

It took more than six months, but Lester would learn how to decipher the scales that his father scribbled on paper for him. From this concentrated effort, he drew the satisfaction of feeling himself freer and less dependent on either his father or the show that he was putting together.

> When I started with the band, I did not read music. I just sort of threw it together, but at least I was with the group. And my sister played too, you see, so I would stick to her, eyeball her part and copy it. We played parade music and all that shit. Finally, my dad comes out one day and says, "Kansas, read your part." God! I knew then I was fried; he knew I couldn't read music. He said it again, "Go on and play your part, Kansas." (Lester hums it:) "Tatatatup—dududatup . . . Go on, it's your turn now. Bam puduboom . . . Go on Lester, take it away!" I couldn't read one of those fucking notes, not the first one! So he yells, "Get on your feet!"—He didn't swear like I do now—"Get on your feet, and go practice some scales on that damn sax of yours. Hit the road. . . ."
>
> I hit the road running. My heart was really broken. I left, shed a few tears, and then I said to myself, O.K., if that's what they want, I'm going to come back and show those bastards

what it's all about. Just like that, see? I went on off on my own and learned to read—all by myself—then I came back to the orchestra and played all that music; and on top of that I was working on the records that I was listening to, so I could really put it to those jerks.

So I took back my old seat in the orchestra that was still playing those damned marches, and I played right on, and everything was perfect. But I couldn't forget how those s.o.b.'s had turned on me and dumped me when I didn't know how to read music. Later they would show up and say, "You wouldn't like to show me how that goes—how you play that?" Oh yeah! Like how, I'll show you that shit—you crummy bastard! So that's how that all came about.[9]

Lester's progress was rapid and clearly noticeable to other band members who looked on him with envy. He proved to his father that music was his domain and that no one, absolutely no one, would ever be able to challenge him.

One day, when Willis Handy was in Amarillo searching for a piano player, he ran into Ben Webster, then a member of the Happy Black Aces. After a spirited discussion, Webster volunteered to play saxophone for Handy. Shrewdly, Willis decided that the offer was not without interest. After all, his daughter, Irma, wanted to quit the sax and concentrate on her voice. Ben could take her place. But he was amazed to learn that Webster had no instrument and, furthermore, that he was unable to decipher his score! Willis bought Ben a tenor sax and took him to Albuquerque where he taught him the basics. It was Lester who, not without a certain feeling of pride, finished the job for his father by agreeing to spend long hours practicing and sharing his new skills with his friend.

So while Ben learned to play tenor, Lester learned alto.

One night, Lester, who was feeling a little intoxicated by the success of his solitary labors, slipped into the ballroom while "Boots" Young was performing at a dance with some other young musicians. Lester jumped up on stage, grabbed his instrument, and began to play, firmly intent on proving his superiority and on dethroning his cousin. Enraged, annoyed, and humiliated, Boots put down his saxophone and attacked Lester; finally Lester's step-mother intervened and kept him from being beaten up in public.

For Lester, this competitive spirit was really a means of over-coming his shyness and testing his limits. It would resurface during his stay in Kansas City, where jam sessions proved to be the best opportunity for him to express his personal musical convictions.

Chapter 4

Trumbauer Was My Idol

Among the recordings that Lester liked to listen to in those days was one of the first cuts by a young white musician from Carbondale, Illinois, Frankie "Tram" Trumbauer.[10] The remarkable Tram was at ease on the violin, the piano, the trombone, the flute, the bassoon, the clarinet, and on each of the saxophones, and he was the inseparable associate of Bix Beiderbecke.

Two recordings fascinated Lester: "I'll Never Miss the Sunshine," containing a breathtaking chorus by Tram and recorded in Camden, New Jersey, on June 14, 1923, by the Benson orchestra of Chicago, and the first recording made by Tram and Bix with the Sioux City Six on October 10, 1924. There Tram plays the soprano sax; he is, in fact, one of the few jazz musicians to have used this instrument throughout his career.

On several occasions in 1925 and 1926, Trumbauer appeared at the Arcadia Ballroom of St. Louis with Bix on cornet, Peck Kelley on piano, and Pee Wee Russell on clarinet. Lester, who at that time was having a rift with his father—who was becoming more and

more intractable in terms of musical technique (Handy is supposed to have threatened his children on several occasions with a
belt)—left the family orchestra, roaming for two months before
going to hear the man who unquestionably exerted the single
greatest influence upon him.

This was neither his first escape attempt nor was it to be his last.

> . . . I remember one time in the south, he ran off to someplace
> in Oklahoma, and we were getting ready to go back to
> Minneapolis, and I don't think they'd seen him for 7 or 8 weeks,
> and my dad had just gone up to the window to buy the tickets
> for us to go back to Minneapolis, you know? And my mother
> (Sarah) was just crying because she was gonna leave Lester
> there—and hadn't seen him in ages, and my dad went up to the
> window and says, you know, "Give me two halves and two
> wholes"—those were tickets, you know—you'd buy them in half
> fare, you know?
>
> And so my mother said to my daddy to look around, and
> Lester was standing over by the door, and he said, "Make that 3
> halves." . . .
>
> "He never did question him—never questioned him. . . .
> We never did know where Lester had been or what he had done.
> But that used to happen so many times—when he would come
> back, it was like he'd never been away. He just picked up where
> he left off.[11]

At the beginning of 1927, Trumbauer signed a contract with
the Okeh company for a group formed around the nucleus of the
Jean Goldkette Orchestra, with whom he had been performing for
three years. A first record was cut in New York on February 4 of
the same year. That recording and the many that followed it
formed the basis of Lester's record collection.

Though he later denied it, Lester also became interested in two
other musicians. The first was a white saxophone player from
Chicago, Lawrence "Bud" Freeman who, together with Tram,
McPartland, Teschemaker, Spanier, Tough, Krupa, Bix, Goodman,
and Mezzrow, was the architect of what eventually was labelled

derogatorily "white jazz"; the same jazz which, in its infancy, delighted Maurice Ravel to the point that he frequently accompanied his musicians on visits to Chicago nightclubs like the Apex and the Sunset.

As much as Trumbauer's personality overshadowed all others in Lester's eyes at that time, being the one role model to be understood and surpassed, it would be an exaggeration to speak of an influence by Bud Freeman on Lester's style. A similarity of timbre between Bud Freeman and Lester does have to be acknowledged, but it goes no further than that.

The second musician who interested Lester was the saxophonist Dick Stabile. Specializing in alto, Stabile played the instrument one octave above its natural register and directed a dance band that would later play in Kansas City. The peculiar sound quality which results from this practice attracted Lester's ear but did not exert any major influence on him.

Other musicians made appearances in the course of Lester's musical adolescence. Jimmy Dorsey came first—who, like Lester, had his start in a family orchestra before working with the California Ramblers—followed by Paul Whiteman and Red Nichols.[12] In reality, Dorsey and Tram were the first two musicians to have truly attracted Lester's ear.

> I had to make a choice between Frankie Trumbauer and Jimmy Dorsey. I wasn't sure which direction I'd be taking, you know. I had those damn records; I'd play one by Jimmy, then one by Trumbauer, and so on. At the time, I didn't know who Hawkins was, dig it? But I could plainly see there were other guys who were telling me stories I liked to hear. I would play a record by the first man, one by the second, so I could understand both of them in depth.[13]

> Finally I found I liked Trumbauer best. . . . I imagine I can still play all the solos of his recordings. He played the soprano saxophone. I have made an effort to produce the sound of a soprano sax on the tenor. That's why I sound like no one else.[14]

The acrobatics, the sense of rhythm, the ruggedness of sound, and the wild effect of Tram's style all combined to outweigh the sweetness and brio of Jimmy Dorsey.

This appreciative "dilemma" occurred again, to a lesser degree, when Lester listened to Bix Beiderbecke and Red Nichols. He admired the personality of crazy young Beiderbecke, followed the fitful alcoholic stages of his career with interest, and listened to his music with a passion. But it was Louis Armstrong who was uncontestably the master instrumentalist.

Those first records constituted an important stage in young Lester's evolution, enabling him as they did to keep abreast of jazz developments in the East. Whenever he had the opportunity, Lester arranged to have the latest releases sent to him, listening to them for hours before trying to duplicate all the solos, transcribing them, too, with the intention of proving to the other members of the family that he was fully as capable as they were, if not more so. Yet the only ones to lend him a sympathetic ear were Sarah and his brother, Lee, who, while daydreaming about baseball and basketball, spent hours stretched out in Lester's room, listening to him practice.

Lester decided that before long he would need to go beyond the confines of the family orchestra, whose interests seemed to him more limited all the time.

During a stopover at a hotel in Bismarck, North Dakota, where he had taken rooms with his family, Lester caught sight of saxophonist Eddie Barefield and pianist Clarence Johnson.

> It was the winter of 1927, around Christmas time. I was in Bismarck ND playing at the Spencer Hotel with Clarence Johnson on the piano. I had just left Minneapolis, where I had founded the Ethiopian Symphonians with trumpet-player Roy "Snake" White and pianist Frank Hines, both of whom were to become Lester's first big admirers. In fact, Snake was to bring about Lester's being hired by Walter Page's Blue Devils. As for Hines, a few years later he would employ Lester in his own Minneapolis orchestra.

So at Bismarck we were housed in the annex of the same hotel as the Willis Young [Handy] band. Lester was young, a little shy, and ambitious. He worked all the time. At that time he was playing alto and would periodically say to me, "One of these days my father is going to buy a new Selmer. . . ." A high class tenor cost around forty dollars in those days.

I had bought all of Frankie Trumbauer's records and had them all with me at the Spencer Hotel, of course. Each record was worth between 50 and 75 cents. You had to go to a music store, leaf through the catalogues, make your choice and wait two to three weeks before your order arrived.

One day Lester came to borrow those that he didn't own, and I noticed that he would spend his afternoons learning all of Tram's solos. I was influenced by Tram at that time myself. I think he was the most original alto of all, and it's a fact that all the saxophone players listened to him.

However that may be, it was then that Lester and I began to play together. We didn't play concerts, we only did practice exercises, rehearsing in our hotel room during the afternoon and sometimes at night. (Eddie Barefield)[15]

By the time the Young family abandoned Bismarck and resumed touring, the economic situation in the United States was starting to deteriorate. Everywhere the orchestra performed, warning signs of the Depression were in evidence, and right along with them came signs of renewed racism toward blacks. Lester's father, who was in the habit of making a tour through the South during the winter and early spring months, informed his wife and children that they would soon have to leave their location in Arizona and head for New Mexico and its surrounding states. Lester tried to modify his father's plans by explaining to him that an economic crisis might occur in the very near future and that those states to be affected first would be the poorest ones, the very same ones he wanted to return to; all of this could only result in problems, both financial and racial, of increasing magnitude. He told his father it would be better to head northward, because work could be found in Kansas, Nebraska, and Iowa.

But Willis Handy wouldn't change his mind, and one evening when the family orchestra was performing at West Lake Park in Phoenix, Lester decided to leave. He was eighteen. After the concert, he laid his old beat-up alto out prominently on the table in his father's room, scribbled a hasty good-bye, put on his jacket, turned off the lights, and closed the door.

"I simply wanted to grow up."

Chapter 5

Salina, Kansas

On December 20, 1927, having just arrived in Salina, Kansas, Lester met Art Bronson. Bronson hired Lester to play baritone in his band. As a result he toured with the Bostonians from January 1928 to January 1929. The group was managed by Lee and Walt Dree, two brothers who owned a chain of nightclubs in Kansas. The band performed regularly in Salina, Wichita, and Arkansas City, Kansas, and appeared also in Missouri, Colorado, Nebraska, South Dakota, and North Dakota, where it played for dances and concerts. Just a few weeks into their association, though, an incident occurred that forced Lester to switch to the tenor sax.

The young musician who was playing tenor when Lester joined the band showed growing signs of self-indulgence; he would spend hours brushing his hair, adjusting the collar of his shirt, smoothing his pants, and re-tying his tie. Worse, and what Lester hated most of all, he would get high and not show up at the concerts when he was supposed to.

Fed up one night, with his instruments (baritone and alto)[16] under his arms, Lester called Bronson over and laid the matter on the line.

"Listen, I told you that things weren't working out with that guy; let's quit giving warnings to that pile of shit. You buy me a tenor and I'll play the son of a gun, and then we'll really be cooking!"

Bronson, it seems, was only waiting for that reaction. The next day he bought a tenor sax, and the same evening Lester made his debut on the instrument: ". . . when I saw the antique tenor he had bought, I almost changed my mind. But after playing on it, I appreciated it."[17]

From then on, Lester played tenor as well as alto and baritone. His new instrument held no surprises for him; he adapted to it easily and preferred handling it like an alto. Whenever he had the time, he continued to do his exercises, but now on tenor.

Lester left Bronson in January 1929. He headed back to Minneapolis where he ran into Eddie Barefield again. Barefield had for a few months been leading a band with the melodious name of "Doo Dads from Ditty Wah Ditty." Lester moved into the Black & Tan, the black neighborhood on the north side of town not far from Sixth Avenue North, where most of the night-clubs and jazz hangouts were located.

> Right away, Lester and I decided to play together, just two saxo-phones, without a rhythm section. You could find work in the afternoon at the dancing schools. The pay ranged from four to five dollars, which was not bad, given that a week's stay at the hotel cost three. I remember that we would spend some after-noons playing billiards with other musicians. At night, when it was pretty late, we would go jam in a club called Upstairs. (Eddie Barefield)[18]

Lester worked non-stop at clubs, at dance halls, and for bands that played at high-school events. For one short tour, Eli Rice asked him to join his orchestra, featuring saxophonist Boyd Atkins and trumpeter Rook Ganz.

For the Young family, which Lester rejoined for a very short while, things were not going as well. The winter of 1929 was hard, and engagements were scarce. The Wall Street crash had plunged the country into a severe depression. Urban areas suffered as unemployment rose, many farmers were totally ruined, and, in some regions the Ku Klux Klan was taking it out on the black population.

In the spring of 1930 Willis moved to California, leaving Lester to his own fate. Once in Los Angeles the family moved into an apartment on Central Avenue, between Seventeenth and Eighteenth streets, next to the musicians' union. Lee was enrolled at Lafayette Junior High School while his father went about contacting Curtis Mosby, the owner of Club Apex, where he signed his first contract.

Lester, for his part, decided to take a vacation and left for the South where his mother, Lizette, still lived and had recently remarried. Lester took along his alto and tenor, and to those who knew him as a child, he did not hesitate to show off his musical abilities. He put so much energy into playing and working his way into every musical event that the rumor quickly spread in both Louisiana and Mississippi that a first-rate musician was traveling in the area.

There was a local musician in Natchez named Bud Scott who was being forced to cancel a tour to some fifteen cities in Louisiana because his tenor sax player was sick. Someone mentioned Lester Young to him, so Scott contacted Lester and explained the situation. A tour, a few jobs in Louisiana, one week, at the most, of filling in. . . . Lester accepted on the spot. So he headed for Natchez and moved in with the Shaws, friends of his family.

His substitution work actually lasted five months; the condition of Scott's saxophonist took a severe turn for the worse, making him unavailable for several months. One night, after a concert in Baton Rouge, Lester and Scott went jamming in a club where, they were told, an excellent guitarist by the name of Persy Sivire appeared on a regular basis. But that night Sivire was absent.

In a dark corner by the stage, Lester noticed a boy hunched over his guitar, paying no attention to the noise that surrounded him as he played. His name was Charlie Christian. He was ten years old. Lester found a chair, drew quietly near, rested his saxophone case between his legs and his elbows on his knees, concentrating on the playing of this boy who wore an odd round hat balanced at the base of his skull. Lester let him play for about ten minutes before remarking, "Not bad!" and asking him to sit with him. They talked for more than an hour, when Lester finally saw the signals Scott was making to him: "The jam session is about to end and you haven't gotten up on stage yet!" Lester quickly climbed onto the stage and began to play. His young friend was fascinated.

And fascination it truly was. Charlie Christian couldn't believe his ears. Without any great hopes of finding him so soon, Charlie had been searching for the sort of original musician from whom he might get moral support; someone who could give him new direction. And there he was, in front of him, playing especially for him on that saxophone.

After this "vacation," Lester headed back to Minneapolis where his path crossed that of another young musician, Oscar Pettiford, who was then making his debut as a singer-dancer in his family orchestra. Like Lester, he first played drums then learned to play piano, followed at last by the cello and bass.[19]

In June of 1930, Lester rejoined the Art Bronson orchestra. But the effects of the 1929 stock market crash were not long in being felt. All over the country, jazz bands were having trouble finding work. Many theaters and clubs closed their doors, the "regional bands" dissolved, and musicians went their separate ways, heading for the large cities where small jobs proliferated. The Bostonians were not spared, and Bronson dissolved his group in September of

1930. Lester had no other recourse but to return to Minneapolis, the only city that was somewhat familiar to him. At year's end, there were 4.2 million unemployed around the country, a number that would triple in the next two years. Misery and hunger had the countryside in their grip, shantytowns were springing up like mushrooms; one in four Americans was in dire straits.[20]

Chapter 6

The Blue Devil

While he was appearing in a Minneapolis club with Frank Hines, Lester received a visit from Walter Page and Buster Smith, both of whom suggested that he join the Blue Devils.

> A trumpeter from Des Moines, Leroy "Snake" White, couldn't stop talking to us about Young. It so happened we had a concert up in that part of the country. So when we arrived, we went to hear him right after our performance. We were so impressed that we literally kidnapped him. . . . He was playing tenor and baritone; matter of fact, he played the baritone so well that Walter Page quit his instrument, saying that he would never play it again. (Buster Smith)

Though thrilled by the proposal, Lester still asked for a few days' time to think matters over before giving his answer. While it was true that the life he led in Minneapolis was not overly exciting, it was worry-free, both in terms of finances and work. Musicians respected him, and club owners regularly made him offers. He knew, on the other hand, that he must stay on the move and meet other musicians if he intended to make further progress, so he accepted the offer and joined Page and Smith as one of the Blue Devils. At that point, the orchestra made its way back to home base in Oklahoma City for the winter.

The Blue Devils were formed in 1925 in Oklahoma City by Walter Page, an ex-member of the Billy King Orchestra and of the Shuffle Along Show. Initially, they consisted of trumpeters James Simpson, Lips Page, Jimmy LuGrand, Trombonist Eddie Durham, saxophonists Buster Smith, Ted Manning, and Ruben Roddy, guitarist Reuben Lynch, pianist Turk Thomas, percussionist Alvin Burroughs, and of course, Walter Page on the string bass, tuba, and baritone sax.

Having spent the winter of 1925–26 in Oklahoma City, the band embarked on a series of tours that took it to Dallas, Houston, San Antonio, Little Rock, Enid, Joplin, and Omaha. . . . Success came quickly, and the Blue Devils easily dethroned rival orchestras like those of Jesse Stone and George Lee. The group's inner workings were simple: each musician was paid the same amount at the end of a concert; Page would lay the money on the table, subtract the expenses, and divide the profits into as many equal parts. The band worked full time, taking only eight days' vacation per year. In 1927, the musicians met William Basie for the first time in Kansas City, where he was taking part in a show put on by the Whitman Sisters. The next year, on July 4, 1928, Basie joined the group, replacing Turk Thomas who had signed on with The Satisfied Five.[21]

A little later, Jimmy Rushing was incorporated into the Blue Devils as well. Their reputation grew so rapidly that Walter Page proposed a "battle of the bands" against Bennie Moten, leader of the region's most popular band. He was convinced that he could easily dethrone him. But the match never took place.[22] The well-established and business-wise Moten turned the challenge down and instead simply chose to lure Page's musicians away with offers of fatter paychecks. One by one the men succumbed to his enticements, and the first to line up with Moten during the fall of 1929 was Basie. No sooner did Basie leave than Willie Lewis stepped in to replace him. There were more defections: Lips Page, Eddie Durham, and Jimmie Rushing. Disappointed, Walter Page then dissolved the band. Yet he reassembled it just a few weeks later with those musicians who had remained faithful to him and hired trumpeter Harry Smith, trombonist Druie Bess, pianist Charlie Washington, and Ernest Williams as vocalist and manager.

So the Blue Devils spent the winter of 1930–31 in Oklahoma City. For several months, the band performed on weekdays at the Ritz Ballroom, a whites-only establishment, and on weekends at Forest Park. Lester became a familiar character on the city streets. He would converse with the newspaper vendors and grocers and often sat down on the elevated shoeshine stands and improvise on his saxophone for the clusters of kids that formed around him. To them he dedicated the first number he recorded in 1936: "Shoe Shine Boy."

At night, Lester would join either local musicians or those passing through town for jam sessions. At Halley Richardson's Shoeshine he got together regularly with Ben Webster and Lem Johnson; at Slaughter's he met up again with Charlie Christian.

Charlie was Slaughter's youngest and most loyal patron; everyone knew and admired him. He did odd jobs to pay the cover charge, and he always came with his guitar under his arm, hoping to join in a jam session. If he lucked into a session with Lester, he noted what importance the older musician accorded each note and recognized the inspiration brimming over in each of the improvisations Young so ably developed along the line of the melody; he sensed a tendency to favor short phrases and an inclination to shift accents within a measure.

Whenever he could approach Lester, Charlie launched into an explanation of his own ideas. But Lester would interrupt, saying, "Go on and play; that's worth more than any speeches." Of course, his technique was still uneven, and Charlie knew it; so instead of playing, he would propose long walks during which they would talk about jazz and its possibilities. Lester encouraged him to get paying engagements as soon as possible, assuring him that that was the best way of getting ahead. So Charlie Christian followed his advice and was shortly hired by Alphonso Trent. When the two friends met again, it was for a recording session.

Aside from those occasions when he went jamming, Lester was a quiet young man. He took care in his appearance, dressed well, parted his groomed hair down the middle, and distinguished himself by his polite manners; the girls liked him, but he rarely asked them to dance. In contrast to his companions, Lester was not a carouser. He did, of course, willingly attend the various social affairs that musicians were asked to attend at night, but he would politely refuse all alcoholic drinks and preferred conversation to flirtation. A few months before, in fact, he had met a girl named Beatrice in Minneapolis about whom he was still thinking a lot; he sent her short letters from time to time. With his fellow band members, Lester liked to talk about music, about his personal tastes, and his admiration for Buster Smith and Walter Page. He would also discuss the band's repertoire and give his opinion on upcoming itineraries. His main interest lay in music, and his whole being was tied up in it.

In keeping with a public that came mostly to dance, the Blue Devils offered two types of repertoire. Their white audiences asked especially for waltzes and rumbas, whereas their black clientele called for blues and jazz numbers. When appearing in hotels, the musicians were forced to change the repertoire entirely and to offer soft selections designed not to disturb either the dining or the conversation of the guests. Also, a number of people in the audience would regularly ask for specific tunes then drop tips in a collection box prominently displayed at the foot of the stage. The tips usually went to pay the cleaning bills or to purchase uniforms, occasionally even to buy music stands or automobile parts.

The musicians gladly went along with these changes in repertoire for, as Buster Smith emphasized, "It's a lot less tiring and the appeal is, for all intents and purposes, the same. I also noticed that if we behaved like gentlemen, we were treated as such." And indeed, there were some cities where, despite the effects of the Depression, the members of the Blue Devils were respected as if they were lawyers or doctors. People gladly offered them meals and lodging, and it was a matter of pride to treat them well.

During a performance in Kansas City, Walter Page was having problems with one of his musicians. He considered eventually replacing him with Jim Youngblood—the pianist in T. Holder's group, the Clouds of Joy—and sent Jim a telegram informing him of the idea. But someone in Page's entourage did not appreciate Youngblood, and a week later he received another telegram from Page withdrawing the offer. Upset, Youngblood filed a complaint with the musicians' union in Des Moines, where he was at the time, demanding damages and compensation. The decision was not long in coming, and Page was sentenced to pay a $250 fine that left him penniless and completely disgusted. Embittered, he simply walked out on the Blue Devils and knocked around for several weeks before receiving an offer from Bennie Moten.

Buster Smith and Ernest Williams became the band leaders and took the group through Texas, Missouri, Iowa, and Nebraska. In the absence of tuxedos, the musicians each sported two classically styled dark uniforms paid for out of their own pockets. They traveled in two brand-new Cadillacs. During a late jam session at Jim Bell's in Omaha, Lester happened to run into pianist Charles Thompson, then appearing with singer Wyonnie Harris. As he would later state, Thompson was impressed with Lester's style, and he invited all his friends to attend another jam session the next day. Among these friends was Jo Jones who, just two years younger than Lester, immediately took a liking to him.

Like most of the musicians in Omaha, Lester stayed at the White House, a small hotel in the black part of town which had a parlor with a piano on the ground floor, and where, for a few dollars, you could buy contraband whiskey. There, Lester met trumpet player Bill Coleman for the first time (with whom he made a recording in December of 1943). Coleman was then appearing at the R.K.O. Orpheum Theater as the accompanist for three tap dancers called the Three Sams. But at that time, Lester had neither the time nor the opportunity to develop his new friendships. Having spent the winter of 1931–32 in Oklahoma City, the Blue Devils once again hit the road, appearing on the road-house circuit across Iowa, Illinois, and Minnesota. In Sioux City, Lester met up again with his old friend Eddie Barefield, who introduced him to Herschel Evans, a young saxophonist from Texas.

> Actually, I think I was the first to lure Herschel out of his native Texas in 1928. I had met him in San Antonio when I was playing there with a small band from Scandia, my home town. Later, when I worked with Grant Moore in Milwaukee and we needed a tenor, I had Herschel come in. Unfortunately, he only stayed a few days; it was snowing and he caught a cold that forced him to head back to Texas. But he returned when the band performed in Sioux City. Then all three of us, Lester, Herschel and I, got back together again. (Eddie Barefield)[23]

Once the Blue Devils had made it into a town, the band would rehearse and work on new selections a few hours before the concert. Lester was usually the slowest to assimilate new compositions, but Buster Smith was always glad to help. Lester would frequently stand slightly to the side, working tirelessly on the same melodies, "Stardust" and "Body and Soul," his favorites. At times he would play baritone, or else, a few minutes before the concert, he might sit at the piano and interpret a series of blues and ballads before reaching for one of his saxophones.

> He's an old alto player, and he never did try to improve his tone . . . to get that tenor tone. He just stayed with that alto tone. . . . And he had a stiff reed, kept it on his tenor all the time. . . . See, most of the time we didn't have but three saxes in the band. Lester Young, Theodore Ross and myself. . . .We had two trombone players and three trumpets. And see, the saxophones tried to blow as loud as the trumpets played. . . . The alto player, we would get C-melody reeds and put them on an alto. . . . Then Lester Young got to getting some baritone reeds and putting

them on his tenor. So they'd blow as loud as the brass section would play. . . . You can't get that big tone unless you got a soft reed. A #2. But a #3, #4, or #5, something like that, that's a hard reed. (Buster Smith)[24]

Having long played alto and baritone, Lester finally decided to opt for the tenor saxophone. The transition was a natural one and wasn't discussed either by Lester or by the other musicians. Playing one concert in Kansas City, Lester found support for his choice and was inspired by the dozen or so other tenors. He even considered settling in Kansas City.

Like most of the bands of that time that wanted to prove their supremacy, the Blue Devils didn't hesitate to challenge other orchestras.[25] It was only a matter of selecting a club and having the bands take turns on stage for two or three hours, each playing about 30 minutes before yielding its place to the next. A group's quality was determined according to its arrangements and based on the "sallies" of its various soloists. The Oklahoma group was undeniably the best. Lester, with baritone reeds on his tenor, joined Theodore Ross and Buster Smith using tenor reeds on their altos and knocked out all of the competitors.

Despite the group's success, engagements thinned out and the distances grew longer and longer. The two Cadillacs bought on the eve of Walter Page's departure began to show signs of wear. Sometimes the musicians arrived several hours late, and, having missed their engagement, they would hit the road again for another city. At last, when their cars gave up the ghost, they had to negotiate for a fresh set of used vehicles. What they really needed was a small bus, but the prices were beyond their reach. They would stop, exhausted, in small towns along the way just long enough to buy bread, ham, and a few cans of sardines to eat by the side of the road.

Shortly before the winter of 1932–1933, the orchestra broke with tradition and headed for Virginia, where it hoped to find work. But once in Newport News, the band members realized that the population there was 80 percent Catholic and that after Easter no one in the state danced. Having spent all their money on the trip, they found themselves stranded with no work. They had a few job offers, but none actually materialized, so they had to sell their cars. Finally, after four weeks of uncertainty, they made arrangements with the owner of a small dance hall: for several weeks, the band agreed to play on Saturdays and Sundays, in exchange for enough money to leave town.

On the way out of Virginia, the band happened onto a black doctor who suggested they play Friday and Saturday nights in a dance hall located above his office. Not being in any position to reject the offer, the musicians accepted.

One evening early in the spring of 1933, a young man from Bluefield, a small town at the foot of the Appalachians negotiated a deal with Buster Smith that changed the fate of the Blue Devils. "Don't stay another minute in this one-horse town. I have a contract that is a golden opportunity for each and every one of you. I run a nightclub over in Bluefield where I'll hire you for several weeks, and I guarantee that you'll be paid nightly." Thinking that they were finally seeing the light at the end of the tunnel, the musicians packed up their belongings, thanked the doctor, jumped into two taxis, and left for Bluefield. No problem; they would pay the seventy dollars the drivers were asking as soon as they arrived and gave their first performance. Sadly, the club they were booked in only held about thirty people, provided they were packed in, and on the first night the band went through its paces for only a handful of people. It was clear to the Blue Devils that they would never make any money under those conditions, especially since the owner wanted to pay according to head count.

The musicians settled into a local hotel and played a couple of nights to pay off their debts to the taxi drivers. Then, Zack White, another band leader, drove into Bluefield alone behind the wheel of a magnificent bus. He had gotten wind of the difficulties the Blue Devils were having and had come to woo certain musicians away and build up his own orchestra.

Seeing the bus arrive, the proprietor of the hotel became alarmed and, thinking the musicians were going to skip out without paying, telephoned the sheriff who, in turn, confiscated all the band's instruments. From that moment on it was virtually every man for himself. Some of the musicians left with Zack White, others had money wired to them so they could get their instruments back from the lawyer who was holding them, still others succeeded in stealing theirs back during the night.

As for Buster Smith, Lester Young, and Theodore Ross—who together possessed exactly $2.80, a knapsack containing a few pieces of meat and some old quids of tobacco—the only way left for them to get back to Kansas City was to hop freight trains.

> . . . We went on down there and caught one of those big freight trains comin' out of Florida or Alabama or somewhere, South Carolina. . . . Yeah, Chesapeake. Chesapeake Bay. It was [one] of them big-big, long trains, about 300 coaches on it, and it was running! . . . And it slowed up and it was running at about 15–20 miles an hour. . . . They said, "Every man get on there and you grab a coach by yourself." Said, "Grab on the front of the coach. Don't grab the back of the coach. When the coach get there, grab the front of it, so if you miss that piece up there and the train throw you loose, you hit against the coach and it will knock you off the track, but if you catch on the back end of it you'll liable to fall in between there and the coach right behind that will run over you. . . . " We mostly got on the flat car. . . . we got on (?) and there coal on it, and we jumped down and got under that coal. We got on it right after dark, and the next day, about 10 or 11 o'clock, we was in Cincinnati, Ohio. . . . I had a white suit, . . . and then it was blacker than them shoes I've got on now. . . . Down there in the hobo city, we ran up on some more guys traveling. . . . Them White boys went out there and got us plenty to eat. Got steaks, brought them back. They already cooked great big pieces of ham, all the bacon you wanted. . . . So we stayed there a day, and then we come on down to Saint Louis. . . . We got there late one evening in the next couple of days after we left Cincinnati. We went down there, and we still had that change left. I had two dollars and

forty cents left, and we went on down there and got one of them 20-cent beds. (Buster Smith)[26]

A few days later, Bennie Moten—who had heard they were there—sent a car to bring them back to Kansas City. As for Lester, unshaven, in a wrinkled suit, and with a faraway look in his eye, he located a musician willing to lend him an alto sax so that he could play a couple of performances for pocket money before returning to Kansas City.

There are those who have always wondered why Lester stayed with the Blue Devils when the situation was getting worse with each passing day. He could have quit the group, like Walter Page before him. But Lester didn't seem to worry about money. He also felt bound by friendship and musical rapport to the other musicians. So despite mounting difficulties, no one considered leaving the orchestra after Page's departure until the day Zack White showed up alone behind the wheel of his fancy bus.

On arriving in Kansas City, Lester had already left the imprint of his musical personality on the future careers of two musicians: Charlie Christian and Charles Thompson. In addition, he had developed friendships with two other musicians who were to play vital roles in his own life: Herschel Evans and Jo Jones.

Chapter 7

Kansas City,
All the Difference

Lester Young arrived in Kansas City[27] early in the fall of 1933; not long after that, Jo Jones, who was hired by Tommy Douglas's big band in November, also came to town.[28] Lester paid a visit to his friend Herschel Evans, whom he had met in Sioux City when the Blue Devils played there. Noticing how unhappy and downtrodden Lester looked, Herschel lent him some money and took him to buy some winter clothes and a new tenor sax. He also introduced him to Bennie Moten.

When Lester met Moten, Moten was ecstatic and gladly offered Lester a place in his orchestra; as it was, Walter Page, Jimmy Rushing, Eddie Durham, Buster Smith, Theodore Ross, Jap Allen, and Bill Basie had already resumed their places.

This massive arrival of southern musicians in Kansas City was to change the face of jazz.[29] The blues played in twelve measures, and variations thereof, quickly became the essential component of

Kansas City jazz. Jazz as a musical form would in turn penetrate the blues and give birth to a vocal style that was melodically richer. Furthermore, as a reaction to the traditional New Orleans style, the Kansas City musicians, headed by bass player Walter Page, would rhythmically emphasize the second and fourth beats, which would later lead Basie to stress them all equally. This accentuation, and the impression of relaxation that it conveys, became the main characteristic of Kansas City jazz.

Riffs—the short, rhythmic phrases that are repeated frequently within variable harmonies—became another characteristic of "Kaycee" jazz. Usually played during the first few measures, such bits of phrases help musicians develop new melodies. As arranger Eddie Durham underscored on one occasion, "You can always write a musical theme off a Kaycee riff." These riffs were to come into more and more frequent use, particularly at jam sessions. This "new jazz," crossed with the blues and punctuated by precise riffs, suited Lester Young's personality to perfection; based on it, and freed from all constraints, he was motivated to develop his own solo skills. Without the historic convergence that brought together Lester Young's originality and the musical innovations of the moment, no such thing would have been possible. It is within, and by means of, that amalgamation that the Young genius took shape.

At the same time he worked with Bennie Moten,[30] Lester found a job with a rival band whose schedule did not interfere with Moten's; it was the Clarence Love Orchestra. Though this band left the city for Dallas just a few months later due to a dispute with the musicians' union, it was at a performance by the Clarence Love Orchestra that King Oliver met Lester Young and offered to hire him. Young accepted, and, after talking it over with Bennie Moten and getting his approval, Young went on tour in Oklahoma.

Since 1928, when Luis Russell had dropped out, the King Oliver Orchestra had been in a steady state of decline. One by one, the musicians kept leaving, and Oliver himself was having health problems that prevented him from playing on a regular basis. He had formed a new band in 1931, but their tours in the South were not successful. The presence of Young was not going to alter that. The country was still in the grip of a depression, and many engagements that weren't canceled remained unpaid. Oliver continued touring until 1935, even though he was hardly able to perform.

Passing through Tulsa with King Oliver, Lester met his friend Buddy Tate at the hotel where all the black musicians stayed; Tate was in town accompanying the Victoria Spivey Review. The two men had met several years earlier when a "carnival" tour in which the Young family was involved had passed through Sherman, Texas: "Their show was called Pap, Sis and Bud" (Buddy Tate).

Right away, Tate informed Lester that there was a room with a piano on the ground floor of the hotel and that most of the local musicians regularly got together there for jam sessions.

> So I went upstairs and I found out what his room number—he was laying up there with pads, some corn pads, two on this one, two on this one.
> (Laughter)
> And it was hot. Didn't have no air conditioning then, you know, windows all up and everything. It was in the morning about 9:30, 10:00—we didn't go to bed, we just went on down there and started jamming. So I says, "Lester, you remember me?" "Oh, yeah, Tate." He didn't call me "Lady Tate" then. I says, "Well,—" He says, "What are you doing here?" and so I told him and I says, "We're jamming downstairs. Would you like to join in?" "Oh, yes." Anytime there was a jam session, man, he was ready, man, and I say in ten minutes, he was dressed and came down there and . . . I wish you could have heard him then. I never heard anybody play tenor like that in my life. . . . He really sounded just a little bit different from an alto. He sounded between an alto and C Melody. . . . I'll never forget it, I'll never forget the sound. So then everybody just— could nobody play. (Buddy Tate)[31]

42

In Oklahoma City the King Oliver Orchestra was performing at the Aldrich, a nightclub located on Deep Second Street. It was at the Aldrich that Charlie Christian and Lester Young met for the third time.

On his return to Kansas City after leaving King Oliver, Lester stayed at the Booker T. Washington Hotel, across from the Elbon Theater where Basie still occasionally played piano or organ to accompany the silent movies. Every day at six, Lester would meet his friends in the hotel lobby. Then they would go to meet other musicians at Eleonora's, an inexpensive restaurant a couple of hundred yards away; the proprietor became one of Lester's most ardent supporters. He would cook New Orleans–style dishes just for Lester—stewed meats, red beans and lots of peppers—which earned Lester the nickname "Red." One night he played with the Bennie Moten Orchestra at the famous El Paseo Ballroom, site of the annual band competitions benefiting Local 627, the regional branch of the musicians' union over which William Shaw presided.[32] That same night he learned that the Fletcher Henderson Orchestra had just come to town. This gave Lester the opportunity he had long dreamed of, to go hear Henderson's first tenor, Coleman Hawkins, the musician everyone was talking about.

> So I hurried over to see him, taking advantage of the breaks between my own sets, but I was broke, so I had to stay outside to listen. At one point, Fletcher announced that his tenor would not be able to play, and he wanted to know if there was anyone in the place who could blow on a sax. Here I had come thousands of miles to hear Coleman Hawkins and he wasn't going to play. Finally Fletcher came out—there were loads of people outside—and repeated his question, "You people in Kaycee don't have a tenor? Isn't one of you suckers able to play?" Herschel Evans was there, of course, he was with me, but he wasn't able to read a line of music. So the fools around me couldn't find anything better to do than to yell, "Red," (that was what they called me) "Red, go on Red, go get your hands on that damned saxophone."

Here I show up to see Coleman Hawkins because of the hype about his abilities, but experience nothing of the sort and end up in this fix instead. They literally pushed me inside. Finally I took a seat, picked up Hawkins' sax, read the parts for sax and clarinet, and played everything! After that I had to dash back to my own job where thirteen guys were waiting. Ten blocks away. (Lester Young)[33]

Late at night, when the last acts were winding down, Lester would make the rounds of the nightclubs in hopes of finding a jam session. After a few weeks, he earned a solid reputation as an improvisor.

. . . it was amazing how, that by word of mouth, these people could become so famous, and so popular. And people would know they're coming to town, and they would crowd out the dance halls. (Sammy Price)[34]

When he couldn't find anyone to play with, Lester would wake up one musician or another, no matter what time of the night it was. Aware of their occasional reluctance, he made sure to show up with a good bottle of whiskey to get them rolling.

Life in Kansas City was tough in those days. All of us were fighting it out like crazy. Saturday and Sunday we would have one or two performances. But then on Monday, Tuesday, Wednesday, Thursday, and Friday there wasn't much to do. (Lester Young)[35]

One of Lester's best buddies on his nocturnal escapades was longtime friend Ben Webster. Ben had recently moved into the city where his mother had just received a teacher's appointment. He was playing regularly with a new band led by Jap Allen and pianist-arranger Clyde Hart, who would play a few years later with Lester at Kelly's Stable in New York.[36]

Together, Lester and Ben frequently visited the Sunset on 12th Street and Woodland. That was where all the saxophonists living in Kansas City congregated: Buster Smith, Herschel Evans, Henry Bridges, Jimmy Keith, Buddy Tate, Herman Walder, Dick Wilson, and, a little later, Charlie Parker. Dick Wilson of Mount Vernon, Illinois, who was a disciple of Coleman Hawkins and Herschel Evans, was Lester's most serious challenger in Kansas City. He joined Andy Kirk's Clouds of Joy in 1935, but died six years later in 1941 from tuberculosis.

The Sunset was a strange place, full of smoke and noise, shaped like a hallway sixty feet long and thirteen feet across and packed every night. The ceiling was so low that a double bass could not be used; only a pianist and drummer regularly provided rhythm for the jam sessions that began around midnight.[37] One night, Ben and Lester were introduced to a young college student who was mad about jazz, Gene Ramey. Every night he crossed the bridge separating Kansas City, Kansas—which remained conservative and segregationist—from Kansas City, Missouri. Then he would make his way through the city to the Sunset where he spent the night listening to his favorite musicians. Whenever he got there early, Ramey knew what to do; he would head for a movie theater or hang around the cafeterias looking for Lester.

> Lester had a very spacey sound. In fact, I still kinda' try to play like that now. He would play a phrase and maybe lay out three beats before he'd come in with another phrase. You know, 'stead of more continuous staying on style, like Bird would play, you know. (Gene Ramey)[38]

At closing time, which generally came between eight and ten in the morning, Ramey returned to college and his music classes, while the musicians had breakfast at the Sawdust Trail across the street and discussed the events of the previous night. Some of them preferred Piney Brown's or the Lone Star directly across from the Sunset, where barman Joe Turner would serve his friends with a guitar strapped across his chest.

These early-morning discussions weren't always to Ben and Lester's satisfaction. Consequently, after a few glasses of cheap wine and several cups of black coffee, they would walk the streets until they were too exhausted to keep going and then sit down in the street, snarling traffic in the process, much to the exasperation of passing motorists—it was 9 A.M., after all! The anger of the motorists merely heightened their determination; sometimes they would stretch out full length, or else defy the drivers with their fists up like boxers. But when the police arrived, they managed to hightail it, yelling and joking like children as they went.

But everything didn't always run such a happy course. Sammy Price tells of an incident one evening when he and Lester courted disaster.

> So the man said we went to work at 9 o'clock and you quit at 3. And in those days, everybody knew that I was from Texas and the people supposed to have a gun. So, after we played all night . . . people liked it . . . and at 3 o'clock Lester and I started to pack up, leave . . . this person supposed to have been a gangster came and said, "Get back on that stand." And I put my coat on and then I said to Lester. . . Lester got his horn and I got my gun out and put it under my coat and said, "Let's go." We walked out. And the musicians are still wondering how we didn't get killed, you know, defying the guy. But that's exactly what happened. He said, "*Get* back on that stand." And I said, "Shit, (you know) you got to be kidding." I said, "I wonder if he know who he's talking to. . . . " The other guy . . . all the musicians standing there playing like hell. (Laughter) Yep, they stayed and played. (Sammy Price)[39]

Jam sessions rapidly became Lester's main preoccupation, his whole reason for living.[40] In a jam session, each musician could play according to his own style without any constraints. As soon as he was able to, Lester descended at night into the Sunset, the Subway, or the Reno, pulled out his instrument, climbed on stage, and measured himself against those saxophonists who were present. The most competitive jamming took place at the restaurant-bar called the Subway, a meeting place for traveling musicians. Lester met Vic Dickenson and Budd Johnson there; he came to hear Thelonious Monk with Herschel Evans, Basie, and Mary Lou Williams before rounding out the night at the Novelty where Thorpe Mern was waiting for him, the only local journalist who was a jazz fan.

On December 18, Lester and a few musicians went to the Cherry Blossom at the corner of Twelfth Street and Vine. Friends had assured Lester that Coleman Hawkins came there to jam after working with Fletcher Henderson. And sure enough, there he was, sitting at a table with a beer in front of him, his saxophone on his knees; he sat there, big man that he was, plunged deep in his own thoughts, just five years older than Lester, but already, and forever, the founding father of the art of playing tenor sax.

Coleman Hawkins had started out with singer Mammie Smith; he left her while in New York in 1923 to join the Fletcher Henderson Orchestra where he stayed for ten years. His reputation started to grow in 1926, the year in which he recorded his first hit, "Stampede," with Henderson. He evolved in a particular musical environment, surrounded by dance music (waltzes, polkas, tangos, popular songs, and, of course, jazz) where the rehearsal of orchestrations and complicated arrangements was as important as performing in public. Due to the time he had spent in Kansas City and the Midwest, Young was known to be better acquainted with the blues and with southern music. On top of that, he played relatively few written scores or arrangements. The Blue Devils, and later the Basie orchestra, were two groups that gave preference to riffs and "top notch" arrangements.

Ever since 1929 when he had recorded "One Hour" with a group consisting of several Chicago musicians called the Mound City Blue Blowers, Hawkins was rightly considered to have given the saxophone its musical credentials. His characteristically baroque style featuring an ample vibrato provided the standard by which the entire saxophone community measured itself. Hawkins himself could hardly have imagined that emerging from his shadow, this evening of December 18, 1933, was another style, antithetical to his own, one that would one day leave an imprint on the history of music that would be at least equal to his own.

In the meantime, the Cherry Blossom had filled up with local saxophonists who were just as ready as Lester to "confront" the uncontested master of the tenor sax. For them, however, it was not a question of challenging him; as indebted as they were to Hawkins, they only wished to show him that they were evolving satisfactorily according to the canon he had established. Understandably, this array of replicas "in the manner of . . . " bothered Lester who, after studying the work of Frankie Trumbauer, had made an effort to develop an original personal style.

The jam session began casually. One tune followed nonstop after another, until around 2:00 A.M. when only four saxophonists remained on stage, Hawkins, Evans, Webster, and Young, each completely absorbed in his task. The rhythm section had changed several times, but at this hour not one hardy pianist remained in the club. Webster, who never ran short of ideas, offered to go wake up Mary Lou Williams, the only person who might still be willing to take on the challenge at this hour.

> . . . around four A.M., I awoke to hear someone pecking on my screen.
>
> I opened the window on Ben Webster. He was saying, "Get up, pussycat, we're jamming and all the pianists are tired out now. Hawkins has got his shirt off and is still blowing."
>
> Sure enough, when we got there, Hawkins was in his singlet, taking turns with the Kaycee men. It seems he had run into something he didn't expect.
>
> Lester's style was light . . . it took him maybe five choruses to warm up. But then he would really blow . . .
>
> That was how Hawkins got hung up. The Henderson band was playing in Saint Louis that evening and Bean knew he ought to be on the way. But he kept trying to blow something to beat Ben and Herschel and Lester. When at last he gave up, he got straight in his car and drove to Saint Louis. I heard he'd just bought a new Cadillac and that he burnt it out trying to make the job on time. Yes, Hawkins was king until he met those crazy Kansas City tenor men. (Mary Lou Williams)[41]

As for Jo Jones, he had remained a spectator that night, and his recollection was of a downcast Coleman Hawkins who, before hitting the road for St. Louis, drowned himself in whiskey while an amused Dickie Wells looked on.

Ben and Herschel were the first to be surprised by this hasty departure. While admitting their own merits, and Lester's, too, of course, they preferred to account for the "escape" as a result of Hawkins' fear of arriving late in St. Louis, 250 miles away. They were nevertheless obliged to admit that Lester was the real force behind the session and that without him they would not, on their own initiative, openly have dared to pit themselves against Hawkins. For it was clear that they, too, had questioned Hawkins' supremacy. But without completely understanding what reasons lay behind Lester's efforts to develop a radically different sound and style, Herschel was no less impressed by the serene mastery his friend had just exhibited.

Lester, for his part, had simply put into practice the Kaycee motto: "Express something with your saxophone; don't just display your virtuosity; tell a story and not a lie."[42] But Young's melodic imagination, the new musical approach expressed by his phrasing, had undone Hawkins. Word of this contest, during which Lester had demonstrated his superiority on several counts to the man whom his contemporaries had consecrated the best tenor saxophonist of all, spread like wildfire across the United States. Writer Ross Russell went as far as to say, "Lester Young's victory marks a turning point in jazz music."

What remained undeniable, regardless of everything else, was the importance that the jam sessions assumed, especially the highly inspiring dynamics that they were able to afford the musicians. What this also proved was that anything was possible in jazz, and that nothing was acquired definitively.

Lester himself emerged unchanged after that famous night, but his reputation grew as a result. Little by little, he drew the attention of those who until then had only had ears for Coleman

Hawkins. During the months that followed, musicians and others who heard him in person would admit that it was possible to play in a different manner and to stake out a new course. But though the artistic significance of this difference was already tangible—recognition would be delayed until the fall of 1936, when Lester made his first recording. There is unfortunately no official record of the night of December 18, 1933.

Chapter 8

Henderson and Heartbreak

By the end of 1933, most of the musicians who had succeeded one another in the various incarnations of the Blue Devils found themselves united for the first time in the Bennie Moten Orchestra; these included Buster Smith, William Basie, Walter Page, Hot Lips Page, Eddie Durham, Jap Allen, Theodore Ross, Lester Young, and Jimmy Rushing.

At the end of January 1932, Basie—who had been the real mainspring in the Moten orchestra for most of the last two years—embarked on a short tour, with Moten's approval, after forming his own group. The musicians threw themselves into the project with more than the usual amount of gusto. They planned to rejoin Moten again in April.

Fletcher Henderson caught up with the band in Little Rock. He had come down from Kansas City to ask Lester to join the Henderson band, which had already left for New York. Coleman Hawkins had filled Fletcher's tenor position for the last ten years but recently had left to take a stab at a European career. Lester, wondering why Henderson wanted someone who played so differently from Hawk, turned to his friend Buddy Tate for advice. Tate advised him to take the plunge.

Lester finally accepted the offer and took the bus for the East Coast before he could change his mind again.

According to some, Lester's choice was determined by the prestige and financial terms offered by the Henderson band, which paid seventy-five dollars a week instead of the scant twenty dollars paid by Basie. But no close acquaintance would have said that. Never in his life did Lester set his sights on financial success. And never was prestige either a means or an end for him. Challenging other musicians in marathons like that with his cousin "Boots" Young or the contest with Coleman Hawkins in December of 1933 was really a form of self-combat for Lester, a continuous effort to master the traps set by his own musical imagination. It all symbolized his desire to bring a strong and original musical personality into existence, first of all for himself and only second for the world.

Convinced that he held the key to his own development, Lester never gave in to other pressures; he always went his own way.

To participate in a tour at the very heart of the Fletcher Henderson Orchestra was for Lester a real opportunity to change his surroundings. He was not greatly looking forward to rejoining his friends in the Bennie Moten Orchestra once the Basie tour was over, either. Not that he didn't have some interest in returning, but he needed to learn other things, to meet other people, and to quench his thirst for adventure. By accepting the invitation, Lester knew he was embarking on a perilous adventure. And having been a stand-in for Coleman Hawkins in the orchestra one night in Kansas City, he was aware of the combined feelings of fear and respect that the other musicians harbored toward him. It was a question of replacing Hawk again; only now it was not just for one night, it was for an undetermined length of time!

I'll never forget the day when Lester arrived at the old Cotton Club and took his place between Russell Procope and Buster Bailey, who were already in the saxophone section. Lester remained faithful to himself, but the orchestra was horrified by his sound. It wasn't the same as Hawkins'![43]

Sure enough, as soon as the first rehearsal was over, the unhappy musicians objected to Fletcher's having hired "a tenor with an alto sound." Yet despite the recriminations, Henderson confirmed Lester's employment agreement and asked him to be ready to travel on with the band. All the way up to the band's first Detroit performance on March 31, Lester couldn't find anyone who would talk to him. The musicians purely and simply ignored him.

As could well be expected, the concert went pretty badly and those scheduled after it followed the same pattern. Lester played well and read the music without any effort, but the orchestra as a whole—with the exception of Henderson—tried to lead him astray and refused to go over new arrangements before a performance if Lester was present. Even as his own doubts grew about being a part of this ensemble, Lester was conforming to his new isolation.

Alone in the various hotel rooms he occupied, Lester practiced his instrument; but whenever he performed in a city and the opportunity presented itself, he would look for a place where musicians jammed until dawn.

Not until he was taken in by Fletcher Henderson, who lived on 139th St. in Harlem, did Lester discover what horror really meant. Every morning at 9 A.M. during his stay, Henderson's wife would wake him up, take him down to the basement where the music room was located, throw a quick breakfast in front of him, and place a record by Coleman Hawkins or one of his imitators on the phonograph. Once the record was over, she would begin questioning Lester: Had he fully understood what he had just heard? No? Then she would put the record back on, and crank it up louder.

Every morning at about the same time, the same routine would start all over again. Lester couldn't get over it.

> Every morning the bitch would wake me up at nine, and try to teach me how to play like Coleman Hawkins. What on earth could that woman have been thinking! Sure, she played the trumpet, the kind you hear at the circus![44]

Finally, when Lester had gone out one afternoon, Fletcher took the opportunity to call a meeting of his musicians.

> So—let me tell you—Jeff said, "One day, Fletcher called all of us together but Lester and says, 'I want you to sit down, fellas, I want to tell you something.' He says, 'I tell you why I called you in,' he says, 'I'm going to fire this boy,' he says, 'because of you. Actually I don't want to. But I'm going to fire him because of you, because he'll never be able to play nothing in here and he'll never have any peace in here. He won't be happy.'"
>
> And the same time, he says, "But before he go—" Fletcher was sort of friendly like Prez, you know, talking-wise, you know. . . . He says, "But before he go, I want to tell all three of you something. He can out play you, you, you and you." . . . And Fletcher told me in later years, he said—we talked about it and this is after I joined Basie. He said, "Buddy, I sure hate to do that, but he never could have had any—he never would have been comfortable there." He said, "But I heard what he was doing," he said, "you know, he wrote all those arrangements and things," said, "I knew he could play." And he says, "He came to me and says, 'Mr. Henderson,' he says, 'thanks for giving me a chance.' He says, 'All I ask of you, would you please give me a nice recommendation?'" And he said, "That's all he asked me for." (Buddy Tate)[45]

The Henderson episode was short and painful. Painful in that for the first time, musicians whom Lester considered to be his peers "beat him out cold" and found fault with his playing, with his style, with his originality. Lester had become conscious of his isolation and of the world that stood hostile guard around him.

Lester alluded to the Henderson incident in several interviews, but as the years went by, he was inclined to modify reality a bit. By his account, he reacted with both strength and determination. His life says otherwise. To François Postif he said,

> Whenever I played, those creeps behind me whispered. I can't stand that. I won't ever talk when you play, not ever—I mean, you hear a bunch of lunkheads whispering. . . . Jesus! So I pulled out. I went looking for Fletcher and I asked him like this, "How about writing me a nice recommendation? I'm headed back to Kansas City."[46]

He was trying to save face, but he wasn't fooling anyone.

After leaving Fletcher Henderson, Lester found himself penniless in a city he hardly knew and with no one he could count on. The only solution was to go back to his adoptive home, Kansas City, where he could count on friends. For several days he knocked around the clubs in Harlem in search of a job, surviving on coffee, sandwiches, and stale cake. But even in those days, the situation in New York was difficult; there were lots of musicians and few jobs. Furthermore, not many people on the East Coast had ever heard of a twenty-five-year-old tenor sax player named Lester Young. There was John Hammond, of course, the critic who, on first seeing Lester perform with Henderson several weeks before, had said, "He's the best sax player I've ever heard." But he didn't come to the rescue when Lester really needed him.

Still, it was in a Harlem club that Lester had the good fortune to meet a young lady who sang the blues, his legendary co-worker Billie Holiday. The meeting was brief; the conversation was about music, especially the jam session in which they had just taken part. Each recognized the other's talent. It was a simple meeting of two musicians who appreciated each other as soon as their paths crossed.

After a painful return to Kansas City, Lester was hired by the Andy Kirk Orchestra for three months.[47] Pianist Mary Lou Williams remembered that he joined the band to replace Ben Webster:

. . . Lester Young joined us in Kansas City, but he didn't stay with us very long because shortly after that he went to Count Basie's band. . . . Yes, we missed Ben Webster on account of sound but Lester was more free and whatnot in solos to play a hundred solos and never repeat.[48]

Kirk's only recollection is of a supercharged Lester Young who would jam all night on the bus on the rare occasion, when the band would have a road trip. Mary Lou and Kirk seem to be the only two people who have any recollection of the time Lester spent in the orchestra; he never referred to this period himself, as though wanting to forget it.

Whatever the case, the first performances were held in a posh downtown nightclub called the Variety Fair Club. There followed a series of performances in a dance hall on Main Street reserved for whites, the Pla-Mor Ballroom, where Kirk had first carried out his new duties as band leader of the Clouds of Joy in the spring of 1929. The band rarely left town; its last tour in 1933 was a true disaster, and no musician wants to repeat that experience: only a handful of concerts took place between Kansas City and Oklahoma City.

Despite his flair for performing, Lester had not quite gotten over the Henderson fiasco, or his wanderings in New York. He took part in a few jam sessions at the Bar le Duc and at the Great Leaf Gardens, where his path crossed that of a certain Charlie Parker (the father of Bird). Kirk had just signed a contract with Fairyland Park, a huge dance hall reserved for whites. The first few evenings, Lester participated, but one morning in November he resigned from the engagement. He was getting bored and restless and decided to go to Minneapolis as he had done several years before.

At this point, the most secretive months of Lester's life unfolded. A short time after having settled into a small hotel on the north side of town, he got to know Boyd Atkins,[49] a saxophonist and violinist who asked him to join his band. Their collaboration lasted for a year, during which time Lester left the city for only a few weeks to do a tour in Minnesota.

In Minneapolis, Atkins and his group established themselves at the Cotton Club and remained the permanent attraction there for several years. One morning, following a night of uneventful music-making, Lester was headed for his hotel when he ran across a young female Belgian shepherd, stretched out on the sidewalk between two trash cans. The dog's unhappy and lonely appearance tugged at Lester's heart, and speaking softly, he approached her. Fifteen minutes later, the two new friends found themselves back in his hotel room after enduring the suspicious looks of the recep-tionist. Lester went back out immediately and headed for the clos-est drug store. . . .

That night at the Cotton Club, Lester took Boyd Atkins over to his dressing room door and said, "I'm going to introduce you to someone. Be nice, she's still a little sick."

The door opened. A pair of startled eyes stared back at Atkins.

> He always had a dog, but he always gave them the darndest names. This dog he had, it was a Belgian police dog, all black, and his name was Tonics, you know, because he used to have a musical saying, "Get your tonics together," so he named this dog Tonics. (Lee Young)[50]

Twenty years later, Lester would brag about having been the only person who could talk to the animals. Critic Leonard Feather reports that Lester had found a small injured bird one night. He took the bird wherever he was playing, fed it between sets and talked to it about its plumage; in short, he was giving it encourage-ment. But one morning the bird disappeared and to explain the sudden departure, Lester elatedly announced, "You see, I gave him back the courage to fly . . . by administering a swig of bourbon!"

The relationship he had with Tonics charmed several musi-cians and club patrons; there was, for example, a young Albu-querque girl named Beatrice whom Lester had already met several times during his tours with the Blue Devils. An idyllic relationship developed between them: Beatrice attended all of Lester's perfor-mances, and he took her to his hotel at night.

A month later, Lester married Beatrice whom he knew nothing about beyond her modest origins and her love of music. She wanted a home, children, a "responsible" husband; he wanted to go out, to play music, to meet other musicians, to travel. The marriage turned confrontational, and Lester was reluctant to go out, feeling guilty about his nightly absences. To make matters worse, he was not making much money, and his wife was asking him to make more of an effort. But what else could he do? In his eyes there was but one solution: to leave. But where would he go?

The only band that still had any appeal for Lester was that of Bennie Moten, where Basie and the best of the old Blue Devils were working. But his hopes of joining them evaporated when he learned that Bennie had passed away in the course of a simple surgical procedure at the time his band was playing Denver. For several weeks, Ira Bus (Bennie's brother) assumed leadership of the band, but the group rapidly lost credibility due to the unpredictability of its new leader. Jobs became scarce, and some musicians began to leave the band. Observing these events from Minneapolis where he was still performing at the Cotton Club, Lester considered heading back to Kansas City as soon as he learned that Basie intended to leave Ira Bus and form a group of his own. He let Beatrice in on these plans, while making it very clear that nothing could be counted on with certainty.

A few weeks later, Lester tuned in to a broadcast, direct from the Reno in Kansas City, of a concert by Count Basie and his orchestra.[51] He sent him a wire immediately, congratulating him, sending his fondest regards, and asking him to hire him.

Several of his interviewers were told by Lester that he sent a telegram to Basie because he couldn't stand Slim Freeman, the first tenor in the band. He proposed to replace him in the interest of all concerned. Basie's reply was not long in coming: Lester would be welcomed with open arms. Overjoyed, Lester told Beatrice, threw a few clothes in a suitcase, got his instrument ready, and headed without delay to the bus station. Tonics went with him. The assumption was that his wife would join him a few days later.

Lester arrived in Kansas City, found quarters in the Booker T. Washington Hotel, unpacked, had a quick meal, changed clothes, and dashed to the Reno where he was given a friendly reception by all the musicians. Basie offered him $18 a week. "No problem," he replied. Two years before, he had made $1.50 in the same club, and with a $3 weekly hotel bill, he felt prepared for anything. Within six days of his arrival and despite the absence of certain friends like Ben Webster and Herschel Evans (who was in California) Lester had resumed all his old habits. Far from economizing, Lester would invite his friends to a restaurant or to Pops Monroe's place, a bar known for selling the best whiskey in town. Lester didn't drink, but he liked to spring for rounds for others. He also took advantage of the regular salary to buy himself a number of new suits and a signet ring that he wore until his death. Once a job was over, he would head out in search of jam sessions at the Subway, the Sunset, and other nightclubs. When he wasn't playing with Basie, he appeared with Margaret "Countess" Johnson, an excellent piano player who rivaled Mary Lou Williams, but who unfortunately died of tuberculosis before she achieved fame.[52]

Lester also played at the Yellow Front Saloon with Eddie Durham, George Hunt, and Jo Jones, who was passing through Kansas City. Every Sunday morning he would take part in the "Spook Breakfast," a sort of gigantic jam session that might sometimes last for ten hours.

In the meantime, the Ira Bus/Moten orchestra was finishing up its last performances. One by one, the musicians were leaving, and the band ceased to exist when Buster Smith finally left it and joined Basie at the Reno.

Chapter 9

Basie

When Basie saw Buster Smith come through the door of the Reno with a notebook stuffed with arrangements under his arm, he sensed the importance of the moment and proposed a new partnership to his friend on the spot. Together, that very evening, they announced the creation of the Buster Smith and Basie Barons of Rhythm. Standing out among the band's components was drummer Jesse Price, former accompanist for Ida Cox and Bessie Smith, along with Walter Page on the bass, Clifford McIntire on guitar, Basie at the piano, Jack Washington on baritone, Lester on tenor, and Buster Smith on the alto saxophone. From time to time Hot Lips Page came in to reinforce the formation and Jimmy Rushing would lend his voice. The musicians worked seven nights a week, from about 8 P.M. to four in the morning; Saturday nights were the exception due to the breakfast jam sessions on Sunday; on those occasions they became involved in real twenty-hour marathons lasting until noon of the next day. Of course, the band did not play without interruptions. In one evening, the Reno offered three or four one-hour shows, featuring singers, comedians, and dancers—all belonging to the TOBA circuit.[53] Intermission would last about two hours, at which time the musicians stepped in to make the public dance.

The weekly salary ranged from fifteen dollars to twenty dollars per person; Smith and Basie earned a few dollars more. This could hardly be called a fortune, but it did enable them to put food on the table and a roof over their heads and to take advantage of the prices at the Reno where hot dogs, hamburgers, and beer went for a nickel apiece, and whiskey cost fifteen cents. The club also had a back room where extensive drug trafficking and prostitution took place.

Despite the frantic pace, the band found time on at least a couple of afternoons a week to rehearse new songs. In contrast to Basie, who showed no interest in them whatsoever, Walter Page devoted himself exactingly to helping several musicians decipher melodies and perfect their technical skills.

The Buster Smith and Basie Barons of Rhythm repertoire was essentially composed of "memorized" arrangements which were tightened up during rehearsals; they originated in the riffs that the musicians performed during their solos.

At the Reno, Lester's most fervent admirer was fifteen-year-old Charlie Parker, Jr., a young man who would go on to accept the Young challenge in the same manner that Charlie Christian had. A student at Lincoln High School, Charlie was fascinated by the saxophone; his mother had given him an old alto that he never stopped fingering. Disenchanted with the lessons being offered at his school, he decided that the best way to learn to play was to listen to those who used the instrument best, the jazzmen in the clubs. In the two years since his earliest nocturnal sallies in the direction of the Sunset, he had lost all fear of the city and went walking at all hours of the night in those parts of town where there was the most activity. Naturally, he picked the club with the most, and best, shows: the Reno. It wasn't long before he came to the attention of Jesse Price, whom he found to be an understanding benefactor with no compunctions about bringing him in through the stage door. Hidden in a stage corner behind the orchestra, Parker found himself on the axis line of the saxophone section, just a few yards from Lester Young.

After three weeks, Parker decided Lester was his favorite saxophonist. There was something undefinable about his playing and his sound that attracted him. When he was certain of not being watched, Charlie would pull the alto out of its case, pretend to play, and concentrate on Lester's music. The musicians who saw him doing it made fun of him; only Jesse Price and Lester showed him any good will. Lester was almost certainly the first to encourage Parker to undertake a musical career. Though he might have wished for it to happen, Parker never asked Lester to teach him to play the sax; he forged his own style by listening to records. For several months the two existed side by side and dealt with each other as friends. Shortly before the Basie orchestra left for Chicago, Charlie attracted the attention of Buster Smith, who became his first serious instructor very soon thereafter.

Six months after his return to Kansas City, Lester learned that his wife had decided to come join him. He had completely forgotten about that side of his existence. So one morning he went to meet her at the bus terminal, took her to the Washington Hotel where he had been living with Tonics, asked about her health and about life in Minneapolis, and finally came around to his own life,

> I go to the Reno around 7 P.M., occasionally with Tonics along. We start to play around 8 P.M. and finish around 4 A.M. Well, that depends, sometimes earlier, sometimes later. If it's earlier, there is always a jam session. Meaning that we make a quick dash for food, then the percussionist heads back and I do, too. The others go to bed. After that we play with a few guys who have come to have a good time. Then I return here and sleep. I take care of the dog a little after that, and then I start the same routine over again. Sure enough, every day. . . . Pay? $18 a week—less if you go on tour, but those are rare because of all

the traveling. No, no other engagements; I have stopped playing in other bands since Basie and Smith got together. No time!

Beatrice and Lester could not live decently on eighteen dollars a week. She suggested he ask for more; he refused. He should do something else! Other performances! He promised to think about it but did nothing. Beatrice began looking for work; Lester came home later and later each day. One morning the crisis reached a head and they broke up. Lester didn't budge as he sadly watched Beatrice leave him. He consoled himself by walking the city streets, Tonics at his side.

Lester never made any express references to this relationship. In fact, no one ever tried to find out what had really happened. He did make one reference to the episode twenty years later, depicting himself then as a hard and pitiless man.

"I was living with a hostile, aggressive woman," he confided to a musician. "Not knowing how she might react to my absences, I would plunk my sax into my case and the case into a garbage can across the street from the house. Amenable, you know . . . . But that way I ran no risks. One day, I had had enough and got mad. You should have seen the broad, down on her knees. . . . "Don't hit me, please! Don't hit me!" "Shit," I said to her, "you've been sharpening your nails on me for a whole year!"

This was to be the only statement he made on his relations with women in his entire life.

The owner of the Reno, Sol Epstein, was an intelligent man. He convinced the producers of a local radio station to record all the Reno soirees. The originality of the show drew a lot of attention to the station and to Epstein's club, as well as to Basie, who gained a listenership for his band many thousands of miles from Kansas City.

One night in December 1935 while on the road to Chicago to attend Benny Goodman's first concert, critic John Hammond, Goodman's brother-in-law, tuned in to the station and discovered the team of Smith and Basie. He parked his car on the side of the road and sat listening until the end of the set before speeding off to Chicago.

> To receive the station clearly, you needed equipment that could pick up police calls, but its signal was strong enough for people to hear it in Chicago. There were times when I could even pick it up in my car around 3 A.M. in New York.[54]

Once in Chicago, Hammond spoke of "his" discovery to Goodman who, by coincidence, had also heard a concert broadcast. Goodman didn't even stop to think; he got on a plane, headed straight for the Reno, listened to a few sets, and hurried right back to Chicago.

Was it coincidence that forty-eight hours after Goodman's stopover in Kansas City Lester developed a sudden love for the clarinet, and that he worked constantly on it from then on? Several people close to him asserted that Goodman himself had offered Lester a clarinet to thank him for playing and to encourage him. Whatever the case, from then on, Lester appeared with a new clarinet, a contrast to his old beat-up tenor.

In New York, Hammond met Fats Waller and praised Basie's qualities. Waller, pleased to learn of the talents of his former student, gave him one thousand dollars and sent him to Kansas City. When Basie's musicians met Hammond at the Reno in May of 1936 they were both surprised and pleased to learn that this person wanted to take them to New York and that in his pocket he carried the sum of one thousand dollars to buy them uniforms, new instruments, and eventually a car. But a few remembered the unhappy experience in Virginia that had caused the Blue Devils to break up; they turned down the offer.

Jesse Price was the first to leave the band. Hammond then suggested that Basie hire Jo Jones, percussionist for the Jeter-Pilars orchestra, who was then in St. Louis. Basie thought it was an interesting idea, particularly since he had already had the occasion to play with Jones several times in 1934. He immediately fell under the spell both of the young drummer's drive and of his swing, hiring him on the spot. But two days after his employment, Jones took off again for St. Louis, refusing to play with Basie.

> . . . they played "After You've Gone" and when Hot Lips Page got through playing, Lester Young stood up and took the second chorus on "After You've Gone" and I went downstairs and refused to accept my money. I said, "I'm going back to Omaha to go back to school," and Basie begged me to stay. I said, "I'm not staying. I can't play with your band, Mr. Basie." My heart went in my mouth when Lester Young got up and took the second chorus on "After You've Gone." I died. (Jo Jones)[55]

But despite this outburst of modesty, Jo Jones did take his seat again in the orchestra a few days later, to everyone's satisfaction.

Basie managed to find a paying organist's position with radio station WHB, assuring himself of a little more money, which enabled him to raise the salary of his favorite musicians, Lester, Jo, and Walter.

Buck Clayton, who was making his way from California to New York, stopped in Kansas City to pay his mother a visit. That night he went by the Reno, got on stage to jam, hit it off with the musicians, and was hired to replace Hot Lips Page; Page had just signed an exclusive contract with an agent named Glaser who advised anyone who would listen that Page was the only valuable component of the orchestra.

But even as Hammond was trying to get a recording contract for Basie with Brunswick, Buster Smith—who was becoming more and more skeptical of Hammond's predictions for the future—also quit the orchestra. He fell in again with Jesse Price and formed an eleven-man band whose existence, unfortunately, was to be ephemeral. Charlie Parker was also a member of that band.

In the meantime, Basie signed, without carefully reading, a contract with Dave Kapp, an agent hastily dispatched to Kansas City by Decca. Whatever the musicians may say, when John Hammond arrived back in the midwestern capital, the situation wasn't very good. One alto position was vacant; Basie had signed a contract that tied him for three years to Decca and forced him to record twenty-four singles for a flat $750, with no additional royalties. Furthermore, one of the contract's clauses forced him to enlarge his orchestra by several instruments.

Fortunately, despite Basie's clumsy moves and thanks to repeated pressure from both Goodman and Hammond, Willard Alexander of the Music Corporation of America came to Kansas City at the end of the summer of 1936 to sign a management contract with the pianist's ensemble. Together they were planning to make a tour of the East.

A few days later, preparations got underway; they had to write arrangements, copy them, find music stands, locate suits that would please everyone, and most important of all hire new musicians.

None of the preparations for departure upset Lester in the least; the prospect of going on tour was something he viewed with great peace of mind. Faithful to his own habits, he spent his nights jamming in the city's nightclubs, beneath the sympathetic gaze of his dog Tonics, always sprawled at the foot of the piano. In tandem with Jo Jones, Lester applauded and encouraged trombonist George Hunt, whose merits he extolled so well that Basie consented to hire him. A few days later, trumpeters Tatti Smith and Joe Keyes, trombonist Dan Minor, and guitarist Claude Williams rejoined the formation.

Around that time, in Los Angeles, Herschel Evans received a telegram from Basie, with whom he had had occasion to play in Bennie Moten's orchestra: "Must have other tenor to play with Lester!" Happily looking forward to meeting up again with his two old buddies, Evans packed his bags and left for Kansas City. The orchestra was ready to begin rehearsing as soon as he arrived. At long last, Couchie Roberts was chosen to replace Buster Smith.

In September of 1936, six weeks before his departure for the East Coast, Lester heard that his father, who still lived in California with the rest of the family, was ill. Lester explained to Basie that he had to take off for a few days, and Basie even went so far as to put the band car at his disposal, complete with chauffeur.

Lester took his instrument, a travel bag, and Tonics with him in the Cadillac. He stayed in Los Angeles about ten days, seeing a lot of the Frank Sebastian Garden. There he discovered his little brother Lee's newfound skill on drums; Lee was then playing with the fifteen-member Eddie Barefield Orchestra.

> Don Byas was with us, playing alto. Me, I needed a tenor and asked him to do that. It didn't come easy. At first, he wouldn't hear of it. Finally, the guy who played Baritone, Paul Howard, and I, we shook him up good. And he became one of the best tenors in the world. Lester came to hear us from time to time, and even though Byas was leaning in another musical direction, he was interested in Lester's progress. . . . I had bought a brand-new beauty of a Ford, and we would go out for a spin nearly every night. It happened so much, that when he left, Lester wouldn't stop talking about cars (Eddie Barefield)[56]

On the verge of returning to Kansas City, and with his mind at rest concerning his father's health, Lester gave his dog to his brother as a gift, stating that he could no longer take care of her. It is, indeed, difficult to see how he could have taken her along on tour with Basie.

Chapter 10

The Confirmation

During the night of October 31, 1936, after headlining with the Duke Ellington Orchestra at the Paseo Ballroom, Count Basie and his orchestra left Kansas City with the blessing of every musician in the city. With them in the bus headed for the East Coast, the musicians took their new costumes; some even had new instruments. Basie carefully cradled a small leather briefcase in his lap, in which he filed the band's repertoire: twelve arrangements!

Lester left the midwestern city with no regrets; for him another episode comparable to that of the Blue Devils was beginning, complete with road trips, small paychecks, excellent musical relations, and the emergence of solid friendships. Just hours before they were to leave, the young Gene Ramey payed him a visit and gave him a magnificent Conn tenor sax.

The band's first stop was in Chicago where Willard Alexander had negotiated an engagement at the Grand Terrace from November 6 through December 3. The Grand Terrace was more of a music-hall auditorium than a jazz club; the décor was luxurious, admission was expensive, and the rather stodgy audience that attended preferred musical reviews to concerts.

That afternoon, when the orchestra entered the room to rehearse, the musicians were taken aback on seeing dozens of dancers going over their numbers for the evening show. At a loss, Basie telephoned Willard Alexander and explained to him that he couldn't see the least purpose for bringing him in; his repertoire was not ready, and they were demanding that his orchestra play light music; furthermore, he really didn't see how he could fit into a musical show. The best thing would be to leave town on the spot. But Willard didn't see things in the same light: the Grand Terrace performances were being transmitted on the air and it was imperative for the orchestra to appear in order for it to get exposure.

The first evening was a true disaster. Fitted into their tight new uniforms and jammed behind music stands, the musicians played without conviction, deciphering with difficulty the parts they were furnished without explanation. The audience let its displeasure be known, and the management of the Grand Terrace threatened to break the contract if there was no improvement.

The first show of sympathy came from the chorus girls who, while amused at the situation, tried to comfort the musicians. Fletcher Henderson, who had just finished a four-week engagement at the Terrace, came to the rescue by offering Basie several arrangements and themes of his own so that Basie could put together enough of a repertoire to please the public. Indirectly, he was also helping a musician whom he admired, but from whom he had been forced to part ways several years earlier: Lester Young.

After going over the material a few times, the orchestra managed to overcome its fears and to familiarize itself with the new arrangements furnished by Henderson. The act was far from perfect, but the ensemble didn't present itself badly.

One morning, after a particularly exciting night at the Terrace, John Hammond entered the cafeteria where the musicians were having lunch. Casually, he took Basie, Lester, Jo, Walter, Tatti Smith, and Jimmy Rushing to one side. He had a simple proposal to make: since he had been unable to void the contract signed by Basie with Decca before it entered into effect, he wanted to make use of the few hours left before the musicians turned in to record them in an independent studio named "Jones-Smith Incorporated."

This was truly a stroke of genius on the part of John Hammond.

> The place was shabby. The studio was one small room measuring 12 by 15 feet. It was much too small to set up a grand piano, and it was lacking both sound-proofing and the acoustical panels you find in studios today. I had one engineer. There were two microphones, but I chose to use just one. The acoustics were so poor that a blow to the bass drum together with vibrations from the double bass sometimes flattened the needle on the record tracks (John Hammond)[57]

So Jo Jones used nothing but a snare drum and a hi-hat.

The situation was entirely new to Lester, Jo, and Smith; here they were about to record for the first time, when only that morning at eight o'clock they had been sipping coffee, recording being the last thing on their minds: "Basie's face was full of energy and conveyed his enthusiasm. . . . Walter maintained his self-assurance, Jimmy too. . . . Tatti was quiet but active; Lester was thrilled, Jo was generous and bossy" (John Hammond).[58]

In three hours (from 10:00 A.M. to 1:00 P.M.), the group recorded "Shoe Shine Boy," "Evenin'," "Boogie Woogie," and "Lady Be Good," a classic written by George Gershwin in 1924.

The discographies of Count Basie and Lester Young give October 9, 1936, as the date of this recording session, but it was really November 9, for the engagement at the Grand Terrace had begun on November 6. Hammond, Young, and Jones also confirmed that the recording took place then. At the end of September and beginning of October, Young was in California and Basie was in Kansas City, making preparations for the upcoming tour. But two contradictory pieces of information do remain: Lewis Porter claims the *Chicago Defender* referred in its news columns to a visit made by Basie to Chicago in September of 1936, and a few years later, Jo Jones "thought" he remembered that the session had taken place on his birthday, i.e., on October 8, 1936.

At that time, there were several Hawkins records on the market, and practically all the saxophonists knew the solo parts by heart. When Lester's recording went into circulation two months later, everyone—except those in his entourage—expected to see more of the musical standards set by "Bean."

The recording contains two major pieces: a highly original version of Gershwin's "Lady Be Good" done in the key of D, and the famous "Shoe Shine Boy," where Lester's chorus is considered by many to be one of the best of his career and one which highlights Lester's originality: First, there are the liberties he takes with the standard four-beat measure. He never ceases to accentuate it at his discretion, sometimes placing the stress slightly ahead of or behind the beat. Then there is the rhythmic accompaniment generated by his very style. The rhythm section guarantees a kind of steady, supple, and continuous breathing effect, with neither interruptions nor special effects. Then he lays out his own rhythmic and melodic ideas on the soft carpeting that has been rolled out for him.

Later, when the full Basie orchestra made recordings, it became more apparent how Lester's style and the aerial effects it created were cradled by Jo Jones' technique. Jones' use of cymbals to mark the beat (instead of the bass drum as before) created a lightness that had not existed until then in the rhythm section, and which was itself driven by the style of Lester Young. One could speak in this regard of a veritable "Lester Young Effect," and its impact was immediate. Lester had broken once and for all with the powerful, turbulent "tidal wave" phrases of Coleman Hawkins. Here, in fact, was a musician more inclined toward simplicity and the restructuring of melody than toward the quest for complex harmonies. This was someone who played more readily by scale than by chord; someone who didn't systematically base his improvisations on harmony, but on fresh interpretations of a single melody. And so in the process of reusing old material, Lester never ceased revisiting both his immediate, and distant, musical past, where Hawkins, by contrast, refused to look back.

Let us also point out that, contrary to the popular opinion of the time—which only took notice of Hawkins' panting vibrato—Lester used nothing but an authentic vibrato. It is a discreet vibrato, to be sure, but it is no less there, affecting the height and the rhythm of the notes, especially when these are repeated (and such repetition is a Young characteristic).

As André Hodeir has reminded us, "all the great jazz improvisors have created a sound out of their phrases, and their phrases out of their sound." And that is exactly what is surprising in Lester's case: this sweet, soft, relaxed sound, a sound that is beautiful and pure, that conveys a preoccupation that is spiritual to start with, one that is no longer strictly physical.

At last, to take up a well-known cliché, Lester was a melodic improvisor who worked on a "horizontal" plane, whereas Hawkins was the prototypical "vertical" improvisor, who relied on the harmonies of a piece. Admittedly, it was not the progression of chords that was of principal interest to Lester; he limited himself to tonics, to dominant chords and to their extensions, showing a clear preference for melodic development. Hawkins, by contrast, organized a whole progression that deviated from the chords, including "passing chords," and a few extensions.[59]

No sooner did this record appear on the Vocalion-Brunswick label than a passionate debate began to rage. Charlie Parker and Charlie Christian were the first ones to buy and decipher it in Kansas City. Gene Ramey remembers having heard Parker around the Kansas City nightclubs: "He would get up and play the Prez' solos note for note; his alto sounded like the Prez'. Bird was so influenced by Young. . . . "[60]

And when Bird left to go on tour with Georgie Lee, during the summer of 1937, the first things he packed to take with him were Lester's recordings.

But if you don't count Bird and Charlie Christian, Hammond,

the Basie musicians, and a few friends, Lester's music received negative ratings in most jazz circles. This didn't prevent Lester from being perfectly sure of his originality; nor did he have any qualms about advertising it.

> I had never heard Hawk, other than on a few records. Everybody copied him. The jazz world was under Hawk's spell. But me, I couldn't imagine myself copying Hawk, or anybody else. You had to have a style that was truly your own. You can't be a stylist if all you do is concentrate on not copying someone . . . , because I meant to be original. Originality, that's the trick. You may well possess tone, technique, and a bunch of other things, but if you have no originality, you don't really go anywhere. You have to be original (Lester Young)[61]

And forty-eight years later, Miles Davis, who was the first to realize a synthesis of the Young and Parker styles, also took Lester's lessons to heart. In an interview granted to Francis Marmande for *Le Monde*, he reminded us of what matters most in jazz, which also happens to be what it currently lacks most:

> The underlying task, the core of the task, is sound. Sound, you understand. Sound is your very own voice; you have to seek it out . . . , sound is in charge of your person. . . . You are the sound. You are your own sound. There is very little sound, original sound, in creative music. Plenty of perfectionism, to be sure, lots of repetition, but very little sound.[62]

But even though that November session may have confirmed each musician in his manner of playing, it certainly did not eradicate the problems that the Basie orchestra was having. The assistance of Fletcher Henderson had been invaluable, but the musicians still needed several days to regain their self-confidence. The time remaining in the engagement was spent getting to know one another and resolving some technical problems in musical placement. In fact, thanks to these explosive moments, the bonds of friendship within the orchestra grew tighter. When Lester was not jamming all night in a Chicago nightclub with Jo Jones and their new friend, Roy Eldridge, he was either in the company of Buck Clayton or that of Herschel Evans, whose personality he grew to appreciate more and more.

The Young-Evans relationship is often presented in terms of a deep rivalry, a real enmity, according to some. Yet this notion is false; the only source of discord among them was their concept of the instrument. Evans was a follower of Hawkins, as was Chu Berry. It is apparent that there was a certain distrust when they first began to play in the Basie orchestra, a certain mutual suspicion, concerning the role each was to assume.

The stroke of genius on Basie's part consisted of having matched these two opposite musical personalities, who were constantly trying to surpass each other for recognition. They both had their fits of pride and their tantrums, but by living and working together, Evans and Young learned how to understand each other better, how to appreciate each other, and finally how to be good friends.

> A quarrel between Herschel and Lester? It was more like a quarrel between two brothers. I was always a kind of messenger between them. . . . I was always trying to get them together in a cafe or a restaurant. . . . In a way, most of the time they were like twins (Jo Jones).

Lester's decision to hold the saxophone at a forty-five-degree angle must be attributed to the outbursts of pride he experienced so often in his youth. "Since Mr. Evans absolutely wants to play in that manner—read: loudly á la Hawkins—since he wants to be noticed and to capture the attention of the public, I am going to hold my instrument so that it is the first thing people see when they look at the orchestra." Footnoting this image probably ought to be the fact that Lester was afraid of not being heard. By slanting his saxophone in that way and by projecting it forward, he believed that the sound was not smothered by the orchestra and reached the audience more freely.

This awkward pose, this impression of levitation on Lester's part, though in no way delivering a better sound from his instrument, did enable him to attract attention. Better yet, as we shall see, his pose was to engender a curious epidemic. . . . The regional press was the first to notice it at the time:

> If you have seen the famous Basie orchestra, the musician who most certainly stood out first before your eyes was Lester Young. He sits a little slumped over, in a strange position at the end of the saxophone section, and seems completely absorbed in his part. When he advances for a solo, you begin to notice something unusual about this fabulous gentleman with the round face. He holds his sax crosswise, nearly horizontally, and plays in the direction of the ceiling.

Such was the way in which Lester was first depicted. The "fractured" neck, the sax borne in quasi-mystical ecstasy (an albatross, they called it), the search for recognition of his completely rethought style of music. And it was original.

Chapter 11

Perfect Harmony

The Basie orchestra gave several concerts, including a series in New London, Connecticut, on its way to New York, where it was to open December 24 at the Roseland Ballroom in tandem with Woody Herman. It was at that time that Lester and Herschel Evans initiated their musical jousting matches. From then on, each began to garner growing numbers of admirers—both at the heart of the orchestra, and among the audience—who made their presence known at every opportunity.

The orchestra's reputation had preceded the musicians themselves in getting to New York, and tickets to their opening performance at the Roseland were in great demand. The owners were anxious about how things might go, and the press was ready to fire its biggest guns. On that night several musicians made an appearance. Among them was Billie Holiday, who had come to see Lester again. Also, there were Benny Goodman, who had come to encourage the new stars of the moment, and Teddy Wilson, a talent scout and admirer of Young.

It was they who madly began to applaud whenever there was a moment of hesitation, hoping to sway both the public and the press with their enthusiasm. And when Lester played his parts for clarinet, Goodman would rush to the stage and oblige the audience to react.

Despite these efforts, their welcome was only lukewarm. Theirs was not exactly the dance music the public was expecting. Other than Basie, Jones, and Buck, the musicians were found to be unconvincing and, what's more, scarcely confident in their own music. The press, for its part, was intrigued. As the days went by, the press even conceded that the orchestra had a certain air about it and that several musicians were endowed with a certain originality. John Hammond praised Basie in *down beat* and underlined the fact that Lester was "undoubtedly the greatest tenor in the country," a belief which most did not share.

New York was not Kansas City; Lester had to convince a public accustomed to the perfectly arranged music of Fletcher Henderson, to the opulent style of Coleman Hawkins, and to the majesty of Duke Ellington. What was the utterly unexpressionistic Lester Young after? Why was he so sparing with the notes which he concealed his vibrato behind? Why did he follow them up with groups of four notes almost obsessively? Why did he lapse into that deep, spare, slightly lackluster sound? It sounded like an alto. But after a week of still unanswered questions, the audience began to enjoy listening to the orchestra, and decided it wasn't so bad after all.

Less preoccupied now with listener reaction, the musicians began paying more attention to the atmosphere that reigned in the Roseland Ballroom. They quickly noticed that black patrons were turned away at the door and that if the Puerto Ricans were not actually shown out, they could find no bartender willing to serve them. As for the "taxi girls," they scorned all but the white and wealthy patrons. Consequently, once their act was over, most of the musicians—the group consisting of Basie, Walter Page, Jo Jones, Buck, Herschel, and Lester—would hurry over to the Savoy Ballroom in Harlem to finish up the night "with the kinfolk."

Soon every musician and jazz aficionado in Harlem was heading for the Savoy to attend the jam sessions during which the Count, Lester, and his "rival" Herschel would outdo themselves, each with a cheering section of his own.

It was in that club, during the wee hours of the morning, that their plans were discussed. Following a suggestion made by John Hammond, Billie and Lester looked forward to recording together. Lester, with a slight note of resignation in his voice, explained to his friend that he would soon be having money problems. He wasn't making a very good living, and the manager of the hotel where he was staying demanded a week's rent in advance. "Don't worry," Billie would answer, "things will work out in the end."

And so, as if Basie had heard her and wished to help these two people get closer, he suggested to Billie that she join his band as a response to Jimmy Rushing. They could open jointly at the Apollo, one of Leo Brecker's clubs, he said. They needed to talk to Willard Alexander about it. He in turn found it to be an excellent idea and promised he would take care of the matter.

Lester's first record was at that time freshly out on the New York market. But despite intense promotion by John Hammond and by Brunswick it enjoyed only moderate success. Still, for all those who had heard Lester, it was confirmation of the genius they had sensed in him. Art Bronson congratulated himself for having had the fortunate initiative; Buster Smith longed for the days of the Blue Devils; Mary Lou Williams smiled when she recalled that famous night in December 1933 when Lester Young had won out over Coleman Hawkins. . . . But aside from a few musicians like Dick Wilson or Herschel Evans, the rank and file of tenor saxophonists turned its attentions elsewhere.

On January 21, 1937, as stipulated in the contract offered by the Decca Company, every member of the Basie orchestra filed into the company studio to record the band's first selections; present were Joe Keyes, Tatti Smith, and Buck Clayton on trumpet; George Hunt and Dan Minor on trombone; Couchie Roberts, Herschel Evans, Jack Washington, and Lester Young on sax; Count Basie on piano; Walter Page on bass; Claude Williams on guitar; Jo Jones on drums; and Jimmy Rushing as vocalist. No sooner were the four tunes in the can, however, than Basie realized that something was wrong. The percussionist had done his job, but that was all; as for Lester and the other soloists, they had shown neither conviction nor enthusiasm. There was no other choice for Basie than to change the makeup of the band.

Two of the four numbers they recorded did receive excellent reviews in the trade papers: "Honeysuckle Rose" and "Roseland Shuffle," a variant of "Shoe Shine Boy."

At that time, the band's repertoire consisted primarily of borrowings, that is, of ideas lifted from the repertoires of other orchestras that Basie and his musicians would rework and develop. This was the case with "Honeysuckle Rose" and it would be with "Jumpin' at the Woodside," "Swingin' the Blues," and others. At another level, some melodies like "Lady Be Good" and "Shoeshine Boy" became a wellspring from which they later extracted ideas for new tunes. Finally, the so-called original compositions emerged from reworking the assorted riffs that were peculiar to the styles of all the different soloists.

On the evening of that first recording session, Lester, Jo, Walter, Buck, Basie, and Hammond submerged themselves in Greenwich Village and entered the Black Cat club where Lonnie Simmons, Frank Clarke, Bobby Moore, Kenny Clarke, and guitarist Freddie Green were performing. Lester was able to restrain himself for only ten minutes; he then strode onstage and suggested they hold a jam session and, without waiting for an answer, pulled out his saxophone, his metal clarinet, and began to play. And while Basie was assuming his position at the piano, Kenny turned his sticks over to Jo Jones. A few minutes later, Harry James, Lionel Hampton, and Benny Goodman joined their friends on the stage; that's when Benny asked Lester whether he'd like to try his clarinet. And by the end of the evening, Basie had suggested that Freddie Green come replace Claude Williams in his orchestra following the Roseland Ballroom engagement.

As it happened, Freddie Green and Lester Young, who did not know each other personally, had a mutual friend: Billie Holiday. They also had a mutual admirer, pianist Teddy Wilson. And it was with the help of Wilson that Hammond set up the January 25 encounter which resulted in the first joint recording session of Teddy Wilson, Billie Holiday, and Lester Young.[63] The American Record Company, which was the principal supplier of juke-box records, quickly took interest in John Hammond's idea of adding a few of the Basie musicians to the Holiday-Wilson duet—the duet had already made several records that could be heard in every Harlem bar. That day the Teddy Wilson Orchestra consisted of Buck Clayton, Benny Goodman, Freddie Green, Walter Page, Jo Jones, Billie Holiday, and Lester Young; it recorded four numbers: "He Ain't Got Rhythm"—which appears on the soundtrack of the movie *On the Avenue*—"This Year's Kisses," "Why Was I Born?" and "I Must Have That Man."

> I had a recording date, my first recording date with Billie Holiday. . . . With Teddy, Buck Clayton and Lester. . . . I expected it to be a really hard thing, you know. But, then we walked in, and Billie would walk in with her own music, you know. Nothing written out, just a piano copy. Songs she'd put on the top of the piano, and Teddy would run over it. And we would go on with it. . . . And, we taped the first chorus and Lester would come in on it. . . . we didn't do many takes on it. (Freddie Green)[64]

From a historical and musical standpoint, this recording had, in many respects, the same importance as the one Lester had made in Chicago. These four melodies testify to the real osmosis which characterized the musical relationship between Billie and Lester from the beginning. The affective vulnerability of each, and of each for the other, was translated into music, became music. Lester's sax followed the lyrics and enveloped Billie's words; they demonstrated the same inspired ability to toy with the melody which, more so than the harmony, was Lester's field of choice. At the conclusion of this session, Billie no longer wanted to record without Lester's participation.

After that—and this is not meant to be critical of the pianist—the best recordings she herself made were those pressed under her own "Billie Holiday Orchestra" label, not those in which she was a participant with Teddy Wilson. Many of his are doubtlessly remarkable, but in them Billie is too often confined to a role of simple accompanist.

After hiring Freddie Green, Basie decided to replace Tatti Smith and Joe Keyes with Ed Lewis and Bobby Moore; in the meantime, Eddie Durham—trombone and guitar player and arranger—had promised to come strengthen the formation in a few months. Shortly before the end of the Roseland Ballroom engagement, Willard Alexander signed a contract for the Basie orchestra, featuring Billie Holiday as special guest performer, with the owner of the Apollo Theater. Before the first night's performance, which was scheduled to take place March 19, 1937, Willard sent the orchestra to Pittsburgh; this left him with just enough time to organize a gigantic publicity campaign at the expense of the Harlem nightclub.

Inside the bus taking them to the William Penn Hotel in Pittsburgh, where, around mid-February they would become the first black musicians to perform, sat Walter Page, Jo Jones, Freddie Green, the Count, Herschel Evans, Lester Young, Jack Washington, Couchie Roberts, Dan Minor, George Hunt, Buck Clayton, Bobby Moore, Ed Lewis, and violinist Claude Williams, for whom these were the last days of playing with the band. Once again their reception was cool. The audience was expecting hit songs of the day, and Basie was obliged to modify somewhat the program to satisfy its demands. Willard had given him advice to that effect, saying, "Hang in there. The important thing is to play; some of these performances will be rebroadcast on the radio. This, and nothing but this is what matters: to make yourselves known, and ultimately recognized."

And their performances did indeed go out over the air. (A number of the tapings survived and many years later the Jazz Archives label put a few selections out on the market; today, they tend to be seen somewhat as oddities). Before leaving Pittsburgh, the orchestra performed at a few more dances in the area. It was during one of these evening concerts that Couchie Roberts informed Basie of his intentions to leave the group. The Count immediately called Earl Warren in, making him the first white musician of the band.

> I remember the first time I worked with Basie; I had a number entitled "Where Are You?" and behind me, the whole band would get up and sing in unison. Instead of singing, Lester got up with his hands behind his back and his lips pursed, and stood on the tip of his toes imitating someone who was singing his heart out. The entire band cracked up, and the audience couldn't tell that he wasn't singing. Me, I broke out in a cold sweat; I couldn't stand to be made fun of! On another occasion, Basie came up with a brilliant idea: from then on, at the end of each performance everyone was supposed to join in a chorus of "Good Night Everybody." But during the finale Lester did so much clowning around that Basie got mad because the audience thought it was a comic number, this after we had just "done them in" with our music (Earl Warren).[65]

Before returning to Harlem, the orchestra gave a number of other performances in nearby states, including one at the Ritz Roof of Boston that established its reputation in the region once and for all.

Chapter 12

Reproaches

On the evening of March 19, 1937, three different audiences responded to Willard Alexander's rallying call to appear at the Apollo Theater: big band devotees, Billie Holiday admirers, and the handful of fans that Lester Young then had. It was a polite success for Basie, but for Billie Holiday—who already enjoyed a certain popularity in Harlem's black community—it was a veritable triumph. And her success with the audience that night was due in large part to the man who had outdone himself giving her musical support: Lester Young.

Lester did not go unnoticed. The audience wondered about his strange posture; when he rose to perform a solo after buttoning up his jacket and approached the main microphone, he bent his neck to the side, his saxophone stretched forward as if attached to an imaginary string. The younger spectators rose to their feet and began shouting to encourage him, and for many, this odd behavior clearly signified that something extraordinary was happening on stage.

Still more astonishing was the response of the young people outside the Apollo. The image of this odd-mannered musician spread through the streets of Harlem.[66] In less than forty-eight hours, dozens of kids were roaming the sidewalks around the Apollo neighborhood in groups of three or four, assuming the "Lester pose," their necks askew, their hands darting up and down an imaginary instrument. At night, still holding that pose, they would gather at the doors of the theater and look enviously at the spectators who would shortly be applauding the man whose name most of those children didn't even know!

Having been won over by Lester, Billie Holiday resolved to give him a nickname that conveyed her gratitude and affection.

> When it came to a name for Lester, I always felt he was the greatest, so his name had to be the greatest. In this country kings or counts or dukes don't amount to nothing. The greatest man around then was Franklin D. Roosevelt and he was president. So I started calling him the President. It got shortened to Prez, but it still means what it was meant to mean—the top man in this country . . . I loved his music, and some of my favorite records are the ones with Lester's pretty solos. . . . Lester sings with his horn; you listen to him and can almost hear the words. . . . (Billie Holiday)[67]

A week after the opening, Basie's musicians recorded four new numbers for Decca. After that, Lester participated in 105 recording sessions with Basie for Decca and Columbia. He is also listed on 50 of Billie's Vocalion labels and on a good number of those completed by Teddy Wilson for Brunswick before his unsuccessful attempt to form a big band in April 1939.[68]

After a series of concerts at the Savoy Ballroom, Lester and Billie left for an East Coast tour with the Basie orchestra. A bus, loads of instruments, close friendships, an occasional rivalry, a little success, a little excess, alcohol, drugs. . . . Lester rediscovered the touring atmosphere he had so enjoyed in the days of the Blue Devils. He had his own reserved seat in the back of the bus; from there he could see every move made by his companions, and he never missed an opportunity to kid them. At night, when the bus was crossing the slumbering countryside, he would sing, and if anyone commented on it, he would candidly ask, "You don't like my singing, lady?"

In fact, "Lady" was what he started calling every musician! Lady Jones, Lady Green. He also found nicknames for everyone.

In fact, the idea was not new to him. A few weeks before, when the orchestra was performing at the Apollo, Lester had spent hours sitting in a chair in the lobby of what would soon become the band's command post, the Woodside Hotel. The Pres had been mulling over the nicknames he could pin on the musicians. And when he saw Harry Edison walk up to the desk one evening, he hurried over to him, put his hand on his shoulder, and looking him straight in the eye, solemnly advised him, "From this day forward we're going to call you 'Sweetie Pie.'" That is how each musician earned a nickname which, in Lester's opinion, fit his personality.

Freddie Green became Pepper, or Squires. Next came Samson for Jo Jones. Then Rags and Big D for Ed Lewis. It became Smiley for Earl Warren, Tex for Herschel Evans, and Weasel for Jack Washington. For Walter Page it was Big-Un, while the Saint, Holy, or Groundhog were reserved for Basie. Moon went to Buddy Tate, Cat Eye to Buck Clayton, and Homey to Helen Humes. Emmet Berry got "Rev," and Little Jim or Honey Bunny Boo went to Jimmy Rushing. Eli Robinson was Mr. Eli; Jimmy Powell's tag was Neat; George Matthews became Truce; and Snooky Young went by Rabbit. Dickie Wells was Gas Belly before he became Mr. Clickers, or Bones; and Benny Morton turned into Morton Gable because of his resemblance to Clark Gable. It was on one of their return trips to New York that the Pres called Billie "Lady Day" for the first time.

> . . . it started in Baltimore. . . . We were leaving the Royal Theater and you know how we used to go in the back to get food, in the house. So we were sitting in the bus to get the food and Freddie Green was sitting with Lady Day. Some guys were

having fun. They had been on Pennsylvania Avenue and they come in and they was using all kind of language. I said, "Wait a minute. You guys can't do that. There's a lady present." So Lester Young and Buck Clayton always sat in the back of the bus, so Lester busts out laughing and says, "What do you mean, lady?" I said, "There's a lady in here. You guys can't do that." So right away he says, "Lady Day." (Jo Jones)[69]

At the end of that first tour, the orchestra once again set off on the studio trail, recording a tune on July 7 that quickly became both a hit and its trademark: "One O'Clock Jump."

I'll tell you how the *One O'Clock Jump* came about. . . . Basie always liked to fool around in different keys every night. One night he was playing along in F (that's his favorite key), and then he took that modulation into C sharp. He looked at me and said, "Set something, Prof," so I started playing that saxophone riff. Lips (Page) set something for the brass, and pretty soon we had it going. We played it for about 30 minutes, and the crowd liked it, so we played it again the next night the same way.

It got its name because of a radio broadcast one night down in Little Rock. We had it on the program lineup, but the name we had on it was one you couldn't use over the air ["Blue Balls"]. The broadcast lasted until one o'clock, so the announcer suggested we call it *One O'Clock Jump*.

It was my tune, but I only wrote one part for it—that was a saxophone part for Jack Washington because the fourth harmony was hard to hear. After Lips and I left the band, Jack taught the new guys their parts. When they recorded it later in New York, they put Count Basie's name on it, and when it became popular, Buck Clayton wrote the arrangement down. . . . I figure I got $5.40 for it. When I saw Basie later, he said, "I don't want you suing me so I'll give you $5, and we'll drink this fifth of gin." (Buster Smith)[70]

According to Ross Russell,

One O'Clock Jump . . . is typical of many jazz compositions. The key phrase originated with pianist Fats Waller. It was reworked and recorded in 1929 by arranger Don Redman, then writing for the Chocolate Dandies, and titled *Six or Seven Times*. A later recording was made by the McKinney Cotton Pickers with whom Redman was associated. Buster Smith heard it on a McKinney recording but only the introduction stuck in his mind.[71]

It was around this time that the public began to appreciate the soloists in Basie's band, and Lester, for his part, owed what success he was enjoying to the handful of ballads that he was permitted to play. One thing seems significant: people no longer came to Basie's performances only to dance, but also to listen. Despite the general enthusiasm, Lester still felt a certain reticence about it. And even though Herschel Evans and Lester became good friends, there remained between them a slight rivalry that was exploited by both men's enemies.

> . . . Herschel had his group. Lester had his group of fans, and when Lester would play, his group would, you know, cheer him on. And then Herschel would play and his group would do the same. And, I think the audiences all over the country, more or less, was aware of this fact, and—that was it. (Freddie Green)[72]

> Herschel was a Hawkins man. That was the difference in our ways of playing. He played well, but his man was Hawk, like mine was Trumbauer. We were good friends and all that, but what I'm trying to say is that there wasn't any shit between us. When we'd get on the stage to play it was like a duel; on other nights, no, it was laid back. You see what I'm trying to say? But essentially, it all stemmed from his way of playing. (Lester Young)

> Lester Young and Herschel Evans in the original Count Basie Band demonstrated two different approaches to the same material. Young developed a light, airy sound on the tenor saxophone which used little vibrato, while Evans developed a heavier, more resonant sound which used a wide vibrato similar to that traditionally used by many black choir singers. Young's style was the fountainhead for the cool style of jazz which would appear two generations later. His subtle lyrical *concepts* style paved the way

for many generations to follow. Evans's style was his personal contribution to the tenor saxophone vocabulary developed by Coleman Hawkins, Chu Berry, and others. Evans's playing was an excellent example of the melodic, harmonic, and rhythmic approach of swing players. (Billy Taylor)[73]

Evans' attire was always so impeccable that people would mistake him for a lawyer. One night he took Lester to one side and jokingly asked him, "Why the heck don't you play alto?" Pres gave him a long incredulous look, and then, with a hint of disdain playing at the corners of his mouth, he pointed at his head and said, "Man, you're never going to understand a thing. There are things happening in here." But that remark, added to other, meaner ones, vexed him. And during jam sessions, he would often notice a tendency among the saxophonists to provoke and ridicule him.

One night, in fact, during a jam session that brought together saxophonists Chu Berry, Benny Carter, Bobby Henderson, and others, Chu decided to have done with Lester once and for all, proposing that they play "I Got a Rhythm," then one of Lester's favorite tunes. Pres didn't have to be asked twice, and went on to play his heart out, forcing Chu and his friends to leave the club in a big hurry.

But then the Pres suddenly decided: "I am going to have a big tone, too."

> . . . this talk about a big tone messed with Lester for months. And me too. So I said, "What the hell, Lester, don't let them make a fool of us. We'll get you a big horn with big fat reeds and things and no damn rubber bands around it holding you back. We'll get us a tone."
>
> So every time Lester could get a dime together he'd get some more reeds and start cutting them up all kinds of different ways. He got him a new horn, too, and thought that would end him up with a big fat growl. But his tone never got any bigger. He wasn't meant to sound like Chu and he soon gave up trying. (Billie Holiday)[74]

The fact that Lester should suddenly decide to achieve a "big" tone with his instrument marked the first true break in his personality. After the paternal conflicts, the hazings in Kansas City, the humiliations within the Fletcher Henderson Orchestra, and the obvious animosity of the East Coast musicians during their jam sessions, there came for Lester a brief moment of doubt in his own playing. He thought he could "improve" his tone without changing his style. He thought this "improvement" would put him on a par with Coleman Hawkins and that from then on he would enjoy the same general acclaim.

But the Pres quickly realized that he could not change his tone, and that the one he possessed formed an integral part of his style; to change the one would be to change the other. And in any case, he did not have the kind of personality that was suited for such an about-face. Unable to change his playing, he went about changing his defense mechanism. Rather than confront a hostile world, Lester chose to beat a slow retreat. In an effort to protect himself, he would soon find refuge in alcohol, drugs, and enigmatic forms of expression.

> . . . Lester was a loner to people who didn't know him, and he only—he kept himself restricted to the people he wanted to know. He only got warm with people he wanted to know, because most of the people didn't understand the music, and didn't appreciate him and showed signs of it, so he rebelled against it.
>
> But a musician who could play fairly well, or who was good enough to make an impression on him, or that he liked to play with, and he heard something he liked, he was very warm. He was not the same cold person that he seemed to be to other people. (Sir Charles Thompson)[75]

Despite all his personal problems, the tour went on.

Every night we would come into town, we'd take a room, we'd shave and take a long look at the bed. Then we'd go to work, come back to the room, give the bed one last look and climb back into the bus. (Lester Young)

The musicians earned very little and had to pay for their own room and board. For Billie, who had joined the orchestra to earn money, these conditions were becoming less and less satisfactory. What little savings she did have, she gave to Lester, who turned right around and gambled them away when all the musicians got together in the bus. She complained to Basie and got a raise; from then on she earned $15; Lester earned $18.50. One day she couldn't take it any more and quit the tour to join Artie Shaw's band; but a few weeks later she came back to the Basie fold.

Unsettled by her departure, Pres began to drink and shut himself up in a room in the Teresa Hotel. He would only come out to meet with Billie, Herschel, or Jo Jones. Lester was to have some unusual experiences in that run-down hotel. One night he found a rat in one of the dresser drawers of his room; he tried to catch it and show it to the manager for some sort of compensation, but the creature escaped between his legs. A few days later drummer Hal West—who was then staying at the same hotel—applied some relaxer to his hair. When he got ready to rinse it off, however, he noticed that their running water had just been cut off. Because the product was beginning to burn his scalp, he ran to Lester's room. Lester saw no other remedy for it than to plunge his friend's head into the toilet bowl. That was when Billie Holiday, in true ladylike fashion, invited him to come live with her.

> Early one morning, after one of these jam sessions folded, Lester went back to Mom's with me to get some of her early breakfast specials. He had been living at a well-known Harlem hotel, and he was almost a nervous wreck from *that*. . . . "Duchess, can I move in with you?" . . . Mom gave him a room and he moved in with us.
>
> Ours was a big old flat, two flights up, with two entrances off the hallway. The front door was my bedroom, with a door opening to the hall and a little room off it we used to call my playroom, where I kept my records and a beat-up old piano. In the back was the living room and Mom's room. In the middle, off the air shaft, were Lester's quarters.
>
> It wasn't fancy, but it beat that damn hotel. And for Mom

and me it was wonderful having a gentleman around the house. Lester was always that.

Lester was the first to call Mom "Duchess"—and it turned out to be the title she carried to her grave.[76]

Lester's spirits quickly improved. He felt surrounded by people who appreciated him and listened to him. His feelings of loneliness slowly evaporated. In the Holidays' apartment he behaved as discreetly as possible. He was considerate toward the Duchess, offering to walk her to the store, and spent long hours listening to her talk about her life. Whenever she prepared those special breakfasts which delighted their circle of musical friends, Lester made sure to put everyone at ease and to direct the conversation in such a way that she would not feel too unfamiliar with the topics.

At the end of the day, before rejoining the orchestra, Lester would throw dice on the kitchen table with Billie and her mother. How he was to handle the instrument, what he would learn during the coming night, everything was revealed to him by the throw of the dice, which for him were much more than tokens of fun. But he would shrug his shoulders if you said anything about superstition to him. "Duchess" would talk to her friends about this mild-mannered, agreeable man who smoked more than he should, but who understood people so well. Those who knew them both wondered at the fact that such a friendly young man had no adventurous flings with women. Perhaps Billie and he. . . . No, she was the Grand Musical Lady, his friend, his confidante, she could not be his lover. Billie thought she had found the man of her life in Artie Shaw. Lester hoped that she was right, but they spoke little of the matter, and when the right moment came, they laughed about it together.

Life went on, serenely, uneventfully. Lester was making records with Basie and Lady Day, and also participating in jam sessions at the Plantation Cafe with Basie, Herschel, and Jo Jones. He got back together with Sammy Price, too, who was now director of the Jazz Festival Society of Philadelphia. With a friend's help, Price had bought a club to hold the festival jam sessions in. Price produced a huge concert at the Academy of Music to which he invited Lester; then he persuaded him to attend a "battle" of the saxophones at the Town Hall.

Back at the apartment in Harlem, Lester would find his clothes washed and ironed. He always paid his share of the expenses, but he was oblivious to the bills; such matters were alien to him. He sincerely wanted to ask the two women out to a restaurant, but worried that the Duchess might take the invitation the wrong way, she who was such a marvelous cook and who never hesitated to fix him the kinds of spicy dishes customary in his native South, the ones that made his forehead break out in a sweat. . . .

He never quite knew how to demonstrate his gratitude. Whenever he discovered that one of his ladyfriends was daydreaming, though, he would discretely grab his tenor and play a few notes of "I Can't Get Started" as an accompaniment to the imaginary voyage being made.

But outside of the concerts and rehearsals, the only joint activities in which the musicians participated were a few short softball games in Central Park during which Lester did his best on the diamond. Sometimes the opposing team was an entire big band, that of Duke Ellington for example, or else simply a lineup of other musicians who enjoyed baseball. They were quite a sight, all in pants and light shirts, the more dedicated ones wearing jerseys inscribed with their names or the numbers of their favorite professional players. After shaking hands, they would decide who was going to umpire—it always turned out to be Basie and Walter Page—then they flipped to see who would go to bat first.

From time to time, Lester allowed himself some moments of solitude; he would hang around the bars in Harlem, or submerge himself occasionally in the red light districts. One day, together with Billie, he discovered the effects of marijuana. Another musician happened to discover the two of them, huddled like truant children, in a room so full of smoke that it was practically impossible to breathe. From then on there were certain musicians and journalists who, succumbing to their taste for sensationalism, would portray the relationship between Lester and Billie as unhealthy.

Not long after that, prompted by his friends, Lester let his hair grow long and grew a thin moustache. On one of his evening outings, he met a young nurse of Italian descent named Mary. For days after that, they were seen everywhere together. And when Lester went on the road with Basie again, Mary waited patiently for him. A month later, while performing at the Famous Door, Lester decided to move in with Mary. He needed to share his life with someone who could understand him. Lester hoped at last to have found the deep-seated emotional bond to which he felt entitled.

Chapter 13

Source and Spirit

Lester moved out of Billie's apartment and settled in with Mary at the Woodside Hotel in Harlem. But he promised the Duchess he would still come regularly to see her. A few days later he made one recording with Teddy Wilson for Brunswick and another with Billie Holiday for Vocalion. January 16, he agreed to be a part of Benny Goodman's Carnegie Hall Concert, both as a sideman in Basie's band, and as soloist in Goodman's orchestra. At the end of their performance, Goodman persuaded most of the musicians to join him at the Savoy, where Ella Fitzgerald and Chick Webb were performing. Webb was considered the club's "big boss" and no one, certainly no musician, had ever dared to challenge him.

But with Basie and his band, things went differently. Lester and Billie sensed a potential jam session as soon as they arrived. Even Benny Goodman called Webb over and asked him if he would agree to "a little jousting match, just for kicks." As the musicians took their places, Basie got some encouragement and a few tips from Duke Ellington, who had just arrived; Billie kept throwing curious looks in Ella's direction; Lester went about selecting and adjusting his reeds, as relaxed as could be. Then, for nearly two hours the musicians jammed with all their might. But when the time came for the audience to choose a winner, the results were inconclusive. In the end, the consensus was that the musicians were all of equal caliber and that they were the best in the city. From that moment on, Basie and his musicians were considered an integral part of the New York scene, and one month later to the day—February 16, 1938—they recorded their second success, "Swingin' the Blues," after renewing their Decca contract for one year only and on much better financial terms.

It was at this session that Lester appeared for the first time wearing his broad black felt hat, creating the second popular image that the public would remember. A hatter with a shop on Eighth Avenue had created it especially for him. Lester had entered his shop one morning and brought out a photograph of women wearing clothes from the Victorian period. He asked the hatter if he could duplicate the hats, without the ribbons, in black.

That was when Lester emerged with his new hat. The felt hat became almost as popular as his music. Viewed by its owner as a comfortable and unique plaything, it was photographed both alone and as an accessory in still-life portraits, alongside the saxophone and the inevitable empty bottle. It was sketched, described, commented upon, and analyzed. How could people overlook the soloist in Count Basie's orchestra after that? Lester and his oblique stance, Lester and his felt hat. . . .

A few days after that session, Billie left the Basie band for good. From that moment on, the relationship between the Pres and Lady Day gradually lost its intensity and their musical appearances together became less and less frequent; when they did work together, however, their rapport remained astonishingly deep and true. As for Basie, he immediately set out in search of another female vocalist. One night, while attending a singing contest at the Apollo, he was charmed by the beauty and voice of the second-place contestant. He sought her out in her dressing room and after a short conversation, suggested she take part in the band's next rehearsal. Within three days he had hired her; Helen Humes would remain with Basie until 1942.

In the meantime, Benny Goodman continued to demonstrate his support and admiration for Lester and the Count. On March 9, 1938, Goodman invited Lester to come and record six tunes with his orchestra, encouraging him at the same time to continue working on his clarinet. More than likely, that was what inspired Lester to record "Blue and Sentimental" with Basie on June 6, a session in which he outdoes himself on his metal clarinet. Another title, "Doggin' Around," demonstrates not only Basie's melodic ideas, but also the rhythmic freedom that Lester indulged in, a freedom which revelled in accentuating the beats at will, beginning his phrasing in mid-measure and prolonging or interrupting it to suit his notion of the melody. Along with the rhythm and the melody, one also senses a nascent concern with form that is at the same time intent on revision. All of this produced a new musical logic that was developing during the first recording sessions of 1936. Yet by 1938 it was scarcely being acknowledged or accepted.

Indefatigable in his efforts, Goodman set about lining up Basie for a Madison Square Garden performance on the night of June 12, an event which Goodman wanted identified as a performance by "[the] Count Basie Kansas City Killers." Unfortunately, his plans did not work out; the Basie name did not appear on the tickets and was hardly visible on the publicity posters. It was Goodman who got star billing instead—and who pocketed twenty-five hundred dollars for the evening—whereas the Count received just four hundred dollars (not counting the accolades), and his musicians even less. But speaking strictly in musical terms, the evening was a total success. After a series of choruses on "Time Out," which was then one of the band's most accomplished pieces, Lester received an ovation for well over a minute from three thousand people. He seemed amazed.

After the Madison Square Garden concert, Lester and Basie had the feeling that they were marking time. Whether in New

York or in other states, they were performing in the same places and for the same audiences. They needed to find a quick means of acquiring a national reputation and a broader audience. Willard Alexander suggested they return to the Famous Door. Why not? In July, the orchestra opened, with new recruit Dickie Wells, at the club, which measured about five hundred square feet in all; they thought they would be staying three or four weeks. They barely grossed thirteen hundred dollars in a week, but the musicians were satisfied. One or two sets were being broadcast every day by a New York radio station.

They were a smashing success. By the third night, people were being turned away at the door. Patrons would line up on the sidewalk an hour before opening time, and when told that all the seats were taken, fifty or more would still wait outside in hopes of getting in.

Fifty-second Street quickly became a subject of conversation. The Famous Door, Basie, and his musicians were making headlines. Their engagement was extended until the end of October. Success so sapped their energies, however, that only four titles were recorded with Decca during their stay at the club. Among them were Basie's third hit, "Jumpin' at the Woodside," and "Texas Shuffle," where Lester's clarinet is again to be heard. At the club itself, though, about a dozen recordings were made.

Lester's importance was steadily growing. A good part of the audience came especially to hear him. He knew this and allowed himself to be stimulated by the applause. He thought back to the days of the Blue Devils when he played for an audience of dancers. To him, both experiences were equally pleasurable.

> In a concert, I'll play in a variety of tempos. I establish my own beat, taking my time as I go. I wish we played jazz for dancing more often. I take a lot of pleasure in playing for dancers because I like to dance myself. The rhythm of the dancers comes back to you on stage when you're playing. That forces you to keep the beat right. After three or four different tempos, you finally find the one they appreciate. . . . (Lester Young)

Within the group, the musicians were according him more and more respect. Lester brought something completely new to the band; he played and improvised as no one, before or since, has ever done.

In September, Lester took a short break and cut a record with Buck Clayton, Eddie Durham, Freddie Green, Walter Page, and Jo Jones under the name of "The Kansas City Six." Together, they recorded five tunes on which Pres used his clarinet; he was able then to enjoy the sort of freedom that he lacked in the Basie band.

"Way down Yonder in New Orleans" had previously been recorded by Trumbauer and Beiderbecke, two musicians admired by Lester. At this point, the tune was one of his favorites; it enabled him to pick up on a few of Tram's ideas and to add some of his own. A first cut without Lester had originally been produced in March by John Hammond, but was turned down by the American Record Company. It was finally accepted for Commodore by Milt Gabler, on condition that it be redone with Lester on the clarinet. Gabler was a fervent admirer of Pres's clarinet style, especially following his recording, two weeks earlier, of "The Texas Shuffle" with Basie.

The songs, "Countless Blues," "Pagin' the Devil," "Way down Yonder in New Orleans," and "I Want a Little Girl," are perfect examples of Pres's genius at reinventing tradition. This type of reinterpretation reached its fullest scope when Lester played the clarinet. The writer Martin Williams is quite justified in describing this as a new version of New Orleans jazz and Dixieland music. As an example, he cites the marvelous clarinet and trumpet duo found in "Way Down. . . . "

Indeed, Lester Young was the most astonishing clarinetist in the history of jazz. The sound of his clarinet, like that of his tenor sax, shocks the ear. He used a metal instrument whose sound differs totally from that of a wooden clarinet. The sound in no way resembles the sound of others of that time, just as no others to follow resemble it. The sonority is tenuous, light, delicate, and subtle with a tender, crystalline purity. And then one day, though he protected it even more carefully than his tenor, someone stole that clarinet, making this recording even more of a gem.

Around the middle of September, Lester teamed up again with Billie Holiday for a Vocalion recording; he used his clarinet again for two of the titles: "The Very Thought of You," and "I've Got a Date with a Dream." But the most memorable score of the session is the masterful "I Can't Get Started," one of the first great ballads that Lester recorded. It is surprising to see him display such great economy with the notes; this later became the principal character-istic of his ballads and blues. This was the only session which included the great Kansas City pianist Margaret "Countess" Johnson, who died soon after of tuberculosis.

Taking to the road again with Basie after the Famous Door engagement, Lester revisited the Midwest. As in years past, the orchestra traveled alternately by bus and by train.[77] In the bus, Lester took care to reserve for himself a certain seat from which he could crack jokes and organize poker or dice games.

> [Lester was] the humorous guy in the band. . . . He had some humor that you never heard before, you know. Funny things that he sings, and what-not. . . . He would say things right off the top of his head, more or less, you know. And whatever it was—you would have to laugh. . . . he kept the whole bus laughing. . . . And, it was always a happy thing, you know, on the bus. Never a dull moment. . . . Buck and I used to be room-mates, and then Lester and I, and Sweets and I, you know, whatever the situation called. (Freddie Green)[78]

Helen Humes took care of the musicians as if they were her own children; they in turn kept themselves amused by keeping track of the romance she was having with Basie. Whenever she found an opportunity, she fixed the meals and ironed and mended the clothes. And she had her hands full on more than one occa-sion. When the orchestra went on tour for a series of single perfor-mances, for example, the musicians ended up staying only a few hours in a given city before hitting the road again, and after a dozen days of that routine, they would each be carrying several pounds of dirty laundry.

As a rule the band stayed in hotels reserved for blacks. If they drove in at dawn, the musicians were obliged to wait until 8:00 A.M. before they could register, to avoid paying for an extra night. In most towns the price of a room was about thirty-five cents. Lester was often the first to jump out of the bus in search of a hotel. Once he had chosen his room, he made himself at home and didn't take long to fall asleep, whereas the rest of the band would still be unloading the bulk of the instruments from the bus. It also happened that hotel owners, seeing the band arrive, would suddenly decide to raise the price by fifteen cents. Again, Lester would be the one to chime in, "Hey fellas, we're sure to find some poundcakes (girls) who'll take us in!" Although according to his brother, Lee, Lester remained monogamous, Buck Clayton spoke of Lester's regular flirtations. Lester himself remained discreet about the matter.

One morning on the bus, Lester announced to the musicians that he intended to buy a car, a Packard. He was also constantly organizing dice games. With his customary luck, though, he would find himself broke half an hour after the game had begun. Then he'd retire to the back of the bus and quietly go to sleep while the card game went on. Occasionally, he might wake up to find that everything had quieted down and his friends had fallen asleep. Lester was not one to give up, though. He would get on his feet, collect the dice, put them in the cup, and start shaking it near the sleeping musicians' ears while singing, "Sweet music, sweet music. . . . " When everyone was finally awake, he would reiterate his Packard idea and suggest another round of dice which, of course, he would again lose in about ten minutes. When he felt bold enough, Pres would turn to his friend Herschel and ask him for a few cents. Evans had succeeded in saving up some money over several months and when another musician needed some cash, he would lend him some at a low rate of interest. But this never kept Pres from losing every game, day after day, month after month.

He never got his Packard.

One morning when the band was traveling by train, the conductor made Earl Warren change cars. Racial mixing was not yet permitted on trains. Lester didn't say anything, but the incident upset him very much. He couldn't understand the reasoning that made certain individuals offend others. His sensibilities were such that he suffered personally when attacks were leveled at people he knew.

Incidents like the one with Earl Warren lead him slowly to distrust white producers, white orchestra leaders, white club owners, and white people in general. He was a solitary figure, isolated in a merciless deaf world. Confronted with that world, he would, within ten years, build himself the "hideaway" we are all familiar with and which still today, forty years later, remains the only image which many retain of him.

Back in New York, Basie and Lester were invited by John Hammond to participate in a mammoth concert at Carnegie Hall on December 23. Baptized "From Spiritual to Swing, an Evening of American Negro Music," the concert was being sponsored by *New Masses,* a newspaper with Marxist affiliations. A dozen groups or so came together for the occasion, featuring among others James P. Johnson, Pete Johnson, Meade Lux Lewis, Albert Ammons, Joe Turner, Sister Rosetta Tharpe, Sonny Terry, Big Bill Broonzy, Hot Lips Page, Sidney Bechet, Tommy Ladnier—for whom this would be the last public appearance—Helen Humes, and the Count. Lester appeared in Basie's band, of course, but also as a soloist in the Kansas City Six together with Buck Clayton, Dan Minor, Walter Page, Leonard Ware, and Jo Jones.[79]

The evening was a huge popular success, but not all of the critics were convinced. "Though it is indisputably quite capable, the Basie orchestra doesn't seem to have anything to say. . . . Page plays the trumpet well. He is one soloist who plays with finesse, a quality lacking in the rest of the orchestra."[80]

At the time, Lester was paying no attention whatsoever to

remarks of that kind; he was more concerned with his friend Herschel Evans, whose health had suddenly taken a turn for the worse. On several occasions, Lester told him to rest and not to worry, that they would find a saxophonist to take his place. But Herschel would not listen. On December 23, Pres was uneasy. He kept a constant eye on his friend, who nearly fainted several times while on stage. Lester walked him back to his hotel and asked Mary not to hold it against him if he preferred to ring out the old year with Herschel.

Chapter 14

The Rift

Herschel's health had steadily deteriorated over the past few months. Toward the end of December, he was having difficulty breathing, he was playing badly, and he looked like a tired old man, even though he was only thirty. Lester also looked ill, as if Herschel had become part of him. His features were drawn, his clothes were wrinkled, and he had been supporting Herschel at all times.

One night in Waterbury, Connecticut, Herschel could barely climb onstage by himself. He turned toward Lester and said, "Oh man! Do I ever feel sick!" While running through scales on his sax, he fainted and had to be carried to the dressing room and stretched out on a table. His chest sounded like a volcanic eruption. Lester called one of his friends in New York to come and get them in his car. Back in the city, Herschel insisted he not be taken to a hospital. He wanted to return to his hotel, where his girlfriend was supposed to join him. Lester said that he could give the girl a message, that it would be better to go directly to the hospital, but Herschel seemed so miserable that Lester did not insist.

The band went on with its schedule, and after a few more concerts, the musicians checked into Harlem's Woodside Hotel for several days of rest. Whenever possible, Pres paid his friend a visit; often he had to wait ten minutes before Herschel would open the door. One night, Lester became worried after getting no response and leaned down to peek through the keyhole. Evans was praying at the foot of his bed, crouching there as if he had collapsed onto his knees, and on top of the bed lay his tenor saxophone. When at last he opened the door for his friend, it was to say to him in a scarcely audible voice, "We can go to the hospital now."

A few hours after arriving at the hospital, Herschel died of cardiac arrest while Lester stood by devastated. For more than an hour he stayed with the body of that irreplaceable friend who had helped him so much, who had forced him to surpass himself during hundreds of concerts, and who had become part of him.

Pres paid the medical expenses, and back at the hotel, he collected Herschel's belongings and paid his last bills. When the musicians saw him arrive at the concert hall dragging a clothes bag and a sax case with the initials H. E. by his side, their conversation stopped. Alone, crossing the heavy silence, he headed for the sidewalk.

Another irreversible separation had just taken place. What Lester had done for Herschel Evans, he would never do again, not for anybody, not even for himself.

Seeing Chu Berry permanently take Evans' place, after he had already sat in for him on the previous February 2 Decca recording session, enraged and insulted Lester.[81] How could they replace a friend with an adversary? Hadn't Chu himself done his best to demonstrate that during numerous jam sessions? During the first few rehearsals, Lester made himself unbearable: his playing was heavy, disruptive, excluding any possibility of dialogue. No deal. Case closed. Berry was literally muzzled and was forced to quit. Pres was determined to show that no one could replace Herschel. Together, they had created some unique dynamics in the saxophone section. On subsequent days, Lester remained upset enough to imitate Herschel's blowing, playing the other's part on top of his own.

It wasn't long before he supplied the public with yet a third image. The orchestra members would be seated with the saxophone section in the foreground. They all wore their stage apparel: the light-colored, pleated pinstripe trousers rising well above the waist, similarly light-colored vests, white shirts, impeccably knotted black and white ties, black blazers reaching down to the middle of their thighs, and a white handkerchief in each breast pocket. Lester would rise and advance toward the mike—people would applaud—Lester would wet his lips and lift his instrument, his neck twisted as usual. Chorus. Lester leaps in. This time the President wore small, round horn-rimmed glasses with tinted lenses; he was cool, a beatnik before there were beatniks. This was how he projected himself onto the collective memory of the age.

News of Evans' death spread quickly in the jazz world and there were many applicants to replace him. After Chu's attempt, Lester discouraged one candidate after another. Basie understood his distress perfectly well and didn't insist. Nevertheless, he sent a telegram to Buddy Tate and set up a meeting with him in Kansas City, where the orchestra was soon to perform after a few concerts on the East Coast.

It was at the Booker T. Washington Hotel in Kansas City that Lester met up again with Buddy Tate. The two talked, and Lester urged Tate to try out for Herschel's seat.

After the first rehearsal, Basie was happy. He could appreciate Tate's playing; Tate was from Texas, like Evans, and he had the same sound qualities. Furthermore, Buddy had shown that he was perfectly capable of playing Evans' parts, to the point of reproducing his solos down to the very last note. As for Lester, he could appreciate not only Tate's personality, but also his playing, and that mattered more to him than anything else.

Like Herschel and unlike Chu Berry, Tate was not a simple generator of notes. He didn't overplay, but placed notes and pauses where they belonged and when called for.

On March 19 and 20, a month after Evans' death, the Basie orchestra recorded its first titles for Columbia in New York City. The second Decca contract had just expired, and John Hammond, who had recently been made a producer with Columbia, hurriedly signed up "his" discovery. Seven tunes were recorded by Buck Clayton, Shad Collins, Harry Edison, Ed Lewis, Dan Minor, Benny Morton, Dickie Wells, Buddy Tate, Lester Young, Jack Washington, Earl Warren, Freddie Green, Walter Page, Jo Jones, Jimmy Rushing, Helen Humes, and the Count. For the first time, the composition of two selections was attributed to him by name. "Rock a Bye Basie" is ascribed to the collaboration of Young, Basie, and Collins, and "Taxi War Dance" is attributed to that of Lester and the Count.

The "war dance" owed its name to a friendly rivalry among the band members as they searched for the perfect taxi girl at each of the clubs where they performed. Among the hit songs of the day, this was one of Lester's favorites. "Taxi War Dance" is a melody in thirty-two measures punctuated by constant riffs and colored with bluesy inflections within the tenor sax chorus. A landmark in the annals of Basie-Young discography, particularly memorable is Lester's introductory chorus, a perfect illustration of his brand of "horizontal" improvisation.[82]

But it was Basie, more than Lester, who reaped the benefits from these compositions, and by the time the orchestra appeared at the Sherman Hotel in Chicago in June, the pianist had become a veritable star. Despite his improved finances, Lester felt ill at ease. He saw his ideas being repeated in concert and during various recording sessions without ever seeing his name credited among the composers. Basie himself recognized what an indispensable hand Lester had had in the band's repertoire.

> Prez had a lot of themes. A lot of things should have been themes. It was just something you played and then you could hear it on the record. . . . But there's some things, some lines that he would play in his solos. And it became a thing that people could whistle and hum his solos. That's the way he

played. I mean all down through the years. I mean, anybody play a record of Prez, everybody could whistle or hum his solo because it's such a melodic line. . . . He was very important. (Count Basie)[83]

Lester felt more and more confined to the role of sideman. On occasion, he would complain about Evans' absence, then get up and walk off the stage in the middle of a set. At that point, he headed for the dressing rooms to pick up his hat and coat. Whenever they could, the other band members tried to hold him back; they needed to get him back to his seat, and sometimes they had to do it forcibly. On the other hand, in cities like Philadelphia where Lester had a loyal following, he was considered the indisputable head of the group. Before the show, between sets, and after the curtain had fallen, his fans invaded the dressing rooms, begging for autographs and talking about his solos.

Some of the musicians were surprised by this success. To meet the expectations of those in the audience who memorized most of the solos off the records, Basie asked his musicians to repeat those same solos onstage, sometimes allowing them five or six supplementary choruses. Everything would run smoothly until the Pres approached the mike. He never played the same solo twice. What he played—and it was always improvised—swept away any expectations the public might have had, but to everyone's surprise, instead of arousing the public's ire, his unpredictability made him all the more attractive in the public's eyes. Often Lester himself would be the most surprised of all at his success, and at moments like these he would question his rationale for being in the midst of this band. Wouldn't he do better if he quit? If he went solo? It would take him over a year to come up with a satisfactory reply to these questions.

During his stay at the Sherman, Pres was introduced to the young trumpeter Lee Castle (Lee Castaldo), a former member of the Jimmy Dorsey Orchestra, and to Gleen Hardmann, an organist whose career had started in Pittsburgh. John Hammond suggested they hold a recording session. The musicians agreed.

Freddie Green joined in for reinforcement. The results were pretty strange and not at all convincing. Despite the skills of both Lester and Lee, the spark just wasn't there, and Hardmann seemed completely ignorant of jazz.

Back in New York, Lester played the Famous Door for two months. In September, as part of a small group consisting of Buck Clayton, Dickie Wells, Freddie Green, Walter Page, and Jo Jones dubbed by Basie "Count Basie's Kansas City Seven," Pres recorded two masterpieces. One was "Dickie's Dream," written together with Basie, the other was "Lester Leaps In," an original composition.

At bottom, "Lester Leaps In" was nothing less than a musical balance sheet where he laid out all his notions about the instrument. It was rare for Basie's piano to attain as it did there what for Lester's blowing was essential: a level of discretion that permitted his phrases to float. This ensemble was undoubtedly one of the best ever to have been at Lester's disposal. The rhythm section was musically and humanly welded together, the trumpeter was prodigious, and Dickie Wells confirms the fact that he was one of the most inventive trombonists in the entire history of jazz.

Pres's genius seemed boundless—his authority was incontestable. Anticipating the harmony, Lester's phrasing attained a new freedom. He gleefully sidestepped the tempos ("Lester Leaps In") and measures, with new divisions resulting from the design of his solos. His rhythmic and melodic esthetics reached full maturity here; they transcended everything that might have existed before them. This was noticeable again several months later (March 1940) when he recorded a new composition of his own, "Tickle Toe," in which he refashioned Trumbauer, Beiderbecke, and the whole spirit of New Orleans.

But with one or two exceptions, the months that followed sparked no new passions in the Pres's life. His private life was uneventful. In New York, whenever he wasn't playing, he would spend his time with Mary at the Woodside Hotel. When her nursing job permitted it, she would accompany Lester on tour. Ever since the orchestra had begun to enjoy a guaranteed success, Basie had suggested to those musicians who wished to that they travel with their wives and children.

Whenever something did not please him musically, Lester never hesitated to say so. One night when the band was playing on Broadway, Lester created a scene that gave all the musicians—except Basie—a big laugh. The Count had decided to create a small scenario around an arrangement called "I Struck a Match in the Dark." Just as the first note of the piece was heard the light man was to plunge the stage into darkness; then Earl Warren was to come to his feet and begin singing, while the other musicians, one after the other, struck matches. Lester considered this idea to be stupid, and one evening he arranged to have every copy of the score on his music stand. As soon as the stage became dark, Earl Warren approached the mike and rang out, "I struck a match in the dark." At that instant, Lester struck a fistful of matches and slipped them under the stack of scores. The fire department had to douse the fire to keep it from spreading. The orchestra never played that song again.

On December 24 at Carnegie Hall, John Hammond organized the second edition of his great *From Spiritual to Swing* concert. On the program were the Count Basie Orchestra, the Benny Goodman Sextet, with Charlie Christian and Lionel Hampton, the Kansas City Five augmented by Charlie Christian, as well as a series of pianists that included Albert Ammons, Pete Johnson, and John Lewis. Hammond not only had the session recorded, but Vanguard also published three titles which today constitute the only testimony to the short collaboration of Lester and his first pupil, Charlie Christian, whose technique displays the same rhythmic and melodic preoccupations as Lester's.

As 1940 drew to a close, Lester was sad to see the departure of his friend Shad Collins, who was fired by Basie. Partial compensation for his friend's departure came with the arrival of Vic Dickenson, with whom Lester established new ties of friendship. But Collins was the second person to have left Lester's sheltered universe, plunging him yet a little bit further into solitude. He began to drink again, and, as soon as he was able to, he left in search of Billie Holiday; with her he would spend hours locked up in a room, smoking marijuana and drinking gin and vodka.

Among other eccentricities, Lester at this time began according an undue importance to the number thirteen. Thirteen became for him the symbol, the portent, and the explanation of good as well as bad luck. As Jo Jones has underscored, "Thirteen was his lucky number. He would only place bets on the number 13. . . . One day he gave Pee Wee Marquette a betting tip and said, 'I gave you $13; I'm going to shake you and lift you up as if you were walking on stilts, you turnip, you. . . .'" Pres also called him a "midget mother-fucker." It was at this time that Lester began to feel he was invested with psychic powers whose merits he began to broadcast.

For Basie, on the other hand, things seemed to be going down-hill. Willard Alexander, the Count's closest ally, had quit the talent agency for which he had been working for years. His replacement paid little attention to the orchestra, sending it to work in impossible places, forcing the musicians to travel several hundred miles between concerts. Everyone was on edge; Basie was threatening to quit the band and rejoin Benny Goodman. Lester felt that quality was going down due to all-around fatigue and irritability. Rehearsals were infrequent and hastily done, and the musicians were assimilating new arrangements badly. Pres felt as unhappy in rehearsals as he had felt in class as a child.

> With Basie it was like at school. I had the habit of sleeping in the classroom because I knew my lesson and as a result, there was nothing else for me to do. The teacher went and told all that to my mother. I dropped out of school. In Basie's orchestra, there was always someone who didn't know his part. It seems to me that if a musician doesn't know how to read, he should say so, and then he gets helped. Or else you explain his part to him beforehand. But Basie didn't do this. I was in the habit of telling him about it, but he never paid any attention to me. You had to sit down and you had to play, over and over. . . . Just sit on that chair and play. . . . (Lester Young)

The arrival of Tab Smith would perturb Lester further; he could not understand Basie's reason for hiring a fifth saxophonist. He made no effort to hide his feelings, and from then on, despite a stimulating tour in California at the beginning of fall, his participation in the orchestra began to wane. He played without conviction and came late to rehearsals. One December morning, Basie telephoned him and advised him of an engagement toward the end of the day involving another recording session. Lester looked at his bed, glanced rapidly at the wall calendar, and then replied in a tired voice, "Hang up and let me sleep. No one makes music on Friday the thirteenth. . . . "

It had all been said. And it was all on record. On December 13, 1940, Lester quit the Count Basie Orchestra. Obviously, his departure came as a surprise, and it also gave free rein to a series of rumors: "He was all mixed up. He's become completely superstitious." "He was drunk and blurted out the first thing that crossed his mind; he'll be back."[84] Not one person thought for a moment that he was not happy with his job, that he had endured too much over the past few months.

> You don't have any real opportunity to play. You go up to the mike for your chorus of eight to sixteen measures, and then head back to your seat. There you sit and all you do is read scores. There's no future for me in that. (Lester Young)

After his departure, it was often said that Lester was not a big band musician. For a soloist, the orchestra was certainly a setting with limited possibilities, and Lester did express himself more freely when he played in a small group—e.g., Count Basie's Kansas City Seven. But to say that Lester was not a big band musician is to forget the role of the Basie rhythm section in the evolution of his style, it is to forget that this same section was only able to undergo development at the heart of a big band, it is to overlook the dynamics produced by the Evans-Young duo and the positive effect this duo had on Lester. What would have become of Lester without the Basie orchestra, which furnished him with a regular job, a certain material comfort, and a relatively peaceful psychological environment? With his style under fire, however, and himself as sensitive as he was to a world whose attacks he was unable to repel, Lester needed this sabbatical more than anyone else; it permitted him to think freely about his music.

On an earlier occasion, he had quit the family orchestra—whose limitations had become more and more apparent to him—by claiming real differences with his father. He quit the Basie orchestra because of the limitations imposed on him as a soloist. Momentarily, Lester was a musician wounded by the departure of certain friends, perturbed by recent management problems, and desirous of enjoying his growing personal popularity; after all, in 1940 he was rated fourth among tenor saxophonists in a poll conducted by *down beat*.

Meanwhile, two months before Lester's departure, Henry Minton, an ex-band director and the first card-carrying member of the musicians' union in Harlem, had opened a small club next to the Cecil Hotel on 118th Street. He put Teddy Hill in charge of the programming, and Hill immediately hired a quartet that included Thelonious Monk and Kenny Clarke. It wouldn't be long before the bebop era would be launched.

Lester Young with his mother. New Orleans, 1912. (Frank Driggs Collection.)

From left to right: Lester Young (alt.-bar.), Odie Cromwell (ten.), Sam Allen (alt.-arrangements): Art Bronson Bostonians saxophone section. Salina, Kansas, 1930. (Frank Driggs Collection.)

Original Blue Devils. From left to right: Snake White (trpt.), Jap Jones (trb.), Theodore Ross (alt.), Leonard Chadwick (trpt.), Lester Young (ten.), George Hudson (trpt.), Ernie Williams (voc.-direct.), Buster Smith (alt.-clar.), Charlie Washington (p.), Reuben Lynch (guit.), Druie Bess (trb.), Abe Bolar (bass), Raymond Howell (drms.). Kansas City, 1932. (Frank Driggs Collection.)

Lester Young, 1937. (Frank Driggs Collection.)

Lester Young, 1938. (Frank Driggs Collection.)

Lester Young, 1937. (Photo by Dunc Butler—Frank Driggs Collection.)

From left to right: Eddie Durham (trb.-guit.), Herschel Evans (ten.), Count Basie (p.), Bennie Moten (tromb.), Lester Young (ten.), Buck Clayton (trpt.), Walter Page (bass). Apollo Theatre, 1937. (Frank Driggs Collection.)

From left to right: Lester Young (ten.), Ray Brown (bass), Harry Edison (trpt.), Buddy Rich (drms.), 1955. (Jazz Magazine Collection.)

From left to right: Teddy Wilson (p.), Lester Young (ten.), Jo Jones (drms.), 1956. (Jazz Magazine Collection.)

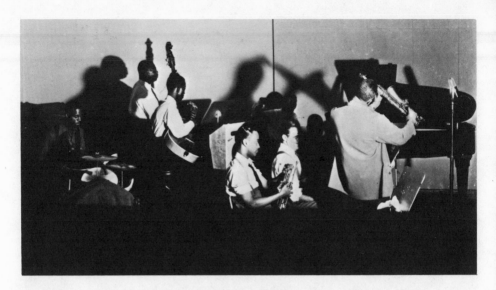

From left to right: Jo Jones (drms.), Walter Page (bass), Freddie Green (guit.), Buck Clayton (trpt.), Count Basie (p.), Benny Goodman (clar.), Charlie Christian (guit.), Lester Young (ten.). Private recording session for John Hammond, New York, 28 October 1940. (Frank Driggs Collection.)

From left to right: Lester Young (ten.), Count Basie (p.), Jo Jones (drms.). The Count Basie Orchestra, Apollo Theatre, 1940. (Frank Driggs Collection.)

From left to right: Nick Fenton (bass), Shad Collins (trpt.), Clyde Hart (p.), Lester Young (ten.), John Collins (guit.). The Lester Young Orchestra, Kelly's Stable, New York, 1941. (Frank Driggs Collection.)

From left to right: René Urtreger (p.), Lester Young (ten.), Pierre Michelot (bass). Club Saint-Germain, Paris, September 1956. (Photo by Marcel Zanini.)

From left to right: René Urtreger (p.), Lester Young (ten.), Pierre Michelot (bass), Miles Davis (trpt.). Lille, November 1956. (Photo by André Joly.)

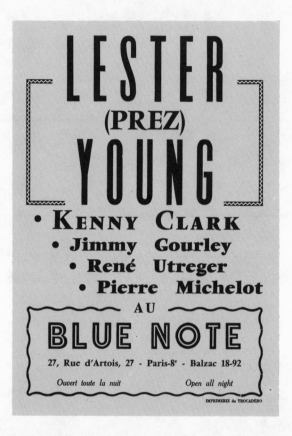

Poster from the Blue Note, Paris, 1959. (Jimmy Gourley Collection.)

PART TWO

Lester Leaps Again

Chapter 15

It's Sad but True

After leaving Count Basie, Pres took part in several jam sessions at the Village Vanguard, Nick's, Minton's Playhouse (where he played with Ben Webster to the point of exhaustion), and at Monroe's Uptown House, where he performed alongside several musicians who were soon to make headlines: Thelonious Monk, Dizzy Gillespie, Kenny Clarke. At around ten o'clock one morning, at closing time, Pres walked out of Monroe's Uptown in the company of another saxophonist and of Monroe himself. They were talking about the previous night. It wasn't long before Monroe and the saxophonist began to disagree over the merits of another musician. The disagreement became so violent that the two came to blows. Lester tried to intervene, but instead received a punch to the face intended for Monroe. While he remained sprawled on the pavement in a daze, Monroe and the saxophonist dashed to the nearest grocery store, bought a steak, then ran back to apply it to Lester's cheek so that it wouldn't swell. Pres painfully got to his feet and exclaimed, "Oh, you caught the Sunday on me!" Then he took the steak off his face, looked at his speechless companions, and said, "Let's go cook this fellow sufferer."

In the clubs, he would often bump into his first two admirers, Charlie Parker and Charlie Christian, and Coleman Hawkins as well.

> . . . we had this after hour place up on St. Nicholas Avenue and everybody used to go up there and jam, they used to serve meals, drinks, so Hawkins just came back from Europe, over there with Jack Hilton. He came back after this "Body and Soul" was real popular. So all the tenor players were just waiting for Hawk you know, Don Byas, Cecil Scott, Chu, Lester, everybody with their tenor. So Hawk he used to go up there every night you know and listen to them play and he'd never bring his horn. So he used to listen to all these guys blowing, so Hawk says, "oh yeah, it sound good, but man, when I went away they were playing those same changes, nothing changed. Maybe a little faster, but they're playing them same changes." So okay, so that went on for about a week, two weeks, so this particular morning, Hawk brought his horn up. So different ones got up there and played, so the last one to get up to play was Hawk. And Hawk sound really good, but it seemed as though Pres says, okay, I'm going to follow you, the rest of you afraid to follow Hawk. I'll play behind Hawk. So after Hawk finished playing, Lester got up and start playing, and it was one of those things where he didn't impress Hawk too much. So it was late and Hawk all the while Lester was playing, Hawk was getting his horn, packing his horn up, he was about ready to leave around about seven o'clock in the morning, and so as Hawk was leaving, Pres walked out right behind him and was playing his horn right behind Hawk as Hawk was going to his car in the street. Oh boy it was funny. (Cozy Cole)[85]

Even if Lester found these impromptu sessions exciting, they did not leave him completely satisfied. Among the benefits of working with Basie had been the regularity of the concerts. Now, deprived of a secure entourage, Lester was left to himself, and for a time, with no clear goals, he succumbed to his own laziness. It was an entirely new situation for him, having no orchestra with which to appear and no immediate prospects of finding one. His musical personality was just as solid, but it didn't allow him to confront the outside world—of which he chose to remember only the racism and opposition to his music—alone. He even appears to have abandoned his intentions of starting a solo career. He was content to have a hotel room, the silent presence of Mary, and, from time to time, a bottle of gin or vodka. Nonetheless, on certain occasions he would demonstrate that he had neither lost his sense of humor nor his sense of reality.

. . . [Prez] was at the Alvin Hotel and Benny Goodman was doing the Bell Telephone Hour. So there was Gene [Ramey], Charlie Christian, Lionel [Hampton], Benny [Goodman] and they wanted a tenor player, so the first one they thought of, and liked him too, was Pres. Let's call Pres. Okay. So everybody said, Man you better call Pres early in the morning so you can catch him before he goes out, because just before noon Prez was liable to go out and get a little gin and wine and scuffle on back in that hotel and go to sleep and you weren't liable to get him. So anyway, Benny called him around about nine o'clock in the morning, phone rang, Prez still sleep, "Hello." "Yeah, Prez?" "Yeah, this is Prez." "Benny." Prez says, "Benny who?" "Benny Goodman." "Oh yeah, how you doin', Pops?" "All right." "So how have you been?" One word led to another and Benny said, "well what I called you bout Prez, we've got this Bell Telephone Hour to do. And Gene, Charlie Christian, Lionel and me. We want you, we haven't worked with you in a long while, I just forget the last record date we did together, we're just looking forward working with you." So Prez says, "yeah, that'll be fine, man, work with all you cats, man, that'll be just wonderful." So Benny kept talking to him and outlining the rehearsal and all that and just where they were going to rehearse and what number they were going to feature him on. "It'll be a good thing for you and there'll be quite a few viewers looking at this, Prez. Mean a lot to your name." Okay, they must have talked about five or ten minutes. So they were about close the conversation, Benny said, "now you understand everything, Prez?" Prez says, "yeah, I got it written all out here, just when it is" and repeated it, going to meet over at NBC and we're going to rehearse, we're going to do this, rehearsals, XX time, one o'clock or whatever it is, and "okay, then, Prez, it's good talking to you and I'll see you Thursday at rehearsal."—whatever the day was. So Prez says, "Okay, Benny," and then he says, "Oh yeah, Benny, look, you talked about everything but you forgot to say how's the bread smell?" I thought that was the funniest thing I'd ever heard. . . . That Prez was quite a character. (Cozy Cole)[86]

What Lester then wanted was his own orchestra. He wanted it badly. As we have seen, the idea had come to him during his last year with Basie, when he thought he saw signs of encouragement in the reactions of the audience. Starting in February he began to canvass Harlem, visiting his favorite clubs, talking to his friends, getting the idea rolling.

He had already picked the club where he might open: Kelly's Stable. Ralph Watkins, one of its founders, was enthusiastic, and he in turn had no trouble persuading his partner, Irving Alexander. If Lester succeeded in quickly forming a group, he might appear by February 27, alternating with Una Mae Carlisle, a singer-pianist from Ohio that Fats Waller had discovered in Cincinnati.

The first musician to sign on for the project was trumpeter Shad Collins. Encouraged by this loyal friendship, Lester also convinced pianist Clyde Hart, guitarist John Collins, bassist Nick Fenton, and another close friend, drummer Harold West. After a few rehearsals in the basement of the Woodside Hotel, the ensemble began its engagement as scheduled on February 27; the audience was more than satisfied.

But whereas more and more attention was being paid to Lester's work among younger musicians, the Old Guard still remained hostile toward him. Furthermore, Lester was participating in the same jam sessions at the club in which saxophonists like Hawkins, Chu Berry, Sam Donahue, George Auld, and Babe Russin were regularly taking part.

Until then, Lester had simply been a sideman. Recently, he

had also refused John Hammond's offer to form a group with Billie Holiday, because he intended to pursue his own career. So the engagement at Kelly's Stable was an opportunity for him to make himself known as a leader and to win those over who were still resisting his style. Working conditions were ideal: the Stable was a warm, intimate place where the audience didn't come just to eat. Lester was in full possession of his means; the sextet was well put together, and the rhythm section rolled out an appropriately red carpet which allowed the Pres to express himself with complete confidence. Full of hope, the musicians felt that it would not be difficult for them to find a producer willing to record them. But Lester, the man in charge, was a bad businessman, and none of the contacts he made ever resulted in anything. He saw this failure as an attack directed at him and his music; worse yet, he considered himself responsible and culpable vis-à-vis his friend Shad Collins and the other musicians. Nevertheless, by inviting the whole ensemble to participate in one of her sessions on March 10, Una Mae Carlisle still managed temporarily to raise the saxophone player's morale; on that occasion, they recorded four melodies, of which one, "It's Sad but True," really had an impact. On March 18, Pres decided to set a limit on the Stable engagement. He felt that the staff did not show him enough respect. And so, despite the quality of the group, the musicians decided to break up.

The invitation to participate in Billie Holiday's next session came just at the right moment. He needed her companionship on this occasion. The musicians got together in the middle of the night after their respective engagements. Lester ran into his buddy from Minneapolis, Eddie Barefield, and also drummer Kenny Clarke. Billie and Pres got along marvelously; unfortunately, the other musicians did not know each other, and none of the four songs they recorded comes across convincingly.

Despite the session, Lester, victim of the aborted Stable experience, began to lose confidence in himself. He lived like a recluse in his hotel, sporadically directing a few words to Mary. In April, Sam Price succeeded in pulling Pres out of seclusion by inviting him, together with Shad Collins, to a Decca recording session for which he served as house pianist. This time, the depressed state in which Lester found himself seemed to take him to the pinnacle of his artistry. He played remarkably. After that session—his third since leaving Basie—another year passed before he set foot in a studio again.

In May of 1941, convinced that New York was hostile toward him, Lester left for Los Angeles. Mary followed him with mixed feelings, and the couple bought a small house in the black section of town. "Little Pea"—that was the nickname Pres had given Lee—found that his older brother had changed. He spoke little, preferred keeping to himself, grumbled about everyone in whom he sensed hostility, and communicated very often in hermetic terms. "He was a very soft-spoken man, and he was an extreme introvert. . . . Lester used a lot of slang and he had his own language—and only the people that he really cared for, that he allowed them to understand him, you know" (Lee Young).[87]

Unlike his brother, Lee was an excellent businessman. As soon as Lester arrived, Lee immediately thought of including him in his own ensemble, of which California tenor saxophonist Bumps Myers was already a member. Count Basie's idea of setting off Herschel Evans and Lester Young to create extra dynamics within the orchestra appealed to Lee, who saw in Bumps Myers a fearsome challenger for his brother. With the help of Billy Strayhorn, who wrote the arrangements for the new combo with Dudley Brooks, Lee was convinced that he would shake up the entire West Coast. He had also just signed a contract with the agency that was to represent the Count Basie Orchestra from then on: The William Morris Agency. They had assured him they wanted to take his interests into consideration.

And sure enough, after several weeks of rehearsals, when on a certain evening in the month of June 1941 the "Lee Young Esquires of Rhythm" opened at Billy Berg's Club at Capri, every amateur jazz fan in Los Angeles was present, from Mel Tormé to Norman Granz, not to mention Hollywood's most respected stars.

Success was instantaneous, but this didn't prevent the local *down beat* correspondent from sharply criticizing Pres, saying that, "Bumps Myers plays more interesting things than his boss." A few diehards, for their part, could not understand why Lester took such pains to blow. The Young-Myers standoff never took place; in fact, there quickly developed a sort of musical complicity between the two men. Unfortunately, the local musicians' union protested the presence of Lester, a New Yorker in the midst of this California band. If he wished to join the group, Lester first had to request that his file be transferred to California and then solicit new membership in the local chapter. In the meantime, he could appear as a "guest star," i.e., play three numbers per set and stand at the foot of the stage, practically in the audience and at a respectable distance from the other musicians, so that no confusion would arise. For nearly six weeks, Lester spent his evenings in this manner, squeezed alongside the bar, slinging down drinks that others bought him and playing cards, while patiently waiting for his brother Lee to "invite" him up, and grumbling about the stupid, discriminatory laws. Once again, he felt excluded and was unable to comprehend the reasons for it. At this time he quarreled with Mary, left the house, and moved into a small family boarding house in the center of town. Most of his days were spent locked in his room, listening to records.

The arrival in Los Angeles of Billie Holiday, who was also supposed to appear at Billy Berg's Club, was like a breath of pure oxygen for the Pres. Together, as in New York, they explored the city and made the rounds of the jazz clubs. Billie could remember taking her friend to the Plantation Club where Billy Eckstine and Sarah Vaughan were performing.

Lester's union difficulties were finally ironed out, and he was able to walk onstage at last. Due to its success, and to Lee's abilities as a manager, the group continued at Berg's Club until December, when it took a two-month rest. Lester and Mary were reconciled, and for a while at least, the Pres's life was serene.

Toward the end of February, still at the same club, Lee and

Lester appeared with Jimmy Rowles, Slim Gaillard, and Slam Stewart, who rapidly became one of Lester's supporters.

> I had heard him on record and, if I'm not mistaken, I saw him with Count Basie, and that was about it. That was about the first time. . . . And when I met him—when I first met him, it was a real thrill to me, you know, like a lot of the cats that I had heard on records. And when I finally met them, it was a big kick, you know. . . . I think he improvised more so than having a lot of pet phrases, you know. He could improvise mostly all the time. . . . I'm sure that Art Tatum was there. And at this one our guitarist, Everett Banksdale, he was on the scene, and I think Duke Ellington was in town with his band also, and Ray Nance was there, I remember this particular session. And if I'm not mistaken Jimmy Blanton came in. (Slam Stewart)[88]

Two months later, Berg moved his club to Beverly Boulevard and renamed it "Trouville." Lester stayed on the marquee until August 1942 and got to be pretty close with Norman Granz. Furthermore, Lester was regularly asked to perform at private parties, and he met George Raft at one of these.

Before leaving Los Angeles and returning to New York, Lester concluded the California period by making a recording that is today considered a classic. Produced by Norman Granz on July 15, the recording session was conducted during an open performance in the back of Music Town, a music store where jam sessions would be held two years later on Sunday afternoons. Lester, Nat King Cole, and Red Callender recorded four songs that would appear on the Philco (Aladdin) label: "Indiana," "I Can't Get Started," "Tea for Two," and "Body and Soul." This was the first record made by Pres as part of a trio and the only one of his career made without any percussion. The producer was Norman Granz, in whom Lester had found a new and precious ally who wasted little time in propelling him to the front of the stage.

The skill demonstrated by Pres on the ballads and found on some of his recordings with Billie Holiday gained full importance at this time. Lester was gloomy, poetic, subject to undefinable dreamy moods, a master musician who surrounded his universe with an aura of sound which today seems even vaster, sadder, and more somber. The Pres was a changed man, and no one could deny it. Something new but still uncertain was emerging, something that could be traced back to the years spent with Basie and to the months that had followed. There could be no doubt that a new period had begun for him, with new spiritual modalities.

Chapter 16

Sidelined

Lee and Lester's band began a five-month engagement at New York's Cafe Society on September 8, 1942; Pete Johnson, Albert Ammons, and Hazel Scott were all performing there at the time. Clyde Hart had replaced Jimmy Rowles at the piano, Red Callender played bass, Louis Gonzalez was on the guitar, Bumps Myers played tenor, and Paul Campbell played trumpet. Having left Mary in Los Angeles, Lester moved back into the Alvin Hotel and looked up his old musician pals. Those who recalled his stint at Kelly's Stable came back eagerly to hear him. A few weeks later, everyone who was anyone in New York knew that Lester had returned at the head of a new group that included his own brother. Lee was the business manager and made sure that everyone had enough money to live on decently; as manager, he was also the one who received the largest paycheck. Lester, for his part, was making good money thanks to the beginning commercial success of his recordings. Though his success elicited plenty of jealousy and scorn among a good number of musicians, it was also a source of inspiration for others. The first saxophonists who came to take lessons from the Pres at the Café Society were Wardell Gray, Dexter Gordon, and Allen Eager. Little by little, the public declared its allegiance to Lester. Yet it would be another year before he was elected fourth best tenor saxophonist—with 491 votes—by the readers of *down beat* in its annual poll; Vido Musso took the lead with 1,203 votes. Other magazines favored Lester, pointing out that he had not made a bad recording since 1936. The future was looking bright.

At Lester's invitation, Charles Thompson arrived in New York to replace Clyde Hart: "[I]n those days the money was very little, in fact I was making $75.00 a week playing with George Clarke, and I was influenced to come to join Lester Young for $55.00 a month—a week."[89]

Surprisingly, Charles Thompson became the Pres's first disciple, even before Charlie Parker and Charlie Christian.

> . . . the fact of the matter is the way I went to New York was I was sent to play with Lester Young, who was my real love. Actually Lester Young was my real love, because I like to play tenor, too. . . . Well it was hard on the teeth, and of course then I'd already established myself as a piano player, and it wasn't really the time to devote to it. And then you know, you can't learn everything at once, but I always loved Lester Young, and really I tried to pattern my playing after Lester Young on the piano, and that's what really established my original style of playing until I, as I said, met Art Tatum who taught me more about the piano itself. . . .
>
> Lester Young gave me the name of Sir Charles. . . . There were three Charleses working in Cafe Society where I told you we were playing. And like they had a phone in the back where the bandstand was, and the rest rooms and the dressing rooms in that area. So when they'd call for Charles one of the guys who ran the elevator's name was Charles, my name was Charles, and another Charles. Right? . . . So nobody knew who it was, and of course I for some reason or another got most of the calls, and so Lester Young said, "listen, we've got to get this thing straightened

out." He said, "listen," my man said "you look like royalty any way, you should have a name so we can identify you" he said. "Baby, we're going to call you Sir Charles, you know." And that's where I got the name. . . .

So I spent all my time there and everything was really great. Then one day there was no more work, can you make that out? And the band broke up. I think Lee must have gone back to California and I believe Lester took a short vacation. Since we had nothing to do, Red Callender formed a trio with guitarist Louis Gonzalez and me.

Lester directed the band with his eyes. He didn't say much beyond "Hey, baby." What he did say usually consisted of compliments. He rarely spoke except with his sax; if you were in tune with him, you could look at his eyes and tell what he was thinking. I would definitely say that most of the words, in terms of discipline and all that, were said by his brother. Lee was more of a businessman and Lester was strictly a jazzman. I'm not saying Lester didn't direct the orchestra, because the fact is, he did. But you see, in a good group like that, you don't need a leader because all the musicians know what's going on; it was enough for a guy to mention a number, or else for you to call a tune out by number, or for you to hum it, or even before climbing on stage, to know what's happening and to simply wait for the beat to begin. . . . Most of the time, Lee would set the tempo. . . . But without a doubt, that was Lester's orchestra, really. He was the leader because he was a great musician and he was undeniably the one the audience came to hear. (Sir Charles Thompson)[90]

The news of Willis Handy Young's death came just as the Café Society engagement ended in February 1943. Lee returned to Los Angeles for the funeral, but his brother remained in Harlem. Fifteen days later, Willis Handy Young's wife also died.

Lester never said a word about either one. Similarly, he would never say anything about his girlfriend Mary. Though distant in everyday life, Lester was very attached to his family. A certain modesty and bashfulness in matters of affection kept him from displaying his feelings. This reluctance of his to let himself be known was painful not only to him, but also to those whom it affected.

In March, the U.S.O. (United Services Organization) signed up a band led by saxophonist Al Sears for a several-week tour of U.S. military facilities. His became the first black band to take part in such tours. Each base was to host two shows, theatrical or musical, every month. Often, a theater group or a band could not finish its tour because several of its members were drafted. At one time a rumor started making the rounds that any musician or actor taking part in a tour would be exempted from military duty. Hundreds of candidates applied, but sadly for them, the rumor eventually turned out to be unfounded.

The U.S.O. decided to get around the problem by searching for a band whose entire membership was married. Marriage was a solid argument for avoiding the draft. All the members of Al Sears' orchestra were either married or already deferred for different reasons, so the band was hired in March. Weekly pay came to $115 for the band leader and $84.50 for the sidemen. All travel and lodging expenses were covered by the U.S.O. As soon as the contracts were signed, Sears hired Lester and Budd Johnson, and the first performance was held April 18 at Camp Polk in Alexandria, Louisiana. Lester found the experience thoroughly distasteful: he didn't like the atmosphere on post, and Al Sears garnered all the applause, while no one paid attention to the other musicians. At night, Lester would play dice with the other musicians, much to the dismay of Budd Johnson: "He had the worst luck possible. I never saw him win once. But he spent all night at it. He didn't want to quit the game. He just loved to see dice rolling."[91]

A few weeks earlier, prompted by the musicians' unions, the Federal government had consented to fight racial segregation in the musical profession by encouraging the formation of integrated bands. Employing Sears may also be viewed as a manifestation of that effort. But in the interim, Lee Young had been dismissed from the radio orchestra which he had just started playing with back home in Los Angeles. In Los Angeles, a black musician could not hold a position in a white band.

In October, the full Count Basie Orchestra began a new tour up the East Coast and, after triumphing at the Howard Theater in Washington, played the Apollo in Harlem from October 8 to October 14. Lester hesitated to show himself, but the urge to see his old friends and to play once again with a formation he had felt comfortable with won out over his fears. Basie welcomed him cordially and immediately gave him a seat in the saxophone section. The reunion lasted less than a week, and when the band hit the road again October 15, Pres stayed behind in New York, where his name occasionally appeared on the bill at several clubs, though he appeared most often at the Fifty-second Street jam sessions.

Over the years, jam sessions changed. As several musicians attest, they were a far cry from the original sessions.

> In fact, in the forties, even jamming came under the control of the Union authority. You were paid to jam; there were official jam sessions at Jimmy Ryan's on Sunday afternoons [they began in 1939 under the auspices of Milt Gabler, N.D.A.], but it was illegal to go out and jam like we used to do in the old days. (Bill Coleman)[92]

> . . . we would, like we went to a town and ran into a couple of bands, and the guys would be in the hotel lobby, starting to talk about playing, and first thing you know you got a jam session going right in the lobby without the piano or anything, just everybody would start playing . . . (Eddie Barefield)[93]

By November of 1943, Basie was in town again, at the Lincoln Hotel. This time, Lester chose to ignore him; his shyness had become pride. But one morning, when he was closing down the White Horse Club with a couple of musicians, he ran into Jo Jones who happened to be strolling down the sidewalk.

> I went round to the White Rose and got Lester and Lester didn't know what I was doing. I bought him a glass of beer. Lester didn't know how to drink no beer; Lester didn't drink at that

time. . . . I went down on the street and told him, "You're due at work tomorrow night at 7 o'clock. You come to the Lincoln Hotel, etcetera." And there he was! Nobody said nothing; he just sat down and just started to playing, and nobody thought about nothing. They didn't say, "Hello, Lester, where have you been?" or nothing. He came back in the band just like he'd just left 15 minutes ago. (Jo Jones)[94]

A few days later, Lester learned that he was replacing Don Byas, who had been fired for excessive drinking. From the moment of his return, Lester was in a good mood and showed enthusiasm for the big band.

Would I like to form a big band? You can bet I would! But I can hardly see myself launching into all that . . . the headaches, the backbiting. . . . I have a hard time forming a quintet! Like the old lady told me, there's always some idiot in the band, and you never know who it is. . . . (Lester Young)

It was at the Lincoln that Pres got his little bell. If somebody missed a note or if you were a new guy and goofed, you'd hear this bell going—"ding dong!" If Pres was blowing and goofed, somebody would reach over and ring his bell on him. . . . Jo Jones had another way of saying the same thing. *Bing—bing— bing* he'd go on his cymbal rod. When you first joined, you would take it kind of rough, but later you'd be in stitches with the rest, and take it as a joke. They'd ring the bell on Basie, too. And if Pres saw someone getting angry, he'd blow the first bar of "Runnin' Wild." (Dickie Wells)[95]

In December, Lester ran into Bill Coleman again and invited him to join the Dickie Wells Orchestra for a recording session that proved to be unremarkable.

I never knew exactly how it came about. Possibly, Buck Clayton, was not available. I remember that the session was a very informal, more of a happy get-together. There was no system for working things out. We all decided that if something was good and could be of use, and did it that way. (Bill Coleman)[96]

By contrast, just a few days later, on December 28, Harry Lim—whose talents have never been properly praised—brought Lester together with pianist Johnny Guarnieri, bassist Slam Stewart, and drummer Sid Catlett in the studios of radio station WOR. The three first titles they recorded are standards, "I Never Knew," "Just You, Just Me," and "Sometimes I'm Happy." The last, "Afternoon of a Basie-ite," which Lester preferred to call "The Afternoon of a Baseball Player" in memory of the softball games they had played in Manhattan's Central Park, is an original composition by Harry Lim. The record announced Pres's comeback, after an absence from the studio circuit of seventeen months.

What had been a premonition in the recording made in July 1942 with Nat King Cole and Red Callender found itself confirmed here. The sound is softer, deeper; it seems to float in the air like an aura. The slight changes that appear in Lester's sound are due to changes in the mouthpiece and reeds. He didn't hesitate to use both a rubber mouthpiece and reeds made of plastic. His blowing was less nervous, and he held his instrument in a more traditional fashion. Still in New York, four months later, Pres made a splendid new recording with Johnny Guarnieri, for whose style, reminiscent of both Fats Waller and Basie, he had a great deal of respect.

> Lester was very kind to tell me that he appreciated my way of playing for him. Most of the time I played the same way I remembered that Basie played for him, but not quite as subtly; I put in a few more notes. (Johnny Guarnieri)

Thanks again to Harry Lim, the session by the Kansas City Five and Kansas City Seven on March 22, 1944, was a total success. Under contract with another company, Basie appeared under the pseudonym of "Prince Charming." In "Lester Leaps Again" (with Lester, Basie, Green, Rodney Richardson, and Jo Jones), Pres's blowing becomes wild again for an instant and seems to follow the piano in a frantic chase up and down the bars. Dickie Wells and Buck Clayton joined the other musicians for "Destination K.C.," during which Lester rendered two superb choruses, "After Theater Jump" and "Six Cats and a Prince."

The session two days later with Commodore was pale by comparison with this one, colorless despite a few great moments. It was easy for Lester to overuse his techniques and he tended to repeat the same notes too often.

Since December, then, Pres had rejoined Basie's orchestra, and in the same month the Count embarked on a long tour organized by the William Morris Agency that took Lester to California in August.

While in Los Angeles, Lester made quite an unusual recording together with his brother and four other members of Basie's band: "A Little Bit North of South Carolina." He appears there as both vocalist and saxophonist. During his career, Lester was fond of vocalizing. With the family orchestra, as a youngster, he was often asked to sing. Subsequently, he was attracted by the "voice" he discovered in Frankie Trumbauer's style. Pres thought every jazz piece was a song into which it should be possible to slip some words. In 1940, he discovered Frank Sinatra, who became his favorite vocalist. The fact that Pres would therefore want to record a title where he would be both vocalist and saxophonist was in itself not surprising. Though it was never realized, one of his last wishes was to cut a record with Frank Sinatra. Unfortunately, "A Little Bit North of South Carolina" is scarcely audible, and no producer ever took the risk of including it on a record. Lester's vocals are faint, and the accompaniment is hard to follow. Despite the bad technical conditions, this one-of-a-kind cut, though totally isolated within his discography, sheds remarkable light on the Pres's secret wishes.

In the meantime, after having participated with Duke Ellington, Count Basie, and Teddy Wilson in the concert that was organized by American Youth for Democracy in memory of Fats Waller, the orchestra played at New York's Lincoln Hotel in May. Most of its performances were broadcast over the air, and the U.S. Army decided to select a few titles for the shatter-proof V-disks it was editing for the troops. These recordings were played in mess halls, reading rooms, and at dances; they also furnished musical programming for the armed forces' radio network in Europe. The red series was designed for the army air corps and the blue one for the navy. The repertoire consisted mostly of jazz and was drawn either from replays or from special recordings produced by the army.

All that month, the army tried to contact Lester to give him his draft notice. Every so often, as he passed through the cities of Pittsburgh, Detroit, Milwaukee, Cincinnati, Chicago, and Cleveland, he would receive letters, even telegrams, urging him to appear at the local induction center in order to take the required physical. He ignored them all and threw each in the trash as soon as he read it. But early in June he began to worry and voiced his concern to Milt Ebbins, Basie's personnel manager, and to Norman Granz who submitted requests for deferment to the selective service board in New York.

At this same time, Lester began to complain of headaches and of various other pains; despite the efforts made by Basie to lodge the musicians in the best possible surroundings, Lester would complain about the hotels and the food. He refused to take the advice of Jo Jones who urged him to see a doctor, and when he appeared at the Orpheum Theater in Los Angeles at the beginning of August, the audience thought he looked pale and drawn.

Lester experienced his first epileptic seizure. Though slight and of little importance, it was only one indication of the poor health he had suffered over the previous years. The depression he often experienced was causing him to lose his appetite. He spoke very little, scowled, and kept to himself and, in order to forget both his occasional pain and the specter of army service, he began to smoke marijuana. He began to drink between performances, and even between sets. Basie noticed this, but said nothing. On the contrary, he tried to distract the other musicians when he sensed that Lester was out of sorts. Whenever he was depressed, Lester could not help but think of all the attacks he had fallen victim to, and of all his unsatisfied desires. Lester wore his large hat, and those around him saw only an expressionless face. To extricate him from his doldrums, Norman Granz organized a jam session with several musician friends of his. Some pictures were taken by *Life* magazine photographer Gjon Mili. Then came the movie *Jammin' the Blues,* produced by Warner Brothers. Lester, Harry Edison, Marlowe Morris, Barney Kessel, Red Callender, Sid Catlett, and Marie Bryant recorded "The Midnight Symphony" and "On the Sunny Side of the Street." For *Jammin' the Blues,* Illinois Jacquet joined the group, and John Simmons and Jo Jones replaced Callender and Catlett. All the numbers were re-recorded to achieve a better soundtrack and also to appear on a record under the Palm label.

Whatever the case may be, this documentary film is an intense emotional experience both for those who never had the opportunity of seeing the Pres in person, and for those who were close to him, but whose memories of him have faded. Although he is surrounded by musicians, one feels he is very much alone. His vulnerability is absolute.

Chapter 17

Guardhouse Barracks Blues

*This chapter has been adapted from Lester Young's military records. The account is accurate down to the last detail.

One mid-September night at the Plantation Cafe, while the musicians were gathering on stage in preparation for the first set, an FBI agent called Lester and Jo Jones aside and handed them their draft notices. The appeals that Norman Granz and Milt Ebbins had made to the Selective Service had not met with success. They were told to appear at the induction center in a few days for their first interview with the military authorities.

On Friday, Lester asked his brother to drive him to the Eighth Street Barracks, and as they took leave of each other on the front steps, one last gleam of hope could be seen in his eyes. While filling out the forms he was given, Lester stated that he smoked marijuana; he thought that would make it clear to them that he shouldn't be drafted. He was not willing to spend that first night at the barracks, either, and managed to elude the officer on duty and rejoin his brother at the Down Beat Club. They spent the night together, and when the sun came up the next morning, Lee discretely brought him back. No one seemed concerned during the next few days about how Lester had filled out his induction papers.

A physical exam revealed a weakness for alcohol. Lester was placed in a solitary padded cell for three days. At last, on September 30, he, along with Jo Jones, was assigned to Fort MacArthur for five weeks of observation. He spent time at several other posts before receiving orders to report December 1 for infantry training with the army reserves at Fort McClellan, Alabama. Lester, who had always avoided the South, now abruptly found himself propelled there, without a single link to the outside.

From that moment on he was Private Second Class Lester Willis Young, serial number 39729502, attached to Company E, Second Battalion, First Training Regiment. His monthly pay came to $50.00, of which $7.50 was deducted for insurance and $22.00 for living expenses. Total net pay: $20.50. A few weeks later he was joined by Jo Jones, who was subsequently assigned to another post at Fort Ord.

Victimized by the arbitrary attacks of his ranking warrant officer, Lester not only saw his instrument confiscated, but was forbidden to play with the 173d Army Marching Band "due to his difficult character." Among the members of that unit were trombonist Jimmy Cheathamm and percussionist Chico Hamilton. It was at this time that he found out that he had been judged the best tenor saxophonist of the year in the poll conducted by *down beat*. Resigned, disgusted, and less and less able to comprehend the absurdity of the world around him, Lester spent his nights in a state of complete prostration. By day he would try to get drugs— even to mix them himself. According to Lewis Porter, Lester supposedly tried to concoct some type of drug with the fermented foods that he obtained while on K.P., a duty to which he was frequently assigned. Luckily, he found allies in the band members, and even among the noncoms who, as a group, would try to change his ways.

At the end of the month, during a training exercise, Lester wounded himself and was sent to the military hospital. Though not serious, his wound was painful; he was given sedatives and an anodyne to lessen the pain. The military doctors took advantage of his three-week stay at the hospital to carry out thorough medical tests. The files that circulated among the authorities are revealing. In a letter addressed to Lester's company commander, the chief of neuropsychiatric services at the Armed Services Regional Hospital mentions that his patient exhibits a strong psychopathic tendency that manifested itself in the absorption of marijuana and barbiturates and has already manifested itself previously in "chronic alcoholism" and a penchant for "nomadism." (Translation: nomadism= permanent state of a musician with no fixed domicile who travels from city to city all year long to play his music.) "It is apparent that he constitutes a disciplinary problem and that measures should be taken by headquarters." It didn't take long for the measures to be taken. On January 30, six days after leaving the hospital, Lester was taken aside by his captain, a young career officer eight years his junior. On inspecting Lester's locker, the captain came across some cigarettes that seemed to contain marijuana and a bottle of barbiturates. Lester was unable to account for the latter with a medical prescription; he was immediately placed under arrest. The man assigned to guard him was none other than the unfortunate Jo Jones. On the day following Lester's investigation, Jo Jones departed for Fort Ord.

The drugs found in Lester's locker were sent to a laboratory for analysis. Then a hearing was held; Lester was suspected of having violated Article 96 of the *Articles of War*. This article can be found with some variations, depending on the political regime, in practically every country of the world. By tradition, it gives military authorities the arbitrary power to discharge any soldier who demonstrates insubordination, or who, judging from his past, could be considered unmanageable. Invoking the article after uncovering suspicious objects, as in Lester's case, permitted them to hold a hearing.

The hearing was conducted swiftly and efficiently. During the three days that followed, it was established that Young's captain had found him in possession of a quantity of pills and capsules of different shapes and colors, of a few hand-rolled cigarettes, and of two flasks containing a pinkish liquid smelling of alcohol. Test results showed that the substances were indeed marijuana and barbiturates.

While the Harrison Narcotic Drugs Law considered the possession of marijuana to be a crime, this was not the case with barbiturates. Nevertheless, in some states it was stipulated that barbiturates could only be administered on presentation of a medical prescription, without which their possession was considered a crime. Alabama was one of those states, and Lester had to admit he had no prescription. Worse yet, he admitted to having smoked marijuana for the past ten years, as he had previously explained on repeated occasions to his draft board, and to the several military physicians who had examined him. Furthermore, he maintained that he could not have withstood the five weeks of investigation at Fort MacArthur—nor the weeks that had followed—without any barbiturates. The hearing was concluded February 9.

Excerpts from the Report.
Pre-Induction Status.

"Age, 35. Race: Negro. Religion: Protestant. Married. Born in Mississippi; moved to New Orleans at the age of ten. Eldest of three children. Father musician. Low educational level; poor adjustment to family circle. Has been drinking excessively for the past ten years. Drug addict with several minor arrests.[97] Legally married, but living in a common-law relationship for the past nine years. Currently suffering from syphilis.[98] Practicing musician his entire life."

Neuropsychiatric Findings.

"Psychopathic tendencies. As a child, he adapted neither to his family nor to school. He was arrested several times and currently has a common-law wife. For years, he has drunken excessively and has used drugs such as marijuana and barbiturates. Given his undesirable character traits and his maladjusted personality, it is unlikely that he will one day become a satisfactory soldier."

It should be noted that only the doctor who signed this examination recommended Lester's immediate return to civilian life.

General Impression and Rehabilitation Potential.

"Civilian and military records of the accused show that he is not a good soldier. His age, as well as the nature and permanence of his undesirable character traits indicate that he can be of no value to the service without appropriate medical treatment and rigorous disciplinary rehabilitation.

"The charges have been reviewed against Private Second Class Lester Young, accused of being found in possession of drugs in violation of Article 96 of the *Articles of War.* The facts have substantiated the charges. This thirty-five-year-old soldier has never received a military sentence. He seems unfit for military duty and the nature of his infraction warrants a much more serious sentence than a simple court of law could mete out. Nothing indicates that he cannot be held legally responsible for his actions.

"He is to be remanded to a court-martial."

The military court convened on February 16, 1945. The proceedings began at 8:10 P.M. The sentence was rendered ninety minutes later. Testimony by the different witnesses was heard after the prosecuting judge advocate had stated his case, and after Lester had pleaded not guilty.

Testimony from the Witness Stand.

The first witness called to the stand by the prosecution was Captain W.C.S., Lester's immediate superior.

Questions directed by the prosecuting judge advocate.

—Do you know the accused?

—Yes.

—What is his name?

—Private Second Class Lester Young.

—Was he under your command on 30 January 1945?

—Yes.

—Did you have contact or a conversation with him on that date?

—Yes.

—Could you give us an account of the circumstances?

—Orders for the day had assigned him to battalion headquarters and on verifying the orders I noticed this man who seemed to be in bad shape. I asked him what was wrong, and he replied that he was "bombed." I asked him for details and whether he had any drugs. He said he did. Then I asked him if he had anything on him that he had taken. He held out some pills. Lieutenant H——— was with me. We searched Young's clothing and his possessions.

—Did you find anything?

—Yes.

—What did you find?

—I found several little white pills, smaller and a little harder than aspirin, three red capsules, and a few marijuana cigarettes, rolled by hand. Two had been smoked; they were burned and a little crushed.

Counsel for the defense: "Objection! We refute the claim that marijuana was involved."

Presiding Officer: "Objection sustained."

Judge Advocate: "You object to the use of the word marijuana, but not to the word cigarettes?"

The Defense: "Absolutely."

Judge Advocate: "I see no objection to striking that from the record."

—Did you find anything else?

—Yes. There were two bottles of pink liquid. One had a strong bitter odor, as if it smelled of alcohol. It irritated the nostrils.

—Now, what did you do with the pills, capsules, cigarettes and bottles that you had just found?

—I took them to Lieutenant H——— at company headquarters.

—When did you begin to suspect that Private Young was under the influence of something like narcotics?

—I suspected it the first time I saw him in E Company.

—Did you ever say anything to him about it?

—No. The man had himself under passable control; there was no problem.

—What made you suspicious?

—Well, his color, his complexion, and the fact that his eyes seemed bloodshot, plus he didn't respond to training like he should have.

—Before finding these things on his person, did you ever speak to him about using narcotics?

—Yes.

—On what occasion?

—Shortly after he had come back from the hospital; he was in the barracks when he should have been outside training and I asked him if he was using drugs. I had just received a report from the hospital.

—What was his reply?

—He said he did.

—Did you say anything else?

—We talked about it and I asked him if he didn't feel it was bad for his health.

—Did you advise him to have himself examined?

—No.

The next person called to the witness stand was the same Lieutenant H—— who had conducted the initial investigation. He confirmed that he had received from the captain the assorted objects found in the locker as well as Lester's clothing. He confirmed having been the one who sent them to the lab for analysis. When it came time to cross-examine Lieutenant H——, the defense tried unsuccessfully to suggest that there had been confusion during the investigation, and that the results were tied to another case that had been ruled on earlier.

—Have you ever led other investigations here in drug cases?

—Yes.

—Following the first cross-examination, I noticed that you took several envelopes out of your pocket. Are you absolutely sure that the envelopes in your possession are tied directly to this case, and not to one of those you investigated in the past?

—There is absolutely no doubt on that score.

A few minutes later, it was established that Lester Young had been in possession of illegal drugs—barbiturates in both capsule and pill form—and of marijuana cigarettes. During his own testimony, whether elicited by the Judge Advocate or by the defense, Lester never denied using drugs. He had admitted doing so to the military authorities on several previous occasions, and they had not taken notice. On this occasion they reacted violently, and everything seemed to indicate that Lester was not so much on trial for his use of drugs, but rather for his existence as a black musician who was hooked on them.

Lester Young is called to the witness stand.

Questions directed by the prosecuting judge advocate.

—State your name, rank and military assignment.

—My name is Lester Willis Young, Company E, 2nd Battalion, 1st Regiment, Fort McClellan, Alabama.

—Your rank?

—My rank?

—Your Army rank?

—Private Second Class.

—Are you the accused?

—Yes.

—Are you a member of the U.S. Army?

—Yes.

Questions directed by the defense.

—What is your age, Young?

—Thirty-five, sir.

—Are you a professional musician?

—Yes.

—Have you played in an orchestra in California?

—Yes, the Count Basie Orchestra; I've played with him for ten years.

—Have you been using narcotics for some time?

—Yes.

—For how long?

—For ten years; this is my eleventh year.

—What caused you to begin using them?

—Well, we do a lot of one-nighters with the band. In other words, I'd stay up, I'd play, then I'd move on to somewhere else. The only way for me to keep going was to take drugs.

—Do other musicians, other members of the orchestra, also take them?

—Yes, all the ones I know.

—Do you remember the time when you appeared for the first time before the draft board, the time when you were drafted?

—Yes.

—Was anyone aware at the time that you were a habitual drug user?

—Well, I'm practically certain they were because before I was actually drafted, I had to take some of those things for my nerves. But I didn't want to take them, and when I laid down, I was completely knocked out and they put me in jail. Seeing as I was really knocked out, they took away the whiskey that I had and chose to put me in a padded cell instead. While I was in there, they searched my clothes. I was there that day, and the next day they put me upstairs, and it was already the fifth army post I had passed through. . . . "

—When you say you were really knocked out, exactly what do you mean? Do you mean because of the whiskey?

—The whiskey and the barbiturates.

—When they took the whiskey from you, did they say anything to you that would indicate they thought you had a drug habit?

—The only thing they did to me was to take the whiskey and lock me up for several days.

—What I want to know is whether there was, at the time you were drafted, any reason for you to believe that the board knew you regularly used drugs.

The prosecution:

—Just a moment. That requires the witness to have an opinion and to draw a conclusion; that is irrelevant.

Counsel for the defense: "All right, I'll rephrase the question: Did you tell them that you were taking any?"

—Yes.

—Have you been to the hospital since your assignment to Fort McClellan?

—Yes, I stayed there for about three weeks.

—To be examined?

—Yes, and they gave me some sort of paper.

—What for?

—During training, I injured myself on the obstacle course, and I went to the dispensary; they ordered me to report to the hospital, and once I got there, they found out. First, I was in room 32, then they took me to room 36 and the doctor gave me the same pills you have there. He would give me one each at 9 in the morning, one in the afternoon and five in the evening, and also at twenty-one hundred hours.

—Were these the doctors at the hospital?

—I think it was Dr. L. B. . . .

—Did they explain the purpose to you?

—No, because I had been in another hospital where they were giving me some pills.

—They didn't explain to you why?

—No.

—How long did you stay at the hospital here?

—From the first of January until the twenty-second or twenty-third of January.

—Then what happened to you?

—Well, I got out and they sent me back to work.

—Did the patient roster list you as being on duty?

—That's not what they told me, but when I went there, I discovered it did.

—Do you know if, to your knowledge, you were being considered as on duty? . . . When you rejoined your company on leaving the hospital, what were your duties, what did you do?

—Um, what Captain S. was saying—I was sitting in the barracks . . . I got permission when I left the hospital.

—What did you do after leaving the hospital; did you go to bed?

—They sent me back out to the field.

—Were you carrying a full pack?

—I don't know.

—Was it a light pack?

—It was a pack with a weapon.

—Were you carrying any ammunition?

—Yes.

—And this took place immediately after your release from the hospital?

—Yes.

—Immediately after your release?

—Yes.

—Do you recognize this witness as the captain that was sitting with you?

—Yes, I recognize him.

—Was this the captain of your company whom you referred to at the outset?

—Yes.

144

—At the time of the events, was he in command of the same company as now?

—Yes.

—Have you ever had any conversations with him regarding narcotics?

—Yes, one morning when I was sitting in the barracks.

—Did you tell him you were taking any?

—Well, he asked me about it and said he knew that I was really high.

—In referring to the fact that you were really high, would you explain that?

—Well, it's the only way I know to explain my condition.

—When you say you had taken drugs, you are not just alluding to liquor and whiskey, are you?

—Yes I am.

—It's not just whiskey that makes you high when you say you are.

—No.

—Now, if you do not take the drugs, if you do not smoke those things, are you affected physically in one way or another?

—Oh sure, it does something to me! I don't want to do anything. I don't care about blowing into my sax, or about being with people.

—Does it have a serious effect on you?

—Only on my nerves.

—Could you undergo the training here if you didn't take anything?

—No.

—Why?

—Because I tried, sir, I really tried.

—Have you had one of these drugs recently, in the last few days?

—Not since they threw me in here under arrest.

—At present, do you feel fairly nervous?

—I think about it all the time.

Counsel for the defense: That will be all.

Cross-examination by the prosecuting judge advocate.

—I believe that earlier on, I questioned the lieutenant to whom you spoke. I think you told him—and this was confirmed during the investigation—that you could procure the drug without a medical prescription, that it was sufficient just to have money?

—Yes.

—Is that how you obtained it? Is that what you told him?

—That's correct.

—And you purchased it without a medical prescription, isn't that correct?

—Yes, sir.

The prosecution:—I have no more questions. Are there any questions from the bench?

Presiding officer:—No questions. The witness may stand down. Does either party have any questions? Do you wish to add anything? Very well, court will retire to reach a verdict.

Since neither the prosecution nor the defense had anything to add, the court retired. By secret ballot, three fourths of those present agreed on the following verdict: Guilty of having violated Article 96 of the *Articles of War.*

The Verdict.

"The accused is dishonorably discharged from military service. He forfeits all prior and subsequent pay. He is sentenced to perform hard labor for a period of one year at a time and place to be determined by the proper authority."

Lester approached the bailiff and signed a receipt for one copy of his court record.

RECEIPT FOR COPY OF RECORD

I hereby acknowledge receipt of a carbon copy of the above described record of trial,

delivered to me at   Post Stockade, Ft. McClellan, Ala.,

this 24ᵗʰ day of   February , 19 45.

Lester young

(Signature of accused)

Court adjourned at 2125 hours [9:25 P.M.], ninety minutes after it had convened. Pending approval, Lester was sent to the stockade at Fort Leavenworth, Kansas. A few days later, the military authorities decided to send him to the stockade at Fort Gordon, Georgia. What happened during the ten months of incarceration he spent in Georgia will never really be known. Lester always refused to talk about it.

We do know he was detained in the section for black prisoners. His guards were white. He was able to save his sax, and he asked to play in the camp band.

By day, Lester would confine himself to the camp's "recreation hall," practicing his instrument along with other musicians, most of them enlisted. But Lester was a prisoner. Every morning, when the other prisoners set out for their work detail, bassist Billy Goodall, an N.C.O., would come to get Lester in the colored guardhouse; he would jam Lester in the ribs with his weapon and order him to march in silence to company headquarters. Though he considered Lester to be the best musician of them all at that moment, Goodall was obliged to maintain the appearances required by his rank and position. It was essential that the other prisoners know Lester was not enjoying preferential treatment. Goodall eventually cracked under the pressure of treating his friend in such an inhumane manner. He was reprimanded, demoted, and sent to another army post: Fort Stewart.

A few days later, he was replaced by a young white M.P. who was a trumpet player and admirer of the Pres.[99] Every morning Lester would endure the same humiliating process again: the young trumpeter, tears in his eyes, would yell at the older man: "Get back to work, you dirty nigger!"—"Yes, sir," would come Lester's quiet reply.

But as the weeks wore on, he managed to put together a band of about fifteen musicians who, one month before his discharge, gave a public performance. What a bitter irony! Shortly before his induction, Lester had said, "Would I like to have a big band? I sure would!"

He is also known to have performed every Sunday night at the N.C.O. Club. That was when he met guitarist Fred Lacey and pianist Gil Evans, who made a special trip to Fort Gordon to play with the band.

The nights wore on like nightmares.

After his discharge, Lester confided to his friend Gene Ramey, "When they threw me in the stockade, at night the guards would be completely drunk and they'd come to hit me over the head." Their mistreatment ultimately resulted in problems of motor coordination from which he suffered until his death.

By a miraculous stroke of luck, Pres found support in the camp's commanding general. Indeed, it was thanks to him that Lester obtained a commendation for good behavior that permitted him to leave Georgia in December of 1945, two months before his sentence expired. The same commanding general notified Norman Granz, who immediately sent Lester a plane ticket for Los Angeles. Jo Jones himself accompanied Lester on the flight to California: "I was at Fort Ord and they gave me a pass to go down to visit with Lester. . . . I went to Los Angeles and I went out to some little hideaway place with Lester and we played. I said, 'Don't worry about it, Pres, everything's going to be all right.' . . . Then I said, 'Well, pretty soon, Pres, I will be coming out of the army.' When I came out naturally I went back with Basie . . . "(Jo Jones).

Lester was free again, but was a physically and morally shaken individual. From that moment on Lester defined his position as defensive—one of passive defense. To wage the war, he withdrew into his shell, going down with survival rations that consisted of music, alcohol, drugs, and hermetic speech, all designed to hold off at still greater distance that which had surrounded and threatened him from the outset. The battle, of course, was lost from the start.

Chapter 18

Watch Your Step

The man who stepped off the plane in Los Angeles had survived but was more alone than ever. And Mary had abandoned him. With no news of her in several months, Lester did not try to look her up. In fact, she had written him several letters that had all been intercepted by the military authorities. Mary, for her part, thought Lester had forgotten her.

Lester rediscovered life, his old friends Freddie Green and Vic Dickenson. He would also encounter a new generation of musicians formed in the bebop school. For them, Lester the misunderstood, the unloved, the eccentric, was the one that had opened the way. He had been the one Charlie Parker, founder of the new esthetic, had listened to with such fervor. The old guard and the new were mingling in clubs and recording studios. World War II was about to end. The world would soon be changing, and with it, jazz.

Lester fascinated everyone, both the veterans and the newcomers such as Dodo Marmarosa, Howard McGhee, Joe Albany, Chico

Hamilton, Argonne Thornton, Roy Haynes, Chuck Wayne, Curley Russell, and Tiny Kahn. Between the winter of 1945 and December 1948, the great Lester also frequented the Aladdin Studios.

The first session took place in Los Angeles in the winter of 1945. It produced only four singles, but of the four, one was the popular "Lester Blows Again," and another "These Foolish Things," which may well have been the culmination of Lester's artistry. It was then that a haggard Lester Young, just returned from his ordeal with the military, produced his masterpiece. Vic Dickenson and Freddie Green, two of Basie's veterans, along with Red Callender, who had been part of his group in 1942, played alongside nineteen-year-old Dodo Marmarosa, who had just left Artie Shaw and was the great hope among bebop pianists.

The second Aladdin session, at the beginning of 1946 and still in Los Angeles, found Lester with a more substantial group, at the center of which was Howard McGhee. The session produced four additional sides with more elaborate orchestrations, including "It's Only a Paper Moon," and "Lover Come Back to Me."

The third session of August 1946 (once again in Los Angeles) saw four additional sides cut, one of which bears a title suggestive of the crossroads at which jazz stood: "Lester's Be-Bop Boogie." At Lester's side stood Irving Ashby, Nat King Cole's future sideman; Chico Hamilton, one of several then experimenting with new rhythms; and most important of all, Joe Albany who would also become one of the most extraordinary figures in bebop music.

During those first six months spent with "Jazz at the Philharmonic" (J.A.T.P), Lester's behavior changed considerably. He wouldn't admit it, but the tour bored him. He didn't much appreciate the principle of an organized jam session, nor the competitive spirit that reigned onstage among the musicians; indeed, he did not participate in the 1947 tour. Nevertheless, he was always the first to show up for rehearsals, the first in his dressing room before a concert; for him, punctuality was a form of respect toward the music and toward the audience.

One night he came wearing his big wide-brimmed black hat

again, the same one he had worn before being drafted. People smiled when they saw him. Then he started speaking in a kind of foreign language known only to him. He punctuated his sentences with "oodastaddis," words he used like a shield. He talked to avoid saying anything.

He was often seen standing motionless, with his hat pushed back on his head and a cigarette in the corner of his mouth; when someone would finally ask what was going on, he'd say, "I feel a draft," which meant that he felt victimized by intrusive eyes. Lester believed that white men, the "gray boys," as he called them, were persecuting him. This idea of a plot would degenerate a few years later into paranoia. He complained of sensing that "Bob Crosby"—the police—was spying on him wherever he went. When asking for news of a friend's family, he would say: "How are your affections?" If a question got on his nerves, he would answer, "Ding dong." If he wanted to succeed at something, he'd say, "I'm going to get my tonics together."[100] If he failed at the attempt, he would grumble, "I'm hit"; but in the case of a success, he would say, "I'm in order, correct." When commenting on the performance of a pianist he liked, he'd refer to the left hand as "the lefties." But this peculiar "language" could become hermetic to such a degree that when Pres went to a restaurant, friends accompanying him would have to translate his order for the staff.

Lester wore a hat and talked hip. Okay, but all musicians talked hip in those days. The one I think used slang more than anybody else was Ben Webster. As near as I can remember, show business people have always used slang. When I was a kid, people had gotten into the habit of speaking a slang that was called "pig Latin" which, incidentally, Lester used. . . . I don't really know why people talk all the time about Lester's hat. It's true that people like to talk about that kind of thing when it comes to musicians. After all, every one has peculiarities that match his personality. During recording sessions, most musicians did wear hats. Look at Lester, Ben Webster, Johnny Hodges, Coleman Hawkins, Charlie Christian. . . . Pres didn't wear his hat in concert. (Eddie Barefield)

The fourth session was recorded in Chicago in 1947. In the midst of Lester's regular orchestra, there stood another strange figure of contemporary piano: Argonne Thornton, who later became Sadik Hakim. That was the day they cut the celebrated "Jumpin' with Symphony Sid," a tune dedicated to Symphony Sid Torin, the well-known disc jockey and great cultist of the new music. This number became a great success and permitted Lester to reach the widest possible audience and rack up substantial royalties.

Lester was retiring, retrenching. He kept everything at a distance. His language, his behavior, his physical appearance, all became weapons of dissuasion. He let his hair grow. It was wavy and carefully combed toward the nape of the neck. Perhaps it was a form of protest, a response to what the army had subjected him to by forcing him to have it cut. . . . He quit wearing the hat. He sauntered in an effort to give the appearance of being drunk. The rumor started that Lester was a junkie. Didn't everything suggest it? His gait, his bloodshot eyes, his way of talking, the spoons and the bits of burned paper he left lying conspicuously about his dressing room. Suddenly, in an assertive move, he tied a ribbon in his hair. He changed his manner. He acquired dainty mannerisms, he would turn a sweet smile on any man that looked at him. At night, alone, he drank in the dark. Gin. Whiskey. He smoked. Tobacco. Marijuana. He would eat curled up on a chair. Crackers. And he was careful not to move, very careful. Not to move a muscle. He was afraid to open his eyes.

"Who needs all the uproar? Not me. I'm looking for something mellow, I need some tender eyes. Yeah, man, I really need some tenderness."

After deciding to end his first association with Norman Granz's J.A.T.P., Lester took refuge in New York. He wore his black hat again (as well as dark clothes) and draped a loose-fitting overcoat around himself. He looked frightful. That was when he met composer-lyricist Charlie Carpenter. A friendship developed between them. More than a passing friendship. They understood each other immediately.

Lester had already reached the point of no return in 1946. He was tired of the responsibilities of this world and was looking for a way out. He was very sensitive, and he had been so hurt by all the people who had criticized his tone. His personal problems didn't help any. He felt misunderstood, and if he was surly or didn't talk at all, it was because he was afraid of being hurt again. At the same time, he liked to be different; he needed to be that way. (Charlie Carpenter)

In New York in 1947, Lester recorded the six sides of the fifth session, among them the superb "I'm Confessin'" and the famous "Jumpin' at the Woodside." At his side stood one of the great technicians of bebop percussion, Roy Haynes.

The title of the tune he recorded at the Aladdin studios in Chicago on February 18, 1948, is significant: "No Eyes Blues." It underscores the pain Lester felt from being attacked and ignored by his entourage and how he wanted the pain eradicated, out of his sight. No eyes for a world that had none for him.

The sixth and last Aladdin session was recorded December 29, 1948, under the direction of Leonard Feather. It included only three selections and featured the accompaniment of a rhythm section comprised of Chuck Wayne, Curley Russell, and Tiny Kahn. Here, the old "Sheik of Araby" draped itself in ominous outbursts of fire.

In December, Lester received both the *down beat* Award and *Esquire*'s Silver Award for best tenor saxophonist of the year despite his recent absence. As Harry Lim wrote in *Esquire,* "If we look back over the last few years, we notice that Lester is the only tenor sax player who has emerged with a style that is exclusively his own. . . . His phrasing is magnificent, never does he lose the melodic line of the piece he's playing, and that's like a breath of fresh air in these frantic times."

In the same magazine, Norman Granz stated: "Lester Young, whom I consider to be the greatest musician I have heard on the instrument, embodies some special stuff: fresh ideas, a marvelous tempo, and always good taste. . . . "

And John Hammond goes on to say, "Lester Young is the most creative saxophonist America has ever produced. . . . "

Soon he would be rich, admired, and copied by an entire generation of musicians; his genius was celebrated worldwide, but Lester was worn out. Recognition had taken too long. He didn't have the strength to wait for it. It stretched before him like a shadow. And while this shadow would attend his music until the end, it also covered him. Pres was taking his leave; he was retiring. His music became allusive and detached.

Early in 1946 Lester signed an exclusive recording contract with Norman Granz, who also became his manager. From then until 1958, Lester would record about 125 numbers on various labels produced by Granz. Granz had had his first experiences in the jazz world in 1943 when he organized jam sessions on Monday night at Club 331 in Los Angeles. These were so successful that he organized others on Tuesday nights in another club. A few months later, in February, he produced a series of concerts in the back room of the Music Town Record Shop; each musician was paid eleven dollars. It was in July 1944 that he organized the Sleepy Lagoon Defense Fund, a benefit for young Mexican prison inmates, which turned into his first big concert at the Philharmonic Auditorium. Just one month later, he organized his first "Jazz at the Philharmonic" (J.A.T.P.) in the same auditorium; he envisioned it as a mammoth jam session with about ten musicians in attendance.

After having signed the production and management contract with Lester, Granz persuaded Billy Berg to open up his club, the Trouville, for Sunday afternoon jam sessions. Naturally, the premiere was held with Lester, whom Granz was quick to advertise in conjunction with Dizzy Gillespie, Willie Smith, Charlie Ventura, Mel Powell, Billy Madnott, Lee Young, Al Killian, and Charlie Parker. However, the management of the auditorium found that the audience was too noisy and unrestrained and refused Granz permission to hold any more concerts.

But it would take a lot more to discourage Granz, who decided then and there to export his idea to other cities. Why not organize a national tour every six months with about ten musicians on the bill? Granz contacted Pres and other musicians and offered each five hundred dollars a week. The idea was appealing, the pay was attractive, and after two other concerts in Los Angeles that brought together Al Killian, Howard McGhee, Buck Clayton, Charlie Parker, Willie Smith, Coleman Hawkins, the Pres, Arnold Roos, Kenny Kersey, Irving Ashby, Billy Madnott, Lee Young, and Buddy Rich, the entire company set out en route for Chicago and New York, where it performed twice at Carnegie Hall (on May 27 and June 3).

> . . . I mean the whole reason for J.A.T.P., basically, was to take it to places where I could break it down, break down segregation and discrimination, present good jazz and make bread for myself and for the musicians as well. . . . We had bad pianos; we had bad mikes; we had bad dressing rooms. . . . (Norman Granz)[101]

In the end America did accept him into her sight, did grant him recognition. Meanwhile, in Europe, criticism reared its ugly head in the trade papers. In his book *Les Rois du jazz* [*The Kings of Jazz*], Hugues Panassié wrote,

> Lester Young has been highly overrated. His phrases are often excessively overwrought in an unpleasantly "modernistic" manner. But he has a lot of imagination and has, in his better moments, considerable swing.

Twenty days after "Jumpin' with Symphony Sid" was recorded,[102] critic Eric Guillod wrote these, for the most part, amazingly uninformed remarks in the March 1947 issue of Brussels' *Hot Club Magazine*,

> Lester Young's tone is wearisome because it is nearly always even, whether in the middle, lower, or upper register. When listening to Young, one has difficulty comparing his style to Hawkins' tone, even in a solo like the one in "Jive at Five."[103] His phrases are much too simple, and harmonic experimentation is virtually nonexistent. . . . In "Oh, Lady be Good," for example, Lester Young comes in immediately after the trumpet

solo with a bad chorus in which he is content to play a few notes in the lower range. It's not pretty, though one can't deny it swings, for he knows where to place his notes, an obvious mark of the black race's superiority over the white. . . . Should this soloist be relegated to the wings because he has a bad tone?[105]

A few years later, Lester Young took that trip and personally made acquaintance with the old continent; he saw Europe firsthand.

Chapter 19

Bebop, Cool, and Swing, Too

Lester was in constant demand as a performer for the two years that followed (1948–1949). He crisscrossed every state of the northern United States from New York to Seattle. His tours were arranged by his new manager, Charlie Carpenter, and by the Moe Gale Concert Agency of New York.[105] "I like to travel," he said. "There's always something new."

He had just cancelled the management contract that tied him to Norman Granz and had chosen Carpenter as his new business manager. Carpenter was convinced that the best way to prevent Pres from lapsing back into periods of depression was to have him play as much as possible. He was right on the mark, and only five weeks after their partnership had begun, Lester seemed to be regaining his strength. But if Lester was enjoying great activity on the concert circuit, his appearances in the recording studios were rare. Thus the only recorded material from 1948 is a studio mix of several radio tapings from New York's Royal Roost.

Another event highlighted Lester's life at this time: first he met, and then married, another woman named Mary. It was the third and next-to-last serious relationship he had with a woman.[106] Mary was a gentle, caring individual who made every effort to create for Lester a serene, familial environment. A few months after the wedding, Mary and Lester had their first child, Lester, Jr.

Shortly before their son's birth, the Youngs settled into a small house at Saint Albans in suburban New York, providing Lester with an opportunity to get his personal matters in order. The income from the next few concerts enabled him to furnish the house, which became his refuge.

Although Pres was back on the road, he scrupulously avoided all southern cities. Unfortunately, his enthusiasm rapidly began to fade; the musicians he had picked for his various groups did not give him full satisfaction: "You have to have some hip guys to make hip music, and there isn't a single one of those motherfuckers in my group."

Depression set in again. He went everywhere with his bottle of gin. From time to time he drank beer, sherry, or Courvoisier. He ate little. "I remember one tour when he was gone for four days and had to be forced to eat" (Charlie Carpenter).

When the musicians' playing did not suit him, Lester would walk off the stage and return to his hotel, a hotel he always chose himself, regardless of the arrangements made by the promoters. Back in his room, he would turn on all the lights, switch on the radio, and put a record on his portable record player, then lie down without taking off his clothes.

Nevertheless, Lester could occasionally count on some quality musicians like Jessie Drakes, Junior Mance, Horace Silver, Aaron Bell, Gene Ramey, Jo Jones, Connie Kay, Roy Haynes, and John Lewis; Lewis was constantly saying, "Lester absolutely must have first-rate musicians to play with." Gene Ramey, who was one of the most popular and most requested bassists of the day, remembers a tense Lester always at his heels trying to convince him that he should join the band. They participated together in a tour that

Moe Gale organized, and after Birdland opened they often played side by side. More than any other musician, Ramey became a true friend to Lester. He attended his wedding, visited him in Saint Albans, and was his confidant and musical companion. In fact, he was godfather to Lester, Jr.

The main difficulty facing Lester was forming a group that was likely to have a permanent existence. When the "ballrooms"—or dance halls—closed at the end of the war, the result was the rapid disappearance of the big bands. The reign of the "star soloist" had begun. Most of the New York nightclub owners preferred to hire a musician with a solid reputation who was backed by chance accompanists, rather than to hire a quality ensemble without any big name soloist. As for the public, it changed with the times and began to attend whenever it felt attracted by the name of a given musician. The situation hasn't changed much today.

It's a well-known fact that Lester was demanding and expected the best from every musician; he also had no aptitude for business. In a system where the principal soloist had to find his own side-men, competition was stiff, and Lester was not the best of recruiters. In addition, many young musicians preferred to express themselves strictly in a bebop context. Thus, given that his man-ager concerned himself exclusively with administrative and finan-cial matters, when Pres was setting up an engagement he was often forced to approach each of his acquaintances individually with the proposition.

Pres didn't understand much about financial matters, and he did not follow the advice of Charlie Carpenter, who told him to carefully examine his contracts. He never knew exactly what salary he was to collect at the end of a performance, and he was often cheated out of money when his manager wasn't with him. If he noticed anything unusual when he was being paid, or in the behavior of the manager at the club he was playing, he refused to say anything. At most, he might say something about it to a friend, who would ask, "And you didn't do anything?" Then Lester would shrug his shoulders. He saw no reason to argue. What for?

That was the natural course of things. The best thing to do was to forget it.

In November 1948, after a concert in Cleveland, Lester headed back to New York. Rather than move back in with his family in Saint Albans, he checked into the Chesterfield Hotel, which stood near a small nightclub between Forty-seventh and Forty-eighth streets on Broadway: the Royal Roost. In the spring, he began a series of engagements there with trumpeter Jessie Drakes, trombonist Tel Kelly, pianist Freddy Jefferson, bass player Tex Brisoe, and drummer Roy Haynes.

When Haynes had to bow out, Pres called in another friend, Connie Kay.

> I met him [Lester] down in Penn Station and asked him what he was doing, and he said, "I'm waiting for the drummer, Lady Kay," which is what he always called me. . . . He was a sweetheart to me. He was very shy. He didn't love crowds or to be around strangers, and he didn't like to eat. All that alcohol. He'd leave home for work with a fifth of Scotch every night and everybody in the band would work on it to keep Lester from getting too drunk. . . . Later, the doctor told him to switch to cognac—a little cognac—so it was a whole bottle of cognac every night. . . . I used to ask him why he didn't play his clarinet once in a while, and he'd always say, "Lady Kay, I'm saving that for my old age." (Connie Kay)[107]

Before he appeared at the Royal Roost, Lester left on a tour up and down the East Coast highways.

> He was of the old school. For professional reasons, he felt himself obliged to be on time. One day, in fact, Al Cooper, who ordinarily organized shows in the New York area, said, "The only thing you need to fear with Lester is that he show up late." One day he missed a train in Washington because he had fallen asleep at the station. He was supposed to be at New Bedford, Mass., to perform that night. Instead of waiting for the next train, he panicked. He took a taxi all the way to Newark, got a seat on a plane to Providence, and once there, took another taxi

to New Bedford. I think it wound up costing him $250. He arrived an hour late and played three extra hours for free. (Charlie Carpenter)

That fall, Lester took part in the annual J.A.T.P. tour and appeared at Carnegie Hall on September 18 with Flip Phillips, Roy Eldridge, Tommy Turk, Charlie Parker, Coleman Hawkins, Hank Jones, Ray Brown, and Buddy Rich. In the press releases sent out by the Gale Agency to many newspapers and magazines around the country, Pres was not referred to as "The Pres" but as the "King of the Sax." In the press photo he appeared donning a ridiculous crown.

After several months of negotiations with the security and law enforcement agencies, Birdland finally opened its doors on December 15, 1949. It was entrusted to the former managers of the Royal Roost, whose doors soon closed as a result. Three ensembles took part in the inaugural performance: that of Charlie Parker, that of Lennie Tristano, and that of Max Kaminsky. Two talented young vocalists named Florence Wright and Harry Belafonte also took part. Pres, who had made a big impression a few months earlier at the Royal Roost, was the guest of honor; he performed with each of the three groups.

After the performance, Lester fell back into a deep depression and a few weeks later sought refuge in the Mark, a small hotel on Forty-third Street. His recent tours and participation in the J.A.T.P. had earned him a lot of money. That year, his income is estimated to have reached fifty thousand dollars. His celebrity was unprecedented. And the money was unspent. Apart from a few suits—always chosen in shades of gray—his booze and his cigarettes, Lester had no expenses. He did regularly stop off in Saint Albans to leave money with his wife, Mary, who remained dutifully quiet and tried to comfort him at each visit.

Instead of settling into obscure, impersonal places, Lester could have afforded deluxe hotels, which weren't lacking in Manhattan.

But he preferred places where he could remain anonymous. Instead of a restaurant, he preferred the cafeteria on the other side of the street, the one where shoeshine boys, newspaper vendors, shoelace hawkers, and all the men who struggled to unload trucks for a few miserable cents would congregate. And even there he didn't feel at home. Whereas his contemporaries plunged headlong into material consumption, Pres owned nothing. He had forgotten all that, even the car that he had cherished in his dreams.

Money and "success" had a negative effect on Pres. By day, he lived in seclusion in his eighth-floor hotel room; he would spend hours caressing a cat that he had taken in and given the name "Philharmonic."

After waking up one morning feeling weary and angry, Lester began to take his feelings out on the animal which, out of its wits with fright, found no better solution than to jump out the window. Lester would avoid his listener's gaze when telling this anecdote.

At night, after hanging around Birdland for a while, he would ask Gene Ramey to walk him back to his hotel. But whenever he thought he'd get some peace listening to his favorite records, someone would softly knock at his door. It was Stan Getz who came to ask him for advice. Pres would patiently confer with him, and after digging around in his boxes, play one of his own records. Next day Getz would be there again, with more questions—and the following days, too, sometimes alone, sometimes with other saxophonists.

Lester experienced a deep uneasiness when making the rounds of the clubs. On the one hand, he would see young tenor saxophonists playing just like him and smile and call them "Pres." But he also realized that most of the musicians were picking up on ideas that he himself had spurned. He felt both exploited and rejected at the same time, as one of his close friends has revealed: "He looked pitiful walking along Fifty-second Street. He could hear all the young guys picking up on ideas he'd rejected. He had come back to find his roots. He didn't find them; you could see him trying to decide which direction to take."

This was about the time people started talking more and more about a saxophonist from Denver who had once played with Nat Towles and Lloyd Hunter: Paul Quinichette. There would never be a musician with a style more like Lester's. They were indistinguishable. Lester Young and his double: Paul Quinichette. The irony of it was that the double did better than his model. He even wound up with the success and the engagements. Lester was somewhere else, always. Yet when the two of them met, they became friends. They were so close that Quinichette became the only musician to whom Lester agreed to lend his sax. On certain evenings, when he was in Paul's presence at a club, Lester would refuse to appear onstage, leaving the honors to the "vice-president" who has today practically fallen into oblivion. But the bitterness crept in when Lester confided in Charlie Carpenter: "I don't know if I should play like myself or like Lady Q., since he plays so much like me."

With that, he said it all.

By that time bebop was causing tremendous excitement in New York, and had been for several years. A number of musicians were turning the rhythmic and harmonic language of jazz upside down. Some of them were credited—often erroneously—with wanting to deny a tradition that they had approved of until then. A few of them claimed that the musical notions of the preceding generation had been outpaced, that it was important to move forward. Yesterday's ideas were quickly forgotten.

A quick technical study reveals that the young musicians who bore the bebop banner had started emphasizing the second and fourth beats, i.e., the weak beats in the measure. In that they clashed with Kansas City musicians like Walter Page, Buster Smith, Count Basie, and Lester, who accentuated the four beats equally, and still more so with the older musicians who favored the first and third beats.

Impelled by Dizzy Gillespie, Thelonious Monk, Charlie Parker, and Kenny Clarke, harmonic experimentation became more complex, and interpretation of the notes took new directions. For musicians of the Swing era, then in its glory days, the success of bebop was a real problem. Even if they wished to, few of them had the ability to adapt. But that should by no means be interpreted to mean that all of them wanted to adapt. Most of them remained loyal to swing and it would, of course, be ridiculous to claim that swing had disappeared with the arrival of bebop.

> . . . They heard about Minton's. So when they came in town, they tear up to Minton's. I remember Prez getting up there because Prez is supposed to be, you know, the President. And they lowered the boom on him with this new music. And Prez had never heard no music like this before. He couldn't get outta the first four bars, man, you know. You gotta have some music in front of you to read or something; your ear will not carry you to where these guys were going. And it was sort of funny and pitiful at the same time, but it was a good lesson. (Budd Johnson)[108]

The reasons for these difficulties were understandable: the various metronome tempos used by the boppers were practically all above 300, black style. During his own career, Pres ordinarily played at a tempo that hovered between 170 and 200, and, as we have said, he played exclusively 4/4. There are one or two exceptions where he accelerates up to 256 ("Shoe Shine Boy") and 284 ("Clap Hands, Here Comes Charlie"). For ballads, he rarely went below 100, contrary to the boppers who, on top of everything else, included numerous accelerated sequences in theirs. As for the "Swing" musicians, their tempos varied generally between 100 and 200.

However, there were very subtle ties between Lester's style and the movement of which Dizzy was one of the champions.

Charlie Parker and Charlie Christian—who was the true linchpin between swing and bop—had developed what Pres described as a "nonchalant, progressive style in which you prefer to relax instead of beating on the next guy's nose." Inspired by his frequent contacts with Young, Christian made an effort to transpose Lester's style onto the guitar.

But this new standard, and the rapidity and profusion of notes found in bop music, left Lester puzzled. He did not answer the call of the new trend but remained faithful to his own rhythmic and harmonic needs. This didn't prevent him from working with several musicians who had rallied to the theories expressed by Gillespie: Clyde Hart, Slam Stewart, Gene Ramey, Dodo Marmarosa, Cozy Cole, to name a few. Cole was, along with Jo Jones, Sid Catlett, Connie Kay, and Roy Haynes, among the drummers preferred by Lester because they maintained a regular base tempo. While giving light touches to the snare drum, they would subtly use their sticks or brushes on the high-hat. As a result, they were among the most able percussionists in all jazz history.

So what was the reason for Lester's loyalty?

German critic Joachim E. Berendt attributes it to a rejection of "innovative exuberance."[109] Berendt believes that Lester's "unreceptive attitude" and the contradiction of ideas that separated him and Charlie "Bird" Parker—both of which led to the development of modern jazz—are fundamentally tied to an "inward struggle between two aspects of Pres' personality: the introverted aspect and the revolutionary aspect. The revolutionary Lester merely allowed the other side to get the upper hand." Berendt is right, of course. But one can go a few steps further and offer a slightly different historical reading.

Lester's concerns were no longer revolutionary at that time of his life. The confrontational ardor had died out. Lester no longer had the necessary strength, either physical or mental, to commit himself to the new course of things, even though he had mapped it out. By clinging to his own style, by preserving it, Lester kept himself alive. He became reactionary. Indifference was his pose. In fact, he was pulling back. But this retrenchment, both modest and tormented at once, placed him "above" what was then bebop in full evolution. On the other hand, Parker, filled with creative ardor, would impregnate bebop with his entire personality; he would become its real powerhouse. Parker's impetus nevertheless retained some of Lester's technical virtues, such as the lightness of sound (without the vibrato), the extension of improvisation beyond the stricture of four measures, a concern for polyrhythmics, and the preeminence given to melody. And indeed, it was the "negative" outlook of Lester's reclusive stance, matched by the opposite "positive" attitude of Parker, which, by way of their successive encounters, sired modern jazz.

When Lester was asked which of the younger saxophonists he liked most, he would cite Wardell Gray, adding "if you're talking about the gray boys, Allen Eager can blow." Not long after that, four saxophonists performed at the Pontelli Ballroom in Los Angeles; their names were Stan Getz, Zoot Sims, Jimmy Giuffre, and Herb Steward. They admitted that Lester had had a direct influence on them. With this first important wave of disciples— i.e., with the emerging piano school of Lennie Tristano, and especially with the school recently formed by Miles Davis that had produced "The Birth of Cool" (first synthesis of both Lester's and Parker's styles), there emerged a new movement that the press qualified as "cool."

Lester did not adapt to bebop esthetics. Something within him resisted this move. On the other hand, he was the founder of cool and was only half conscious of his offspring. In his youth, he had blueprinted the bebop design by working the legacy of Frankie Trumbauer, then he had developed it unconsciously in his personal evolution, via his thought patterns, his pastimes, his lifestyle. In effect, the traits he had discovered in the music corresponded to several traits in his own personality. People speak of introspective musical sentiment, of intellectualism, of false lethargy, and of a tonal quality that supposedly corresponded to his spiritual quest.

Lester always denied having any ties with bebop; and as for "cool," he never said a thing about it. It was with a veiled pride that he discerned his influence on certain young musicians, but he never made an issue of it. In response to a world intent on putting him in some "class," Lester would use only one adjective: swing. And he didn't mean a trend or school by that; it was simply meant to describe his concept of tenor playing: "I play swing tenor. I don't play swing, cool or bop, I play swing tenor."

Pres also categorically rejected the term "honk" used by the critics to describe certain embellishments he included in his music, favoring instead the term "swing." The notion of a "swing" tenor is actually closely tied to Lester's fondness for dancing and melody. But after repeated use by him in 1950, the expression took on more dramatic connotations.

Despite the hostile world in which he was evolving, despite his sometimes acerbic critics, Lester had always clung to the notion of enjoyment. But it seems that after his discharge from the military, Pres lost his sense of pleasure in playing. What kept him going afterward were surges of desperate energy. Sometimes his grasp of the instrument was vigorous, sometimes the saxophone appeared to be the only thing holding his fugitive body in place.

The first quarter of 1951 saw Lester's every wish fulfilled. For three months he performed at Birdland with a solid group made up of several of his favorite musicians: John Lewis, Gene Ramey and Jo Jones. With them he recorded about ten numbers for Norman Granz. Jessie Drakes who, next to Buck Clayton, was Pres's choice on trumpet joined the group around mid-March; he played regularly with Lester's ensembles from then until 1957.

> I really like John Lewis' playing a lot. The Modern Jazz Quartet is very nice, but it has to play in a quiet place for people to be able to hear it. Those short things they play are original compositions. It's a novelty. Aside from them, I've never heard anybody play like that. . . . I like Jessie Drakes because he plays his way and doesn't try to imitate anyone. We've been playing together for so long that I barely have to start a piece, and we're on our way. Things like that mean a lot. (Lester Young)

Aside from Birdland, which gave him the security he needed, Lester did little else. He had finally given up the depressing hotels in Manhattan and moved back home to Saint Albans where he began to spend some time with his son. He remembered his own childhood and the virtually nonexistent relationship between his father and himself. Aside from certain family friends and the musicians with whom he played, Pres didn't want contact with anyone; he preferred to keep to himself. Not long before, when visiting Carnegie Hall, he had had words with the administration which refused to give him access to a dressing room he might have occupied alone. Charlie Carpenter recalled it as follows,

> He never got dressed in a room with the rest of the guys, unless it was really the only available room. . . . Most of the time he kept to himself. They always wanted to pair off and chase the girls. Not Lester. In fact, his relationships with women seemed strange to me. Those I saw were like him, same size and delicate. The only guys he would hang out with during a tour were strange, anti-social types. One of them, a drummer, had a style Lester didn't like; but they hung out together like bugs in a rug.

Lester stayed in New York most of that year; Birdland had definitely adopted him, and Pres made it his musical home base. Reacting to one of Lester's gigs at the club, on a night when he shared billing with Dizzy Gillespie, a certain magazine emphasized its preference for Lester's group, but concluded—and this is important: "This is but one of several evenings which prove that Lester without Granz is a good formula." Indeed, aside from their finances and their publicity, Lester got little musical satisfaction from his participation in concerts at any of the J.A.T.P. levels. Their joint recordings attest to this. He was more apt to find the musical conviviality he needed in groups he could form himself. Yet as pleasant as it was, life in a small group drew quickly to a close. The problems he faced as band leader were distasteful to him, and if no one intervened to take the reins in his place, Lester was lost. It would certainly have been preferable to see a Lester in command of himself, confident, basically optimistic under all circumstances, and an excellent business manager to boot. Reality proved otherwise. And so despite the "good formula," it was difficult to imagine Lester without Granz, for in a sense, Granz had been his tutor. In the eyes of many, therefore, the first-rate performances of Lester and his band (and there were some exceptions) constitute the last select moments offered to the public by the Pres.

It was 1952 before Lester undertook the first of his transatlantic voyages. When Norman Granz informed him of an upcoming J.A.T.P. tour in Europe, Lester caught the ball in mid-air and accepted the invitation on the spot. He did, however, request an exemption from having to complete the entire tour; he was only interested in Paris and in one or two other cities. And yet on April 6, 1952, onstage in Paris at the Salle Pleyel, Lester was disoriented. Some excellent musicians were backing him up: Hank Jones, Ray Brown, and Max Roach. But the Pres was not with it. The audience that had come to attend this particular concert to close the Salon du Jazz was disappointed. His first European trip was only half successful. The French magazine *Jazz Hot* gave a laconic account of the evening in its May issue: "It was quite a disappointment for many jazz lovers." But the respect the specialized press had for Lester prevented any more vehement criticism.

Even though the Pres was not "with it" when these opinions were expressed, he was aware that things had not unfolded the way he had wanted. Coleman Hawkins had come seeking glory in Europe before he had, and Hawkins had had no trouble in finding it. The general public had been favorable toward him. The audiences had been charmed by his assured personality and by his remarkable playing. For Lester, things worked just the other way. Disappointed, he placed the fault on the operating procedures of the J.A.T.P. and showed no objections to accepting the invitation of several musicians to go jamming in a Parisian club called Le Ringside. His first contact with French musicians proved to be excellent, and on that occasion, Lester came away satisfied: "I value a certain number of musicians that I played with in Europe. There were some towns where I'd play in two or three different places the night after a J.A.T.P. concert. I was surprised because here, you hear some funny things about what goes on over there, but when you go to Europe, you find out that those people play very well, too" (Lester Young).

When it came time to leave Paris, Lester promised to return. But before returning to New York, he took off for a gig in Brussels. This was a concert organized by the Hot Club of Belgium, and it was a carbon copy of the Paris concert, but no one was pleased. It was a relief for Lester to return to the United States, and there he immediately sought out the security he enjoyed at Birdland.

It was like old times in January of 1953. Lester appeared for three weeks at Birdland, both as part of a quintet, and as the special guest of the Count Basie Orchestra. He asked for $125 a week, but John Hammond, program director at the time, refused. Lester got angry, called the producer every name under the sun, and resolved never to speak to him again. For several days after that, whenever Lester saw him in the club, he would taunt him saying, "Here comes the tightwad again." Feeling uneasy about the matter, Hammond made an effort to win back the esteem and friendship of the Pres. He was never to succeed, and Lester avoided him no matter what the circumstances. In fact, to show his displeasure, Lester played a trick on the orchestra musicians.

He slipped a water pistol into the breast pocket of his jacket. Standing in front of one of the other musicians, he reached slowly into his jacket; suddenly, the movement accelerated, and fifteen seconds later, Lester stood looking happily into the same face, now dripping and torn between a smile and a grimace. No one knew how to take these practical jokes; some were amused, others were irritated.

At the end of the Birdland engagement, Lester flew off on a six-week tour of Europe with the new J.A.T.P. lineup. After one concert in London, he made the acquaintance of a budding new saxophonist called Ronnie Scott. Impressed by the older man's playing, Scott voiced regrets at not having Lester for a teacher. "Too bad we can't do anything about it," said Scott to him. "Oh, but we can," said Lester, who then turned down the invitation of his pals to visit the city in favor of dedicating several hours of his time to coaching Scott. The founder of the famous Ronnie Scott's Club still recalls Lester as a man who was gentle, generous, and attentive, and who deeply loved kindness.

In 1953, during this second of Lester's stays in Europe, Henri Renaud, then pianist and band director at the Tabou on Dauphine Street, met the Pres:

> Norman Granz had offered his musicians a one-week vacation in Paris after the J.A.T.P. concert. Lester was staying at the Claridge on the Champs-Elysées; Jimmy Gourley and I would go pay him a visit every afternoon: it was like going to see God!
>
> I can still hear Pres answer the phone in that odd affected manner of his; he would pucker up his mouth—which was already round to start with—and say in a very soft, studied voice: "This is Dr. Willis. . . . " He'd say a few words into the receiver, come back to you and confidentially reveal, "It was Ella [Fitzgerald]. She is a lady, too. . . . "
>
> One day I had brought along copies of the 78 RPM's recorded by Pres with Billie Holiday and the Teddy Wilson Orchestra at the end of the thirties. Apparently, Pres had never listened to them again. Listening to his solos, he would indicate astonishment and he'd gasp with surprise, as if he were listening to a saxophonist other than himself! After we had listened, he asked me to leave the records with him; I agreed (though secretly dismayed) to do so, and he remarked, "It's because I'm going to cut an updated version of those numbers."
>
> Someone had told him we were working the Tabou and had invited him to come join us some night. He said, "Write me the address on this paper, and tonight Lester will arrive." We didn't dare believe it. But that very evening, at midnight precisely, a taxi drove up in front of the club. And under the famous hat . . . in walked Lester with his tenor sax! We had let the word out to a number of friends, and they were there expecting him: Léon Cabat, Sacha Distel, Charles Delaunay, etc. There's a picture showing Pres giving the orchestra a surprised look: "Why isn't the guitarist marking the beat?" he cried with a sharp note of reproach. It was Gourley, apparently, who was standing with his

guitar held like a saxophone. I suggested Pres drink something; he refused at first, saying, "Look at my hair. See? It's kinky; I'm a negro; isn't someone going to slip something into my drink?" And he could plainly see that everyone at the *Tabou* loved him. He had a whiskey; he asked a girl to dance; and after a while, "I'm going to play with you some." One picture really captures the scene. You can see Jimmy looking at Lester as he would an idol! We played standards, notably "Somebody Loves Me." We were in seventh heaven. . . .

Our little group of musicians consisted of people for whom playing jazz meant trying to play like Lester. Nowadays, this also has to be made absolutely clear: Having been cut off from the United States by four years of war, we had gone straight from Django Reinhardt to Charlie Parker; and we were then discovering the man who had transformed jazz in the interim period; it was Jimmy Gourley who played a crucial part in that regard. Arriving from Chicago, Jimmy Gourley moved to Paris in 1951 and became what amounts to our jazz "courier." He introduced us to the style of jazz which had had much influence on great numbers of American musicians in the early 1940s, but with which we were not familiar, due to the events of the period.

When you tally them up, it's wild how many American musicians of my generation decided to play jazz after hearing Lester—Lester with the Basie orchestra, that is. At the top of the list is Dexter Gordon, who renders such beautiful homage to Pres in the Tavernier movie *Round Midnight*. In 1939, while still in high school, Dex saw a poster announcing that the Basie orchestra was playing in a movie theater, during the intermissions. He went. All he saw was Lester! Dex was amazed! He attended every single performance. When he got home he announced to his parents, "I'm finished with school; I'm going to be a tenor saxophonist." And lots of other people did the same thing! Jay Jay Johnson, the trombonist, told me that he and his musician friends, whatever their instrument, would learn the solos Lester played with Basie. George Wallington the pianist, too. He was born in Palermo, Sicily, but his parents settled in the United States. One day when he was about twelve or thirteen, he turned on the radio and happened to hear a recording of Lester, with Basie. For George, it was a revelation!

He decided immediately to become a jazz musician. Gil Evans has told me how much Lester also influenced Miles at the beginning of his career. Then I think of John Lewis and of Jimmy Rowles who had the incredible good fortune of playing with Lester while still very young; John was fourteen. It was in Albuquerque. When Jimmy was about twenty, he worked in a small band with Lester and Billie Holiday, and did so for over a year. From him I know to what extent Pres was a man brimming over with vitality, as was his music.

We needn't even mention the saxophonists who were deeply shaped by Lester and that everyone knows. I'll just quote this statement by Kenny Clarke on hearing Charlie Parker for the first time: "Hey, there's an alto that plays like Pres."

In 1952 and 1953 at the *Tabou* we modestly presented music akin to that which had inspired young American musicians during the forties. For them as for us, Lester was the master player. He had his own brand of humor, of course. One day (I don't remember any more if it was in '53 or '54), Daniel Filipacchi took him sightseeing in Paris. They went to the Arc of Triumph to take some pictures. Lester looked at the dates inscribed on the Tomb of the Unknown Soldier, and thoughtfully remarked, "1914–1918. That one sure didn't live long!"

I can still see myself with Lester at the home of pianist Eddie Bernard's mother in the city's Trocadero section. Eddie commented on the fact that his mother was a pianist, too. Lester immediately said, "Then you must play something for us, madame." Very graciously she then opened a collection of Fats Waller arrangements and started playing "Shoe Shine Boy," with its left-handed *stride;* Lester was crazy about that style, and he listened, cigarette in hand, to this woman playing things by Fats Waller. It gave him a real thrill.

To conclude, John Lewis is known to have made a superb statement concerning Lester Young. It was in 1956, when Pres, the M.J.Q. [Modern Jazz Quartet], and Miles gave a concert in Paris. We were in the large auditorium of the Pleyel Music Hall when we suddenly saw Lester come in; John turned to me then and said, "Here comes the greatest American poet." (Henri Renaud).

Yet Pres was not as calm as he appeared. Traveling was starting to get on his nerves, planes upset him, and he glared suspiciously at all the stewardesses, never responding to their smiles. After a landing, he would hurry onto the passenger ramp and take a deep breath; a few yards beyond that, his hands deep in his pockets, a cigarette in the corner of his mouth, his left eyelid drooping slightly, he would look absently at the immigration officials. They were white and Lester had his memories.

In New York, from his office on Forty-eighth Street, Moe Gale was preparing Lester's comeback. Charlie Carpenter had just arrived; they were discussing the text of his new press release. One version was intended for local producers. It read like the following:

> Your nearby car rental agency will gladly cooperate with you. Place banners on the sides of your trailer and equip the car with loudspeakers. You can circulate in the city and crisscross the suburbs. Play records by Lester and announce the date and place of his concert in your city.
>
> You may suggest to restaurants, cafes, and similar establishments in your community that they offer a "Lester Young Special," a special Lester Young sandwich, a special Lester Young beverage, a special Lester Young ice cream. . . . Placing several banners at key places in these establishments—in exchange for a few free tickets—should maintain in people's minds Lester Young's name, and the date and place of his concert; they will constantly remind your future clients of the event.

Attached were one or two photographs of Lester. Light suit, dark stripes, black tie, white shirt, small mustache, big smile; ten years younger. Not counting Birdland, the Boston Hi Hat, and Philadelphia's Peps Musical Bar, the Lester Young of 1953 didn't sell well. In the fall, he participated in the traditional J.A.T.P. concert at Carnegie Hall and finished the year in Boston with Ella Fitzgerald and Earl "Fatha" Hines performing in producer George Wein's Storyville club.

> It was the first set of the first night. There weren't any customers yet. I went onstage with the rhythm section. Lester was watch-

ing; he had found himself a chair at the foot of the stage and was waiting for me to play. It was just like an audition. I played one chorus, a second, a third. Finally, he said, "You and me, we can get along, Pres." He called all the people for whom he worked, "Pres." The musicians, he called "lady." I have the feeling that if Lester had not appreciated my playing, he would have left. . . . (George Wein)

A lackluster year, an uneventful year. One year more, one year less.

Chapter 20

You Stupid Sonovabitch

The last five years of Lester's life were chaotic. He had irreversibly cut off all ties with the outside world, leaving only one or two access points for his closest friends. Behind the serene exterior, those who did approach him found a tormented man who spoke bitterly of his past, yet who would also crack an occasional joke.

He took on concert offers without fuss and traveled non-stop from the East Coast to the West. From 1954 to 1955, he played with a regular group, but unfortunately they recorded very little; its members were Jessie Drakes, first-rate pianist Gildo Mahones, double bassist John Ore, and Connie Kay, "the lady from the Modern Jazz Quartet." There is no record of the people he met or the cities he crossed. Gliding like a sleepwalker through the world, Lester saw only what he wanted to see and heard only what he found convenient: "His was a world, fully constructed with all the loose ends tied up, that created reality could not and did not puncture . . . " (Bobby Scott).[110]

And with it all, always those jokes. For instance, there he was on stage in Montreal, Canada. Puzzled, he cocked his head. Why in hell did Oscar Peterson insist on playing so many notes so fast? The only way to find out was to go over and ask. Pres headed for the piano, unnoticed by the audience which was concentrating on Peterson's chorus. The piano cover was open, hiding the microphone; Oscar's hands were dancing on the ivories; Pres leaned over, carefully protecting his sax with his left arm: "Pssst." Peterson raised his eyes. At a distance of four inches from the hidden mike, Pres asked, "Hey, where are you at, you s.o.b.?" Peterson stared at him, nonplussed. Backstage, Granz blanched. Pres turned around, his shoulders slumping, wondering why the audience had just burst out laughing.

At Birdland, Lester would begin the sets by reminiscing, strolling down memory lane with the bassist and drummer. Peacefully sitting on a chair, he played for his memories' sake, withdrawing for a moment before rising to give himself over to the audience. Just long enough to have a cigarette and a glass of gin.

A few notes floated above the noise; only trumpeter Jesse Drakes and pianist Gildo Mahones caught the first measures of "Jive at Five." That was the signal for the other players to rejoin Pres. "And here comes the great LESTER YOUNG. . . . " The audience responded approvingly. Lester never interfered with his musicians' playing unless he felt called to do so.

> I never interfere in their manner of playing, that way they don't interrupt me when I play. Otherwise your spirit is unsettled. That's the reason why I always let my guys play their solos; it's so they don't bug me when I do mine. Matter of fact, sometimes I get chewed out by some audiences who want to hear me play more; I think that if you pay a guy to play and this guy's on the stage and really can play, then he should have a chance to tell his story. (Lester Young)

Not having had such freedom, many of his accompanists, most of whom were much younger than he, were thrown off by his policy. You'd frequently hear the Pres say to a hesitant musician who couldn't understand why he was being allowed to play several choruses in a row: "Don't Ever Give Up."

Charlie Parker died.

On April 2, 1955, Pres delivered a eulogy to him on the Carnegie Hall stage. The lights went out; loudspeakers crackled; 2800 friends listened motionlessly to Parker's theme song, "Now is the Time." A mixture of applause and sobbing met Lester when he stepped forward onto the stage in a halo supplied by one of the projectors. "I Can't Get Started." He was followed by three hours of music by Billie Holiday, Horace Silver, Stan Getz, Kenny Clarke, Lennie Tristano, Dizzy Gillespie, Thelonius Monk, J. J. Johnson, Gerry Mulligan, Lee Konitz, Charles Mingus, Al Cohn, Art Blakey, Oscar Pettiford, and Jo Jones. Pres left the scene modestly. What more could he say or do? A taxi took him to Manhattan.

The 1955 J.A.T.P. European tour was an absolute triumph. Everywhere they played, they were sold out: Zurich, Geneva, Basel, Paris, Lyon, Frankfurt, Munich, Stockholm, Copenhagen, Berlin. The only event to dampen their spirits was when Stan Getz contracted a disease that required his hospitalization in Sweden. On returning to the United States, Granz' first concern was to find a replacement so that they could go ahead with the autumn tour. He called Pres and explained the situation to him. Pres agreed to participate in the tour and fell in again with Roy Eldridge, Dizzy, Illinois Jacquet, Flip Phillips, Oscar Peterson, Ella Fitzgerald, Herb Ellis, Ray Brown, Buddy Rich, and the young Bobby Scott who, at eighteen, was the band's youngest member and very rapidly surprised everyone by becoming Lester's sidekick.

> What struck me most was his openness to younger musical talent. It wasn't patronization. . . . It was genuine, and his interest constant. (Bobby Scott)[111]

> I have to give a gig to these young guys, he'd say to me. So we had to use some of his men. Afterwards, he'd often admit that

the records weren't as good as they'd have been if we had chosen better-known musicians. (Norman Granz)

There were several occasions, right from the outset of the tour, when Lester felt that the musicians were preventing him from expressing himself, and he criticized the percussion section for splitting his phrases. On the stage, a little to the side, he would await his turn, looking absentminded. He would approach the microphone, walking obliquely. Suddenly, he'd stand erect, make every effort to hold his instrument upright, and seek inspiration by playing around the melodies. The audience loved him for the ballads he played using a bare minimum of notes. But as soon as Lester noticed the lack of conviction surrounding him, he'd let his shoulders slump and withdraw, his head low, as if begging their pardon.

During moments like those, Scott had the impression that Lester "was in every way an outsider. . . . Even the respect shown him was often perfunctory, and too many musicians seemed merely to suffer him. (Illinois Jacquet was an outstanding exception.) I was suffered too, reminded by the musicians in an exquisitely subtle way that at my age I was not entitled to an opinion. I've often thought I came by Lester's friendship as a result. We were both suffered (Bobby Scott).[112]

The musicians made a stopover in Houston, Texas, where for the first time an important "mixed" concert was to be held; mixed not just on stage, but also down in the audience. Many of the city's inhabitants were outraged by this, but no one could prevent Granz from renting the hall. However, they used a different strategy: a few moments before the beginning of the show, Lester, Illinois, Dizzy, and Granz met in Ella's dressing room to shoot dice. The stakes were one dollar apiece. Pres had barely rolled the dice when the dressing-room door was violently kicked in by three plain-clothes policemen brandishing large flashlights and their revolvers. They arrested all five performers for gambling.

Everyone was shocked. Granz was very upset; he threatened to cancel the performance despite the two thousand spectators. "You won't just have five people to arrest, but two thousand. Because if there's no performance, you're going to have a riot on your hands." After a quarter of an hour of tense negotiating, the police chief came in person to extend his apologies.

The days stretched on, and one night, Lester, Dizzy, Buddy Rich, and Bobby Scott attended a world boxing championship match that pitted Archie Moore and Rocky Marciano against each other. Moore, who had had occasion to exchange a few chords with most of the musicians on the podium, was their favorite. The betting got underway. Lester bet on Rocky Marciano. All the other musicians challenged Lester, but at the end of the evening, Marciano retained his title. Lester earned a few dollars, yet the attitude displayed by his companions so upset him that he withdrew from the others. Whenever he emerged he would break out in what many took to be humorous expletives.

> For a reason I have never been able to isolate, he shouldered the burden of being resident jester on that 1955 tour. And he was good at it. His brand of story-telling was unique. it was littered with so many "motherfuckers" that it was shushed down, and out, when we found ourselves in the company of the general public. . . .
> He would have mock fights with Roy Eldridge and other "shorter" fellows who would grab his arms as if to do him up. "Midget motherfuckers!" he would cry in pretended desperation. "Lawyer Brown, Lady Pete!" he would call to Ray Brown and Oscar Peterson. "Socks! You gotta help me with these midget motherfuckers! . . . *Those . . . midget . . . motherfuckers!* Socks, I could take 'em—one at a time! But the midget motherfuckers gang up on me! They gang up on ol' Prez!" . . . Sometimes, when he was on a roll, it went on for days. Not jokes or one-liners, although he had a few of those. No, it was always situational. . . . (Bobby Scott)[113]

One can easily imagine what kinds of situations they were. Back in the dressing rooms, before the unbelieving eyes of his fellow musicians, just before going on stage, Lester would sit, fully absorbed, listening to the latest release of his favorite crooner, Frank Sinatra, or to a new cut by Jack Sheldon, whom he had only recently discovered.

In a Texas airport, Lester came off the plane, wearing his felt hat, lost in his oversized black trench coat, saxophone case in hand, and found himself being stared at by two Texas rangers in their oversized Stetsons. "Socks, go tell 'em I'm a cowboy."

The misgivings that Lester had long been developing toward whites now took on quite different proportions: he became paranoid. His paranoia manifested itself in mood swings that frequently took on humorous aspects. He grew to hate all airplane flights. It was Bobby Scott who first noticed the effects:

> Lester felt a huge surge of anxiety if a very ill person—or worse, one in a wheelchair—got onto our flight.
> "God damn it, Socks," he'd groan, "it's Johnny Deathbed!" His eyes would remain fixed on the plane's entrance—until he saw a child, or an infant, board. If it was an infant, he eased immediately, noticeably. Though he never talked about religion, Pres let me know that the Deity was to be taken for granted. He obviously believed in the fair mercy of God, for the presence of the infant on our flight ruled out any chance that God would take out the entire flight to collect the Johnny Deathbed. The implications that vibrated outward from this view amused, and stimulated, me greatly. It was Lester's conviction that people about to take the Big Journey ought to be in their "cribs" waiting, not out here where innocents might have to share their fate. . . .
> Often, if we boarded a flight at the last minute, the seats we got were served dinner last. Too often we were just digging into our food when the plane began its descent. Lester trotted out his paranoia, blaming everyone from the Midget Motherfuckers to the White House. I couldn't eat for laughing. He'd squinch up his face in a deviltry that could bring me near to wetting myself, and mumble, "You see this shit, Socks? You see *this*?" He would shake his head, glancing furtively toward the back of the plane where "the enemy" sat. His voice, still softly clandestine, would push out, "they're tryin' to *get* us, Socks." And I of course had to go along with him. . . . When I arrived at the airport apron one

morning, I made my way through the small group of passengers and found Pres with a perplexed and doom-filled face, eyeing our aircraft. It was a DC-3, slightly worn-looking but otherwise apparently fit. "Socks baby, it's a *two-lunger!*" Pres felt much safer in a four-engine craft. "We gotta have a *four*-lunger, Socks! Shit! You lose one, you still got *three!* One of *these* motherfuckers goes, an' we only got *one* lung left!"

Moments later, having accepted the inevitable, he was sitting next to me, back in his groove, snapping his fingers at the engines outside the window, and hollering (to the chagrin and embarrassment of the tour members): "Get it! Get . . . *it!* God . . . damn . . . IT!"

He talked to the engines, shouting his encouragement as we barrelled down the runway. He was still hollering, to the shushing sounds of Ella Fitzgerald and Norman Granz, when the creaking weight of metal lifted up out of the uncloroxed clouds into the sunshine.

He smiled then. He had fortified himself with Dewars. He whispered, "It's only gettin' here that bothers me, Socks." (Bobby Scott)[114]

Though subject to these crises, Lester did not lose his nonchalance. When he spoke to the musicians, most of the time he did so calmly. His attitude contrasted sharply with the general excitement and the nervous edge that preceded all performances. For him, there was no reason to hurry for any purpose whatsoever. According to Scott, "his speed was that of a sleepwalker."

He was a sleepwalker who now moved in a world he himself constructed, a world from which he stood aloof, protected by a wall of scotch bottles that he stacked higher day after day, night after night to the point where the life he was defending began to take on the appearance of death.

Once the tour had ended, Lester went back to Saint Albans. He was exhausted, drained, and showed no interest in the things that went on around him. Other than taking part in the recording of a Billie Holiday concert on May 6, 1955, at Carnegie Hall, and in a J.A.T.P. recording on October 2 at the Chicago Opera House,

Lester cut only one record that year, on December 1 in New York, accompanied by Harry Edison and a few members of the last J.A.T.P. After that session, Lester accepted an invitation to form part of a quintet at Birdland, and he remained there until December 21. But he was not convincing on stage; he placed more value on the bottle and neglected his instrument. At his place in Saint Albans, he would absent-mindedly push aside the meals prepared for him by Mary, preferring scotch instead.

One morning, out of concern for her husband's state of health, Mary alerted a physician who immediately prescribed a period of hospitalization at Bellevue Hospital. Though short in duration, it nevertheless signaled Lester's irreversible decline.

Alcohol abuse, exacerbated by poor nutrition, was causing problems in Pres's nervous system: his step had become ungainly, and his movements were more and more awkward. Ironically, just as Lester was entering the hospital, an advertisement for Dolnet saxophones showed him in perfect health four pages from the cover of the French magazine *Jazz Hot*.

During his stay at Bellevue, he quarreled with his manager, Charlie Carpenter.

> We talked about his comeback in my tours as soon as he got out. To begin with he accepted the usual $750 weekly fee, then he called back to ask for $850. I okayed it. Ten minutes later, he called again to ask for $950. Okay. Finally he said he ought to have $1000. This was very strange behavior for him. However that may be, we argued and he toured with another group instead.
>
> Lester punctuated his statement with, "I'm still warm and they're already coming to pick my bones." (Charlie Carpenter)

Though short, the separation from his manager gave Lester a fit—who would take care of his business, his concerts, and his money? He couldn't ask either John Hammond or Lady Granz. He asked his close friends, Jo Jones, Buck Clayton. No luck. He called Walter Schaap,[115] then translator for *Jazz Hot*, and asked him to take care of matters. He also refused. Lester was upset; he imagined himself to be the victim of a plot. Reluctantly, he resigned himself to putting off solving things until his release from the hospital.

After two weeks of intensive treatment, Pres returned home again. He seemed to be calm and in good spirits. He listened to his records, watched television, spoke to friends who were concerned about his health, took walks with his son Lester, Jr., and played with his dog "Concert"—"I picked him up after a concert," he would explain. No one knew him in the neighborhood.

One morning, Lester and his son were quietly tossing a ball around outside. Behind the hedge that separated their two yards, perched on a bench, two neighbor ladies sat observing the family scene. Father and son gave the impression of enjoying themselves. After about twenty minutes, Lester came to a standstill: "Okay, Little Lester, let's go in." The boy retrieved the ball and followed his father. Standing at the door, Pres tried in vain to turn the door-knob. The door was locked, and there was no way of getting in. Lester turned to his son, and in the iciest of terms said, "See there, you stupid sonovabitch, you locked us both out of the house."

That same week Nat Hentoff paid Pres a visit. Lester was relaxed during the interview.

> Of all the tenors, I like the younger kids. I like to hear them play. The best sounding ones were on a record by the Four Brothers. Do I notice my influence on what they play? Yes, I hear a lot of little things out of what I may have played, but I won't say anything. I mean there are a fair number of little riffs, things like that. . . . But I don't want to give the impression of thinking that I influenced everybody. . . . There are certain young brasses I like a lot. Miles Davis is the one I've listened to most; him I respect. And Jessie Drakes, who has played trumpet with me since 1949. I like him because he plays his own way and doesn't try to imitate anyone. . . . I thought Bird was a genius. . . . Every musician should be a stylist. . . .
>
> This year, if I could find one, I'd like to pick a clarinet for myself. Out of the records by recent clarinet players, I pick those by Jimmy Giuffre. . . . He plays like me for sure, especially in the lower registers. Among clarinet players, I'll always mention

Benny Goodman, him and Artie Shaw. . . . It feels funny to listen to my own records. I think I like all of them. The danger is that I'll repeat them when I play, that's why I don't like to listen to them forever and again. If I listened to them too much, I might think back to them when I'm performing or when I'm recording new ones. Among my favorites are, "Lester Leaps In," "Clap Hands," "Here Comes Charlie," "Every Tub," "Swing the Blues," "One O'Clock Jump," and "Shoe Shine Boy," the first record I made. . . .

After all these years, I still have some tricks up my sleeve. I don't rehearse because I think I've been playing long enough. But I like to play. (Lester Young)[116]

On January 22, 1956, Lester cut his first record with Roy Eldridge: *The Jazz Giants of '56*. Participating in that session were Teddy Wilson, Vic Dickenson, Gene Ramey, Jo Jones, and Freddie Green. The next day, he recorded seven numbers with Wilson, Ramey, and Jones, among which was "Pres Returns."

To emphasize his return, Lester went back on the road in February for a tour organized by the Gale Music Agency. Among the "Birdland Allstars" traveling up the East Coast were Count Basie and Bud Powell. Much like the year before, Pres's role was fairly restricted. He appeared as a guest of the Basie orchestra and played only a few songs with it. In March, he was invited back to Basin Street on Fifty-first Street in Manhattan prior to setting off for Chicago, Detroit, and Toronto.

Apart from these concerts, Pres kept to himself. Every night, after the last round of applause, he would tiptoe up to his room in a second-rate hotel, carrying his saxophone case and the red bag in which he had carefully deposited his whiskey bottle. No one said anything to him—he asked for nothing.

The next meeting between Lester and Count Basie took place August 24 on stage at the Randall's Island Jazz Festival (in New York), produced by Don Friedman and Ken Joffe. Ten thousand fans assembled in a huge stadium; nearly half of them had to use binoculars to see the musicians. Again, regrettably, Pres appeared as guest star of the Basie orchestra. He only played a few selections. Short as it was, however, his performance constituted one of the highlights of the festival.

In the fall, after a month spent at Birdland with Jessie Drakes, Pres was sent to Europe by the Gale Agency. The new Birdland Show tour consisted of the Modern Jazz Quartet, Bud Powell, Miles Davis, and Lester. It was an opportunity for Lester to revisit a stage that he could appreciate: the Pleyel auditorium in Paris, where he played accompanied by René Urtreger, Pierre Michelot, and Christian Garros. The tour traveled to Strasbourg, Lyon, and Marseille. It scored a real triumph at the Teatro Manzoni in Milan. Lester also went to Frankfurt, where he played with the local musicians; one of these evening performances was recorded by a local radio station. A few days before returning to New York, he appeared in Zurich with the same rhythm section that had accompanied him in Paris.

> It's hard to get back into the mood of that era (1956) when we were young musicians. Our frame of mind was completely off the wall; we listened to jazz, read about jazz, talked about jazz, drank and ate jazz, we even made love jazzy. . . .
>
> In October of 1956 I had formed a small "traditional" jazz band of the kind Boris Vian called Niou. We had been invited to the opening of the Storyville, a Frankfurt nightclub that an American—a crazy ex-G.I.—had just opened. Now you have to imagine the city scene, the mood that prevailed then. . . . A mixture of science-fiction and of apocalypse. We had just arrived from Paris, which had remained more or less intact in the wake of the war. But in Frankfurt, there were neighborhoods where the ruins had only recently been swept out. Whatever happened to be under the supervision of the American forces was more or less operational, but the rest. . . . You had the impression of waking up in another world, of straddling the fence between reality and a dream—or a nightmare.
>
> The young did their best to think of other things; they were trying to make a new start in life. For many, jazz represented not just music, but above all a new way of thinking, of living. It was

a serious subject. So you had to be "serious," meaning that you had to play furiously and non-stop. When the Storyville closed around 2 A.M., we'd go see if anything was still going on at the Jazz Keller, a wine cellar that had doubled as a shelter during the bombing raids. But it took us forever to make our way to the Keller because they were in the process of rebuilding the neighborhood and the landmarks would change from day to day. Still, we did our best to make out our location according to certain stretches of wall, certain piles of debris, or newly erected scaffolds.

One night as we stood at the door of the cellar there was total silence—something unheard of. Ordinarily, the atmosphere was supercharged and you could hear people yelling up to 50 meters from the door. We went down, and there, on the podium, was Lester. Lester Young. We could hardly believe it. What on earth could he be doing there?

For us he was like a legend that you often invoked but could never corroborate. Olympus was at our fingertips! Lester was playing with two other Americans who were living in Frankfurt, bass player Al King and a drummer whose name I've forgotten—then there was a German piano buddy with whom we jammed a lot: Horst Omerth. We stood there transfixed for maybe an hour without even daring to applaud for fear of disturbing him. Around five A.M. Lester wanted something to eat. He knew a fellow from Frankfurt whose name was Gunther, I think. He asked Gunther if he could go to his place and eat. I found out later that Gunther had been cooking for Lester for two days. But Willi, the owner of the Jazz Keller, finally took us to his place. He was living in a kind of large studio-dive on the edge of town. There were about a dozen of us who finally landed at Willi's.

. . . Lester was sitting on a big cushion and holding his saxophone case between his knees. We didn't speak English well, and we hardly dared speak to him at all. I wonder, in fact, if he'd have heard us. From time to time he'd say something and we'd quiet down—not understanding—and look timidly at one another. He must have sensed our uneasiness.

At one point he got up, went over to the kitchenette and sat down on a chair. I think it must have taken him five minutes to get his instrument out of its case. Then he blew into it with little puffs, as if he wanted to arouse it. Everyone went silent; he immediately stopped and went through the motions of putting his sax away. We understood that it would be better to continue talking without paying him any attention; I think he was embarrassed for us to listen to him. We were talking, all right, but we had never before been as intent on listening to a musician. He would play so few notes—all those silences loaded with swing. . . . Oh, it didn't last long, maybe 15 minutes. Then he lit up a cigarette and looked at Gunther. Five minutes later, they were gone. . . .

A few years later, in '59 I think, when he was playing the Blue Note in Paris, I was able to go listen to him one night, but I couldn't get close then, and the atmosphere was different. (Armand Gordon)[117]

After that trip, Lester was tired; he was becoming less and less able to stand that kind of touring. Still, he got up the courage to appear in Washington and at the Café Bohemia in New York.

At the Olivia Patio Lounge in Washington, D.C., he was accompanied by pianist Bill Potts, bassist Norman "Willie" Williams, and drummer Jim Lucht. Though not very well known, they were musicians for whom Lester had considerable appreciation.

Because their nights were ticking away, the trio was finding the thought of getting a tape recorder more and more attractive, so that they could have a memento of their marvelous time together. I was personally in possession of all the professional equipment necessary to record. On Friday, December 7, I set all the equipment up on the stage. As soon as he walked into the club, he took one look at the stage with its three mikes, two professional tape-recorders, sound-mixer and earphones, scowled and looked at me with a very sad face saying, "Oh no, Billy. . . . No. Norman will kill me."

Willie, Jim and I got together and after a quick talk, decided on a possible solution. We dug up the largest Hennessy cognac bottle we could find, and wrapped it in a gift package with a card that said "Thank You." The trio was thanking Lester for the pleasure of knowing and playing with him. Lester smiled, and then said, "I don't think Norman will really kill me." Then we all dashed down to the stage to adjust the tape recorders, and we played. (Bill Potts)[118]

The seven numbers they recorded would not be released until 1980; they were "A Foggy Day," "When You're Smiling," "I Can't Get Started," "Fast Bd Blues," "D.B. Blues," "Tea for Two," and "Jeepers Creepers." It was Norman Granz himself who published them under his Pablo label.

Bill Potts should certainly be thanked for his initiative; the record is outstanding in every way, and it provides the last recorded version of a danceable "D.B. Blues." It is the last great recording made by the Pres.

Sadly, by the end of December, Lester was physically run down again. After talking to him at length, Mary finally succeeded in overcoming his stubborn resistance to treatment, and after further discussions with his friend Jo Jones, Lester agreed to another hospitalization: "Lester would not go to a doctor or nothing unless he consulted me . . . " (Jo Jones).[119]

At the hospital, Lester received a visit from Charlie Carpenter; their old friendship seemed rekindled.

Despite this second "rehabilitation" which put him temporarily back on his feet and the birth in December 1956 of his daughter, Yvette, the new year would be a sad one. For Lester, everything was cause for depression and isolation. His friends tried to help him. They tried to recreate the original musical atmosphere which he seemed to need more and more to feel at ease. But few could handle playing with a sick man who was already so far gone.

On July 7, George Wein invited Lester to join the Count Basie Orchestra at the New York Festival. On October 25, after having him record seven titles, Norman Granz introduced him on stage with the J.A.T.P. alongside Roy Eldridge, J. J. Johnson, Sonny Stitt, Illinois Jacquet, Coleman Hawkins, Stan Getz, Flip Phillips, Oscar Peterson, Herb Ellis, Ray Brown, Connie Kay, and Ella Fitzgerald.

He took part in several other performances of the tour, but his heart wasn't in it. He no longer had his reserved seat in the back of the bus. His strength was gone. One day, as Lester tried to sleep, Sonny Stitt stood up, meandered down the aisle with his instrument, and began blowing a rapid chain of nervous notes right into Lester's ear. Lester looked up at him with sad eyes and said, "Very cute, Lady Stitt, but sing me a little song instead." Then he sank back into his dreams.

In December, Nat Hentoff and Whitney Balliett produced a television show for CBS called "Sounds of Jazz" which aired late on the afternoon of December 6. This was an opportunity for thousands of television viewers to discover Lester Young, Coleman Hawkins, Jimmy Rushing, Count Basie, Roy Eldridge, Doc Cheatham, Big Bill Broonzy, Pee Wee Russell, Red Allen, Jimmy Giuffre, Billie Holiday, Vic Dickenson, Jo Jones, Mal Waldron, Danny Barker, Jim Atlas, Ben Webster, etc.

During rehearsals for the show, Billie and Lester also had the opportunity to trade a few memories and to share for the last time some of their old anxieties. Though they saw each other only infrequently, the ties that bound them were deep and very much alive. Billie chose to sing one of his blues compositions called "Fine and Mellow." A dozen or so musicians accompanied her, each successively taking two or three choruses; among them were Vic Dickenson, Coleman Hawkins, Ben Webster, Gerry Mulligan, Roy Eldridge, and Lester. On the video tape that is currently in release, Lester appears manifestly fatigued; contrary to the others, he remains seated, and when he does stand, it is to play a chorus of only twelve measures. Yet it is he who enjoys the warmest response from Lady Day, whose reactions to each of the musicians around her were captured by the camera. Of course, she also expresses admiration—slightly bemused—for the vitality of Hawkins and for Eldridge's pluck, but with Lester it's different; she tilts her head and approves and gently makes silent comments to each of the three phrases ("Three Little Words") of his brief solo, whose tenderness has become so fragile. That's Pres, all right, that's always been the Pres. . . .

During the last rehearsal, there was a woman standing off to one side. She was inconspicuous and dressed all in black. The musicians knew her well; it was Elaine Swaine. For several weeks she had been following Lester's every step. She was to be his last companion. Tenderly, dotingly, and silently, she would attend to Lester, keep him from feeling lost, talk to him in moments of depression. That afternoon, Lester was, in fact, sad. He withdrew, oblivious to the people joking around him. He played very little and that with difficulty. But despite that, Columbia recorded a few numbers, and in one of them, "Fine and Mellow," one clearly detects the respiratory difficulties from which Lester was beginning to suffer.

A few days later, in *down beat's* annual poll, Lester was classified as the sixth best tenor saxophonist, garnering few votes and placing far behind Stan Getz, Sonny Rollins, Zoot Sims, Bill Perkins, and Coleman Hawkins. John Coltrane placed eleventh. But Lester had not concerned himself with his reputation, nor with his health for years. At the end of the year, the situation was more serious than ever. Lester had continued to drink and was still smoking excessively. He had discovered new pleasures in which to overindulge, one of which was a mixture of gin and sherry. His playing was completely altered by new respiratory problems. And when anyone spoke to him of medical treatment, he'd respond: "You're joking!"

Chapter 21

Critical Reviews

At the end of 1957, Pres was hospitalized again. He spent six weeks at King's County Hospital, where doctors tried their best to get him back on a normal diet again and to bring his continuous need for alcohol under control. His liver was diseased. His nervous system was under siege. Day after day, the nurses surrounded him with attention. But Lester was absent; he neither saw nor heard anyone. He would stare at his saxophone for hours and smile at the pictures of his children. From time to time he'd enjoy visits from his wife, Mary, from Elaine, from other musicians, and from Norman Granz.

A month later, his health improved. He seemed ready to resume his musical life. Only the hospital's chief of staff and a few nurses knew that it was really his swan song. Norman Granz, who constantly watched over him, convinced Lester to record seven numbers in New York for which he used a new metal clarinet. He was surrounded by excellent musicians: Roy Eldridge, Harry

Edison, Hank Jones, Herb Ellis, George Duvivier and Mickey Sheen. Many consider this session to have been a failure—not to say a disaster—and indeed, only five selections were made public. And yet, perhaps never before was the infinitely fragile, aerial grace of Lester's art as moving as on that occasion, enhanced as it was by the amicable confrontation with trumpeters Roy Eldridge and Harry Edison, whose phrasing was sharp and trenchant. In any case, Pres withdrew into his shell again, using alcohol, marijuana, etc. Six weeks later, he made another unsuccessful recording in a New York studio; none of the four titles he cut was made public.

In February, Pres appeared at the Cork 'n' Bib in Westbury, and then at Small's from which he was summarily ejected. He had repeatedly fallen into the audience after attempting to lead his band perched on a chair.

One morning, after returning to his home in Saint Albans, he explained to Mary that he could no longer live so far from the New York jazz scene: "I can't concentrate anymore; I can't get with the program because I really can't get around when I'm at home. This is a real nice place, with the lawn around it and all, but I want to be back there so I can watch my friends go in and out of Birdland" (Lester Young).

Lester collected a few things, packed his record player, picked out his favorite records, and returned to Manhattan where Jo Jones was waiting for him. They pulled up in front of the Alvin Hotel on Fifty-second Street. After his friend had filled out the registration slip for him, Pres chose a room on the fourth floor from which he could observe the entrance to Birdland: "At that point Miss Jones, Lady Jones, came to my rescue" (Lester Young).

At approximately the same time, Reverend John Gensel, who was then taking a course on "Jazz and the Cultures of the Present" with historian Marshall Stearns (who had founded the Institute of Jazz Studies in 1951), began to envision creating a ministry for the New York jazz community.

From time immemorial, music in all its forms has been used for a variety of reasons. The music used in India for religious purposes is different from that used here for the same purpose. At the beginning of this century, jazz had not developed much and sacred music conformed to the period; it consisted mainly of classical European music. Today, we say matter-of-factly that jazz is our contemporary music and that there are many who express themselves through it. It is therefore quite natural that there should be people who wish to express their religious feelings by way of jazz. Just look at Duke Ellington, Charles Mingus and others who have written in that vein. Jazz is also a way of expressing deep religious feelings. . . . In fact, it all depends on what you put into the music and on the way you use it. Jazz was not used in churches because it was associated with bordellos; it was considered profane music, the devil's music. But in reality, it can be used in churches as easily as any other music can.

So the idea of creating a jazz ministry started making the rounds, and musicians started to come to me and lay out their problems; there were funerals, marriages. . . . Then one night, in a club on the East Side (the Black Cow), I met Lester Young. He was playing with his quartet. I also remember that Carmen McRae and Gerry Mulligan were in the audience. Then I got into the habit of visiting him at the Alvin Hotel on 52nd Street. He had a room on the fourth floor and I would regularly go up and we'd talk. At one point he said, "I have a cool house over there on the island, but I prefer to be here, where I can see my friends coming out." He was living on the fourth floor, from where he could see the entrance to Birdland. I doubt that he went very often to Long Island, where his family lived.

Lots of women tried to approach him and engage him in conversation. One day he said to one of them, "I know your name." She was clucking with pleasure, "Oh, really?"—"Yeah, yeah, your name is Mary, but I don't know which one anymore, Mary-Magdalen, the mother of Jesus, or one of my wives."

He also said something very strange to me: "When I'm dead, I'll be laid out somewhere and people will walk around me and say, 'That was Lester,' but I'll be able to hear them all. I won't really be dead. But as soon as I am, they're going to bring out a whole series of albums in memory of me, and they'll make all that money on my back."

I don't know if he had some sort of premonition about his death. Contrary to what some people say, Lester and I never spoke about religion. . . . Oh yes, he drank and he was really sick! . . . He made one remark to me pertaining to drugs: "When someone talks to me about drugs and asks me if I take any, I answer: 'Sorry, I've never auditioned. . . .'" (Reverend John Gensel)[120]

During the months that followed, Pres appeared regularly at Birdland. When he'd go out in the morning, he would suffer anxiety attacks; clinging to the sides of the buildings, he would hide beneath his black hat, clutching the gin bottle he had just purchased. In the afternoon, to avoid the restaurants and the necessity of talking, of ordering, he would hide out in the cheap movie houses on Forty-second Street, staring at westerns, horror movies, and comedies without even seeing them. By the time he came out, night would have fallen. With faltering steps he would go back to his room, light another cigarette, a glass of gin in hand, and pour his troubles out to Elaine when she came to see him. Late at night, he would walk across the street to Birdland. Inside, when he ran into one of his remaining friends, his appearance would change; he would talk and joke as if nothing bothered him. But he would pay no attention at all to the audience that gazed at him with admiration. His reputation and what he stood for in the eyes of hundreds of musicians and fans mattered nothing to him.

Lester's state of health had a number of his acquaintances worried, in particular the historian Marshall Stearns who, after a quick visit to the Alvin Hotel, decided to notify a friend of his, Dr. Luther Cloud, who subsequently kept up with Young until the time of his death.

On July 5, George Wein invited Lester to take part in the Newport Jazz Festival. First, he appeared with Jack Teagarden and Pee Wee Russell in a Dixieland band which the press reviewed as "a horrible and embarrassing configuration." Luckily, the next day he was joined on the same stage by several friends of long standing: Billie Holiday, Benny Goodman, Georgie Auld, Buddy Tate, Buck Clayton, Walter Page, and Jo Jones. For Lester, it was the perfect setting. These were musicians who understood and appreciated his music. Despite all that, Lester withdrew between sets, sitting on a chair to one side, ignoring his entourage.

So Prez was—he was sick then. It was getting to him, you know, he was really failing. He was short-winded, he didn't have any stamina, couldn't hardly fill his horn, you know what I mean? Sound—couldn't control his sound. So that day, we had a rehearsal, rehearsing things with Billie. . . .

So anyway, we were there playing. So Prez couldn't find the place. The hall was really hard to find. And Prez is sincere about everything. I mean, like he didn't even want to be late, you know. We'd been playing about an hour, rehearsing about an hour and a half, just going over some things to play for her and little riffs and things we was going to play behind Billie, you know. So man, when he came in, when he found that place, he came in and he ran—when he walked to the door, like he'd come in from that foyer there and he stops and he spies us and he got this big wide hat on and the crown's about that high. And he really looked comical, you know? And man, everybody broke down and started laughing. Said, "You finally found us, Prez." And man, it hurt his feelings, you know, because everybody was laughing at him. He says, "I don't see what's so fucking funny with you ladies." He says, "I've been looking for this fucker for two hours and a half and there ain't a damn thing funny." . . .

He said, "Now, I don't see nothing for you all to laugh about." So we says, "Oh, Prez, we didn't mean anything like that," you know, "we just—" You know. He told me later on, he says, "Hey, Tate, you know, I was really surprised that you were laughing at me."

—"But we weren't laughing at you. I had a devil of a time finding the damn hall myself." But anyway, I was with him—he asked me, says, "How are you going home?" . . . he had his lady and a friend that had driven him there and a Cadillac. He's sitting in the back in the middle of the seat like the way those big engines ride down in Oklahoma, you know, big hat on. So he says, "You ride with me." I said, "Well, I'd love to, Prez." He says, "You've got to. You don't go back over there. You ride with me." So I says, "Okay." He says, "And as a matter of fact, I want you to be my manager today, to take care of my business for me, pick up my money." He was playing at the Birdland. He says, "They docked me, you know. They're not going to pay me for the night." He said, "But that's all right." . . . He says, "I haven't done too well, you know." He says, "I've been down right to rock bottom." . . . So, you know, I tell you when I got in the car that night with him, first thing he did, he opened his wallet like this and turned me on, you know. He lit up. He said, "Now, let's review the books." . . .

So he says, "I haven't done so well, you know." I says, "What do you mean?" He says, "I never really made it on my own." I said, "What do you mean, you haven't made it?" I says, "Man, you're a legend." I says, "You and Hawk." He says, "Yeah, but all the other ladies that they say play like me make all the money." So I says, "Well, I don't think you're a good business-man. . . . I can even book you. . . . But maybe you just don't take care of business." . . .

You see, to tell you about Prez, if you once do him a favor, he never stop paying you back. . . . Flip [Phillips] told me he got nine cigarette lighters that Prez had given him. . . . Because he'd fix his horn, he fixed his horn for him all the time. . . . He'd come to Flip and say, "Lady Flip? My baby ain't acting right." They'd be on a jazz—said, "You better do something for her." And Flip said he was standing over him watching him and Flip said, "Look now, Prez, if I'm going to fix it, take your ass on in the other room somewhere." He says, "I know what the fuck I'm gonna do. Leave me alone." . . .

We got lost and it took us nine hours to get from Newport. I'm glad, because those last nine hours was the last time I spent with him and we talked all night. So I picked up his money for him and took care of his business and everything. He told me, "Just send my wife a hundred dollars. Just say Lester—don't say nothing." . . .

He carried me to my apartment uptown and everything. So he says, "But I'll tell you what I'd like for you to do." He says, "If you know anyplace where I can get me a bottle," he said, "I'd appreciate it because there's not going to be anything, tomorrow's Sunday and I won't be able to get me a bottle until late, you know?" He said, "And I'll pay some dues." . . . there's a guy walked all night right on my corner . . . with bottles in his pocket and he's selling them. . . . and she said to me—she called me—she said, "If you do, the doctor done said any drink, he might start hemorrhaging to death." She says, "And I know he would die if you bought him a bottle and he did it," you know, started hemorrhaging. So I wouldn't do it.

And sure enough, you know when we pulled up to that corner, the first guy I saw was that bootlegger. I could have went right to him and got it. But you know, when she told me that, I would have—you know, I would have felt badly all my life . . . he lived about eight or nine months longer. . . . That's all he wanted me to do for him and I didn't. And you know, sometime that bugs me. . . . So that was my last time with him, those nine hours in Newport. . . . (Buddy Tate)[121]

Toward the end of July, several journalists and musicians decided to celebrate Lester's thirtieth year in the business by putting together a party in his honor. July 27, the Black Pearl Club organized a special show with that intention.

But appropriately enough, it was a month later on August 27 that the event was celebrated at Birdland during an evening affair planned by Nat Hentoff, Marshall Stearns, Symphony Sid, and Morris Levy, the owner of the club.

Lester had come with his friend, Elaine. He called her the "girl in black." Like Lester, she wore a black felt hat. Lester had decided to appear with a new combo just for the occasion; it consisted of trombonist Curtis Fuller, pianist Nat Pierre, bassist Doug Watkins, and drummer Willie Jones. During the first two sets, Lester played several of his favorite tunes. The audience was ecstatic, and so was Dan Morgenstern.[122]

Can Prez still blow? Oh, Baby!

But parties must proceed on schedule. Big cake and champagne brought in. Lester attempts cake-cutting ritual from stand. Impossible. Descends into space between stand and front table. Big cake. Lester blows out candles, smiles, shakes hands. Symphony Sid announces members of party. Includes a Dr. Cloud. Nice name for doctor. Lester cuts cake. Birdland camera girl, instructed by official-looking gentleman, takes picture. Pop! goes flashbulb. The band watches. "He didn't look up" says cameragirl, plaintively. Lester plays a few bars of *I Didn't Know What Time It Was.* "Got the message?" asks Prez. Picture is ordered retaken. Lester picks up knife, makes like cutting cake, looks up and says "Cheese." Flashbulb goes pop. Success! A toast. Bubbly and exchange of pleasantries. Lester is perfect gentleman. Excuses himself. Climbs back on stand. . . . Prez beats off *There'll Never Be Another You.* It is nostalgic: wistful and tender but somehow removed.[123]

The evening came to an end several hours later when Bud Powell took a seat at the piano behind Lester. Pres packed away his sax, donned his hat and, following this one moment of joy, this ray of lucidity, sank back into the night. His night. The President's night. On his arm was Elaine.

Thanks to the constant attentions of Elaine and Dr. Luther Cloud, Lester was slowly recovering his strength. No one forbade him to smoke or drink; he was simply cutting his alcohol with water and sometimes replacing it with wine. From time to time, Elaine would prepare his meals; he was back to eating normally, albeit irregularly. The club circuit opened up for him again. During the fall, he signed a contract with the United Artists Record Company. With the assistance of Norman Granz, he appeared in November at the Five Spot, at the Brooklyn Academy of Music, and at the Newark Kiosk. It was to be the last time Lester and Eddie Barefield, his friend from younger days, would see each other.

A few weeks before he died, he was playing the Five Spot with Valdo [sic] Williams on the piano. After he saw me come in, we went over to a table and sat there talking for hours. . . . Every time we saw each other, we traded our impressions on life. Yes, there was a deep spiritual relationship between us. That night, I remember clearly, he was really very unhappy. He was telling me about the problems and the aggravation he was having, . . . how his manager was mistreating him, how he was having financial worries. . . . (Eddie Barefield)[124]

In the December readership poll of *down beat,* Lester was ranked eighth best tenor saxophone player with 138 votes, far behind Stan Getz who received 1722 votes and who ranked first in all the polls for that year.

Then one morning Pres decided to leave for Europe again. He remembered having been well received in Paris. "That's where I'm going to go," he told his brother, who had come to visit him in New York. Lee didn't understand him; he pleaded with him to control himself, and especially to stop drinking and smoking. No. He was bound for Paris. And if he was drinking and smoking like his brother and Dr. Cloud said, it was because he had worries.

He did, in fact, have plans. He especially wanted to nullify all his existing record contracts so that he could sign a new one with Dot Records. That way a new phase in his artistic life could begin, during which he could do what really made him happy. He was thinking, for example, of recording an album with his favorite musicians, Miles Davis, Harry Edison, Freddie Green, Jo Jones, and also Frank Sinatra. As he envisioned it, the group would not perform in public; he would be happy just recording his favorite tunes with it. He was even thinking of another record already, with a group of string instruments. Lastly, he dreamed of undertaking a tour across the entire United States once he had returned from France. Therefore, he had them put together a new press release and demanded that they take a photograph of him looking his best so that a poster could be printed. Elaine tagged along with his enthusiasm, while at the same time urging him not to overdo things.

Before leaving for Paris, Lester made a quick stop in Saint Albans, hugged his children and explained his plans to Mary. As he left New York, he knew that several clubs would welcome him back on his return—him and his ensemble.

Chapter 22

Paris, La Louisiane

Paris, January 23, 1959—Le Bourget Airport. Seconds after the airplane came to rest in front of the terminal, the ghostly silhouette of Lester Young appeared. Black hat, black overcoat, small white briefcase with brown leather stitching; for an instant, there was a glint of joy in his tired gaze.

Several people came to greet him, among them Ben Benjamin, that corpulent American boxing and jazz fanatic who managed the Blue Note on the rue d'Artois where Lester was soon to open. At the time, he greeted everyone like a gentleman. Yes, he had had a good trip; yes, he was happy to be in Paris. The reporters? Let them come later.

That same evening, he went by the Blue Note to take a look. While there, he ran into the members of the quartet who were to back him up and with whom he was already familiar: Kenny "Klook" Clarke, who had permanently settled in Paris, and Jimmy Gourley, the guitarist with whom he had often come to play at the Tabou in 1953 and 1956; with them was René Urtreger at the piano and Pierre Michelot on bass, both of whom had already accompanied Lester during the Birdland European tour of 1956, during which Christian Garros was drummer for the trio. These were musicians who admired and respected him, musicians who knew who he was and who loved him. Yes, they would be able to do good work together. Charles Delaunay and Henri Renaud also came to say hello. And then there was Stan Getz, who was still on the bill and who was just wrapping up his engagement.

Contrary to everyone's expectations, Lester had not brought his instrument along. He had no desire to jam; he was tired from the trip. He preferred to watch Getz, who played like a President, on stage. He brought news from New York, joked with Kenny Clarke and Jimmy Gourley, and promised to consider making a record there in Paris with French musicians. The atmosphere was cordial, and he was already familiar with the club, having come there on a previous trip.[125]

His life fell into place. During this visit to Paris, Lester stayed at the Louisiane hotel, 60 rue de la Seine, close by the Boulevard Saint-Germain; it is a busy neighborhood, especially in the morning around the rue de Buci market. First he occupied a room on the second floor; but very soon he ended up sharing the room of a young German woman, Erika, whom he had met in 1956 and who came to look him up in Paris. She kept him company during his stay in Paris. Jimmy Gourley, who was also staying at La Louisiane,[126] recalls that Pres's movements around Paris were otherwise very limited:

> In one sense, a day for the Prez was quite simple. We'd leave for the Blue Note at night. By taxi as a rule. Where I was concerned, that was a little problematic because it was on the expensive side, but Prez who, after all was very tired, avoided as much as possible having to walk; he didn't even want to go to the taxi stand on foot, and that was just a hundred or so meters away, at Mabillon. So the car would come get us at the hotel door, and to come back—at about four-thirty or five in the morning—we did the same: we took a taxi. The only time Prez

ever went out in Paris was when he did a little grocery shopping at the Buci market, and that was on the sidewalk across the street.

Lester cooked in his room, on a little hot plate, just like other guests did in the hotel. It was New Orleans cooking, red beans, fatback, etc. This was La Louisiane, after all. When Jimmy Gourley knocked on Lester's door one afternoon, it was a surprisingly hard, brutal voice that answered, "Who the fuck is it?" He then identified himself: "It's me, Pres, Jimmy." And immediately everything changed—the same voice took on humor and affection, the sort of sweetness that always seems to parody itself slightly. "Oh! Lady Jimmy! Come in!" So Jimmy entered. At times Lester and Erika would be in bed, and to this day, Jimmy can still picture the couple, sheets pulled up to their chins, Lester's hair straight out on the pillow, his eyes full of mischief. At other times, Pres would be in his bathrobe while a particularly appetizing dish finished cooking on the hot plate; but Lester hardly ever ate any of it. Kansas Field would eat it all, he complained in fun; Kansas Field, the drummer, would often stop by to see him and trade verbal insults. So Field ate what Lester prepared, while Lester looked on and cracked a few jokes. He smoked one cigarette after another and drank one glass after another. Non-stop. The day would pass; soon it would be night. Pres dressed, always elegantly, impeccably, as recalled by René Urtreger, who sometimes also came to get him at the hotel. Then he would take a taxi, speedily crossing Paris on a cold February night to the Blue Note where he would stay until 4 A.M.

According to statements made by René Urtreger and Jimmy Gourley, the recording made March 4 in Paris provides faithful testimony to the repertoire that the quintet had played every night at the club; it consists of standards, the Pres's favorite songs, including "Oh! Lady Be Good," "I Didn't Know What Time It Was," "Indiana," "Three Little Words," "I Cover the Waterfront," "I Can't Get Started," and even a new "D.B. Blues" that reminded

Pres of that awful year spent at Fort Gordon between 1944 and 1945. In one sense, every ingredient was there—tone, the airy lightness of the phrasing, whimsical contours of inflection—but everything seemed suspended in a state of exhausted grace, ready to disappear once and for all. Everyone at the club was fully aware of this, but there you had him: it was Pres, complete with style and a presence all his own, and the four musicians who accompanied him chose to play entirely, integrally *for him*. Among them was René Urtreger:

> We all loved him. I sincerely believe that I have only wept once when listening to music played like that, live; it was in 1953, in fact, at the Pleyel with the Prez. If my memory serves me correctly, it was "I Cover the Waterfront." What he was playing was just incredibly beautiful. I was present in the auditorium for the J.A.T.P. concert, but it was, above all, for him that I had come. When he appeared on the stage, there was an ovation like I have never heard for any musician. Prez was a kind of poet, you know. He seemed so different, almost incongruous, among all those showmen who had their numbers down perfectly. He was something else. You knew that just by looking at him. And back in 1959 he was happy playing. Of course from time to time he spoke of himself in the third person, but he did it in fun. He never took himself seriously; there was nothing "unhealthy" about his attitude in that respect.
>
> During the entire engagement, Kenny was terrific. Each time he sensed that he [Lester] was taking off on an idea or a rhythm, he would encourage him: "Blow, Prez, blow!" And here this "bopper" whose percussion style tended to be vigorous, energetic, even "interventionist," would infuse his accompaniment with flexibility and an incredible lightness, with everything, generally speaking, that might relax Lester and put him at ease. Because you also got the general feeling that he needed to be helped, that he needed support. And then there was Jimmy Gourley, who admired Lester enormously and could play back all of Prez's solos; stylewise, he played exactly like Lester. As for Michelot and me, we had already accompanied Lester and

Miles during the 1956 tour. You can imagine how many memories I had of him already. . . . Traveling on that tour, I had seen how much Miles respected him. Every evening, the second part of the program was covered by Bud Powell and the Modern Jazz Quartet; the first part would begin with Michelot, Garros, and me as a trio, following which we'd back up Lester and Miles. Miles always insisted that the place of honor go to Lester, so he would step up first (even though he was already an important performer himself) to allow Lester to conclude the first part. Later on he would reappear to play a number with him—"Lady Be Good!" if I remember correctly—before the intermission. Lester was also the only one from whom Miles would take a less than pleasant remark. I remember a very revealing anecdote in that connection: we often traveled by bus and had a very precise schedule by which everyone had to abide; usually everything worked out well, except for one morning, when we all had to wait for Miles for nearly half an hour. All the other tour members were present on the bus, and as the minutes ticked by, we were beginning to get really ticked off. After half an hour had passed, Miles finally showed up, casual, relaxed, smiling; no one dared say a thing to him, except Lester who, in that somewhat pinched manner of his—not raising his voice, but so that everyone could hear him—said, "There are some *stars* in this group. . . . " Miles sat down without uttering a word, but he never arrived late again!

That reminds me of another episode that was really funny during that tour. Prez drank a lot, as you know. Every morning, as we were getting ready to leave, he would ask us, "Where are we headed for today?" We would reply, "Milano, Frankfurt, Geneva, . . . " as the situation warranted, and every time he would give us a big smile and say, "Ah, Milano! That's my town, that's my favorite town!" And he would take a big slug of whiskey or gin to celebrate the occasion. One day, we took a plane; we were in Germany, headed for Scandinavia, I think. So after everyone got on board and found a seat, luck would have it that Prez found himself alone on a row of seats that faced each other, two by two. Shortly after that, three Germans took the seats next to and facing him; these were three businessmen, really business-like, super-serious types, complete with their Tyrolean hats and their portfolios brimming over with papers— you know the type. . . . It really seemed as if two planets had suddenly met on a single row of airplane seats! The rest of us were two or three rows away, and just to see Prez, his black felt hat, that allure of his, and those three incredibly *korrekt*, clean-cut individuals, gave us a fit of laughter. Especially since after takeoff, we noticed Prez doing his thing with them: "That's my town!" Pulling out the bottle, uncorking it, and drinking to Stockholm's health. Then he offered a sip to his neighbor. The other guy was obviously very surprised, but after a moment of hesitation, he accepted and took a drink. Prez repeated everything with the second man and the third. When the bottle came back to him, chug-a-lug, he took another slug, passed the bottle to his neighbor, and so on. . . . To make a long story short, all four of them were pretty plastered by the time they reached Stockholm, having themselves a ball, and slapping each other on the belly. Real pals! I tell you, seeing them together was a scream!

This didn't at all prevent me, back in '59, from being very impressed by playing with him (as I was by playing with Kenny, too). Especially since I was young in those days. So naturally, I was a little intimidated and didn't at times dare take but one chorus; that's when Prez would look my way and exclaim, "You gave up!" Jokingly, of course. Prez was the kind of guy who never stopped joking, even during that last month in Paris. I'll give you an example. There were several times when Jean-Louis Viale was brought in to take Kenny's place at the club. Jean-Louis, who died last year, was in my opinion the French drummer who had in those days best assimilated a black American drummer's "swing," and Lester liked him a lot, although he would occasionally beat a little too loudly, at which time Lester would call him "Big Bomber!" Fittingly enough, Jean-Louis was also physically rather big. So when Jean-Louis was present and Lester was about to set a nice, light, swing tempo, he'd turn to him in advance and say, "Soft eyes, Big Bomber?" It was his way of indicating that the bass should keep a low profile! He had loads of expressions like that, a whole language of his own, always in jest. At that time, he'd add Italianized endings to words (similar to "Blue Nottini," for instance); he'd change the titles of tunes. "All of Me" became "Oil of Me." Girls who were on the heavy side, he called "Long Distance!" Women in general were "Miss Wiggins"—essentially birdbrains; Erika had the privilege of being "The Original Miss Wiggins!" (René Urtreger)

Jimmy Gourley's recollections are entirely in the same vein:

Prez was what English speakers call a "compulsive talker"; he talked and joked incessantly. One night when we were playing at the club, he called out, "Now let's take 'Justice'!" All four of us gave each other blank looks. "What'd you say, Prez?—*Justice*, 'Just Us,' you mean, right?" The same thing would happen with "Three Little Words," which might turn into "Three Little Turds," to which he'd add, "and I'll bring the paper." Prez might well have been really and truly ill, but he'd never stop cracking those jokes. And he'd always create some sort of parody to set the stage. Just the way he'd approach the mike with tiny steps and a slight swing of the hips—that must have been what made some people think he was a homosexual! One day when I said something to him about it, he answered, "Showbiz, Lady Jimmy, it's showbiz!" And when we'd arrive at the Blue Note at night, he had a way of picking up his sax (which he had invariably left on the piano "as is" after the last set—never even putting it back in its case, as if he were only leaving it for five minutes), lifting it to his lips, playing a descending arpeggio down to the lower register, always the same one, absolutely the same, and then saying to himself with a look of (apparent) surprise, "Oh! Iceberg!"

One time Don Byas came by the club at night. He wanted at all costs to jam, to perform; so the Prez quietly says to him, "Okay, Lady Don, you can play . . . if you know 'my songs. . . .'" And it was clearly not a matter of repertoire. . . . Of course, Don played after his fashion, i.e., at top speed; and Prez sat there listening, unperturbed, waiting for it to end!

You should have seen him call the bartender while we were in the middle of a song: He'd blow a deep note, foghorn-style, then he'd make this elaborate ceremonial gesture, cracking everyone up in the process; and the bartender, who had immediately understood, would bring him his drink. He had a code: "a soft one" was wine; "a hard one" was vodka and Pernod, for example, or Pernod with wine. He drank and smoked like crazy. Really nonstop. He always had his "red dog" (his bottle of whiskey) in his saxophone case. But as strange as it may seem, this went on absolutely undramatically; invariably, it took on a sort of humorous appearance. I practically never heard the Prez complain—except once, when Kenny had brought us back to La Louisiane at 5 A.M. in his little [Renault] Dauphine, and the Prez had a lot of trouble extricating himself from it; and one other time, too, when he complained about his stomach being shot to hell. . . .

Even so, never would you catch him laid up in some corner, or coming in late; he was not absent a single time during his engagement. The only recollections I ever heard him mention occasionally were those he had of his stint in the army, which had left him deeply scarred. In that connection, I'd like to make one clarification: According to what Prez told me at the time, it hadn't just been a case of drug use. From the outset, I mean as soon as he set foot in the barracks, he had had an altercation with his captain. When Prez had been drafted, he was in possession of a fairly large amount of money; so he went looking for his superior officer to give him the two or three thousand dollars he had for safekeeping, plainly thinking that the money would be safer there; and the other guy could find nothing better to say than, "Where did a nigger like you come across two thousand dollars?" *A nigger.* . . . Prez punched the guy squarely in the kisser, and that, of course, immediately landed him in the slammer. There was also the other story he would tell me, one that certainly didn't help his situation any either: One day, during maneuvers in the woods, while his captain stood on a tree stump reviving the troops' fighting spirit by announcing the regiment's upcoming departure for the front in Asia, Prez said to him, right there in front of everyone, that he certainly wouldn't keep the captain from going, but that as far as he personally was concerned, he'd rather abstain. . . . And there was also—it's coming back to me now—another episode of racism that involved a marine in the New York subway early in the 1940s: There was Prez, minding his own business, when at a certain stop there's a marine who boards the same car and walks over to him saying, "Give me that seat, nigger!" Prez looked at him and, pulling a knife out of his pocket as he spoke, said to him in that coded language of his, while at the same time making a practically untranslatable pun (combining the words "seat," and "set" in the sense of what musicians play during a nightly show), that boiled down to this: "You say you wanta set? Then you'll have to get on it while I make you dance to it!" In any case, the episode ended badly. At the end of the line, the police were waiting, and Prez was the one who had to pay a $500 fine! When he'd tell me stories like that, he'd always finish by saying, "But with you, it's different, Lady Jimmy; you're a Christian gentleman!" And I'd answer him, "Gentleman, maybe, but as for Christian, that's another matter!" More often, though, we'd joke around talking about the present; or about the Alvin Hotel, where he'd soon be returning, opposite Birdland. . . . (Jimmy Gourley)

All the rest aside, Pres had been playing in Paris for a month by then, and there wasn't much of a crowd at the Blue Note any more; during the last week there were a dozen people there on average. On February 18, Lester granted François Postif a long interview. On the afternoon of March 4, he recorded for the Barclay label in the Avenue Hoche studios, the last recording of which mention has already been made (*Lester Young in Paris*). As remembered by Jimmy Gourley and René Urtreger, Pres seemed normal: no more sick than usual. The day was simply more exhausting, for after the recording session, they had to return to the Blue Note for another evening's work. Jimmy Gourley had made the contacts, and since he was concerned, Lester tried to reassure him: he had promised; he would come; he was staying in Paris especially for that purpose.

And sure enough on March 11 Pres was there as agreed, with Jimmy Gourley. Gourley was to witness a very embarrassing scene, which graphically illustrated the difficulties Lester could encounter as soon as he was away from the network of friends who were apt to provide him with a favorable environment:

The plan was for Prez and me to play with the rhythm section of trumpeter Idrees Sulieman [sic], who was also scheduled to perform during the broadcast. And lo and behold, when we got to the studio, Sulieman started creating a fuss, claiming that he and his musicians played with tricks of their own, and that he could not make them available to anyone else. Right then and there, I blew my top: "But this is not just 'anyone else'! This is not just anybody! This is the Prez, Lester Young! And if he hadn't existed, you wouldn't even be here!" Prez witnessed the scene without saying anything; he was standing a little to one side, apparently busying himself absent-mindedly with his sax; he heard everything, obviously, but he didn't say one word. Finally, Sulieman's pianist took me aside to tell me not to get upset, and that they would be playing with Prez no matter what. Sure enough, we were able to record after all. We played "D.B. Blues" and one other piece whose title I don't recall any more.

We certainly had our doubts about whether that would be the last time. . . . When we heard about his death, just a few days later in the papers, something very touching happened. After Prez had left, the young German woman, Erika, had stayed behind at La Louisiane; as soon as the news reached her, she who was so blond went out to buy herself a black wig, and she also dressed completely in black. . . . (Jimmy Gourley)

Everything happened very quickly then. No matter how many jokes he told, it was obvious Pres's condition had taken a serious turn for the worse. When Ben Benjamin suggested he see a doctor as soon as possible, Lester answered that he didn't speak French and the doctor would not be able to understand him. He would see about it in New York. March 14, he left Paris; he looked terrible, and the photographer, Chenz, who accompanied him to the airport, confessed that he had the impression of dealing with a dying man.[127]

The night before, Pres had sent Elaine a telegram announcing his return. It was a Friday, Friday the thirteenth. Just like the time he had broken with Basie, in December 1940. . . .

Thirteen. Quite a story, isn't it?

The sum of one lifetime.

Notes

1. Willis Handy is also said to have been the principal of a high school, probably at Bogalusa, Louisiana.

2. Along with minstrel and variety shows, black choirs and chorales were having an enormous amount of success. Their repertoire was founded on the gospel music of the churches to which the vocalists belonged. Willis Handy belonged to several of these choirs.

3. During this period, the Youngs performed on the Theater Owners' Booking Association (T.O.B.A.) circuit, also known by the nicknames "Tough On Black Acts," or "Toby Time." TOBA offered the best booking opportunities for traveling musicians. The organization made its appearance just after World War I, and, in keeping with its variety clientele, specialized in handling variety and vaudeville bookings on other circuits, such as the Keith, the Orpheum Theater, and Pantages. In the twenties, some one hundred theaters were affiliated with this network, and from it came their playbills. No sooner did the jazz orchestras make their appearance than TOBA was managing the tours of King Oliver, Fletcher Henderson, Louis Armstrong, Duke Ellington, and Bennie Moten, as well as tours by blues singers such as Ida Cox, Bessie Smith, and Ma Rainey. The organization disappeared just as quickly in the early forties. Its principal claim to fame is that it fostered the exposure of black orchestras in this country, and that implies in turn that it promoted jazz.

4. Interview, National Endowment for the Arts, Jazz Oral History Project, Rutgers University, Institute of Jazz Studies, Newark, New Jersey.

5. Lester Young gave one last interview to François Postif in Paris in 1959. Twenty years later a transcript and a translation of the interview were published in numbers 362 and 363 of the French magazine *Jazz Hot,* with the following remarks as to their background: "The story of this last interview is strange in and of itself. Published initially in number 142 of this publication, it was included in a brochure to accompany Verve's triple 'Lester for President' recording set (VEV 0020/21/22). Not long after that, all trace was lost of the original tape, which had been

loaned by François Postif to the American critic Nat Hentoff. Recently, one of those small twenty-four-hour jazz stations that spring up here and there on the East Coast aired a copy of the tape made by François Postif. It aired very late at night, in order to keep young ears from hearing the graphic language with which Lester Young expressed himself. Luckily, one Danish jazz lover recorded the broadcast, and finally by way of a third party in Copenhagen we succeeded in recovering the phantom interview."

6. Postif interview.

7. Cootie Williams (born July 10, 1911) never actually appeared in conjunction with the saxophone orchestra. His position was in the orchestra pit, and his duty consisted of announcing with a few runs on the trumpet that the band was about to change sets. Cootie and Lester paired off thick as thieves, and they often made such a din that the orchestra would mix up the order of its numbers. All the Lackman and Carson shows were performed under a big tent.

8. Interview, National Endowment for the Arts, Jazz Oral History Project, Rutgers University, Institute of Jazz Studies, Newark, New Jersey.

9. Postif interview.

10. Trumbauer was influenced by saxophone virtuoso Rudy Wiedoft. Benny Carter acknowledges having been influenced by "Tram" to the point of buying a soprano saxophone. He finally dedicated himself to the alto, since the orchestras with which he wanted to work had no arrangements for that peculiar instrument. Other musicians such as Adolphus "Doc" Cheatam who began on the soprano, Eddie Barefield, and Buster Smith were influenced at one time or another by Trumbauer. Trumbauer died in Kansas City in 1956.

11. Interview, National Endowment for the Arts, Jazz Oral History Project, Rutgers University, Institute of Jazz Studies, Newark, New Jersey.

12. Jimmy Dorsey talked his friend, bootlegger Joe Helbock, into opening the Onyx, a club on Fifty-second Street in Manhattan that was to have enormous success.

13. Postif interview.

14. "Pres," by Nat Hentoff, *down beat,* March 7, 1956.

15. Unpublished interview with Eddie Barefield, New York, June 13, 1984.

16. Lester also played alto in Bronson's band.

17. Informal conversation between Lester Young and some other musicians reported by Alan Morrison in *The Jazz Record,* July 1946.

18. Barefield interview.

19. Oscar Pettiford was born September 30, 1922, on an Indian reservation in Okmulgee, Oklahoma. His father was of Cherokee descent, and his mother was a Choctaw. The family band earned its reputation with a repertoire made up largely of original compositions influenced by Cherokee and Choctaw folklore.

20. President Herbert Hoover was unable to handle the crisis, and it was left to Franklin D. Roosevelt to begin corrective measures in March 1933 with the New Deal.

21. William Basie was born August 21, 1904, in Red Bank, New Jersey. He began to train on the drums at the age of thirteen, then turned his attention to the piano. While playing with local bands, he took lessons from Fats Waller. From 1925 to 1927, he went on tour and figured in assorted "variety acts." He joined the Blue Devils in July 1928 in Dallas.

22. Bennie Moten was born November 13, 1894, in Kansas City and spent most of his life there. He made his professional debut with the Lacy Blackburn Orchestra and only subsequently began to study the piano. At the age of twenty-four he was conducting his own trio, hoping to form a bigger group with a ragtime repertoire. A few months later, the pianist introduced a sextet in the black section of Kansas City. The group was an instant success, and in 1923, accompanied by two local blues singers, Bennie Moten cut his first records on the Okeh label in St. Louis. These comprise the first documented record of the nascent Kansas City style.

After several sessions with Okeh, Moten moved over to Victor Records in 1926. From then on he led a ten-man ensemble that was the pride and glory of Kansas City. In the fall of the same year, he undertook a tour on the East Coast that brought him to Camden, New Jersey, where he made his first recordings for Victor. The band became one of the most popular at the dance halls, and its records enjoyed a huge success. But to improve its quality, the group needed musicians with a wider range, musicians like those in the employ of Duke Ellington and Fletcher Henderson, or like the Blue Devils. Returning to Kansas City after another tour, Moten issued his first invitations to the budding talents of the Blue Devils.

23. Barefield interview.

24. Interview, National Endowment for the Arts, Jazz Oral History Project, Rutgers University, Institute of Jazz Studies, Newark, New Jersey.

25. In the days of the Blue Devils, bands were customarily made up of two alto saxophones and one tenor, two trumpets, one trombone, a banjo or guitar, drums, a double bass, and sometimes a violin.

Certain ballrooms disposed of two stages, one intended for the "house" band, the other for traveling ensembles. This arrangement favored the organization of band contests.

26. Interview, National Endowment for the Arts, Jazz Oral History Project, Rutgers University, Institute of Jazz Studies, Newark, New Jersey.

27. Situated at the crossroads between the eastern and western United States (where the Kansas and Missouri rivers meet), Kansas City was an important river port, a major rail terminal, and a burgeoning industrial center. In 1933, the city had more than half a million inhabitants, of which 10 to 15 percent were black. Although twelve million people in the region were unemployed, only a minute segment of the work force was affected. The fact of the matter was that "K.C." was then in the hands of a more or less corrupt family of politicians—the Pendergasts—who for thirty years had maintained an extended network of powerful business ties. At the same time, they exercised a corruptive influence.

28. From 1930 to 1942, saxophonist and clarinettist Tommy Douglas led a big band which several musicians later quit to form the core of Harlan Leonard's Rocket.

29. When Prohibition was repealed in December of 1933, liquor went from black-market to legal sale. The bootleggers and gangsters on Pendergast's payroll became honest businessmen. Bars, nightclubs, theaters, and dance halls continued to prosper, attracting growing numbers of musicians who had lost all possibility of employment elsewhere. Kansas City became a true musical capital, so much so that it gave birth to what would later be called the Age of Swing.

30. Before Bennie Moten's band had arrived, Jesse Stone's Blue Serenaders—who came to Kansas City in 1928—were the sole black band in the city to have a repertoire contained on sheet music.

31. Interview, National Endowment for the Arts, Jazz Oral History Project, Rutgers University, Institute of Jazz Studies, Newark, New Jersey.

32. Williams at one time played flute for Noble Sissle.

33. This excerpt from the interview given by Lester Young to François Postif appears exclusively in the French version of *Jazz Hot,* no. 363. See note 5.

34. Interview, National Endowment for the Arts, Jazz Oral History Project, Rutgers University, Institute of Jazz Studies, Newark, New Jersey.

35. Informal conversation between Lester Young and some other musicians reported by Alan Morrison in *The Jazz Record,* July 1946.

36. Before his association with Allen, Hart had been a pianist with Mac Kinney's Cotton Pickers—also known by the name Chocolate Dandies through its Parlophone recordings—an orchestra directed by alto saxophonist Donald Redman.

37. The regulars were Pete Johnson on the piano and Murl Johnson and Baby Lovett on drums.

38. Interview, National Endowment for the Arts, Jazz Oral History Project, Rutgers University, Institute of Jazz Studies, Newark, New Jersey.

39. Ibid.

40. Kansas City was recognized as the capital of jam, and most musicians who passed through town did their best to participate in a jam session. Duke Ellington and Cab Calloway were exceptions; they forbade the members of their orchestras to jam. Of course few paid attention to the injunction, which they considered "anti-musical."

41. Mary Lou Williams, *Hear Me Talkin' to Ya,* eds. Nat Shapiro and Nat Hentoff (New York: Rinehart & Co., 1955) 292–93.

42. Musicians often repeated these remarks to one another before starting a jam session in an effort to ready themselves to surpass their own limits.

43. Hilton Jefferson, *down beat,* November 2, 1955.

44. Postif interview.

45. Remarks made by a former Henderson musician, Hilton Jefferson, to Buddy Tate and reported in an interview, National Endowment for the Arts, Jazz Oral History Project, Rutgers University, Institute of Jazz Studies, Newark, New Jersey.

46. Postif interview.

47. Andy Kirk was born May 28, 1898, in Newport, Kentucky. He studied music in Denver, Colorado, with Wilberforce Whiteman, Paul Whiteman's father, and took his first paying job at the age of twenty in the George Morrison Orchestra. In 1925 he went to Dallas and joined Terence T. Holder's Clouds of Joy, becoming the band's leader during the winter of 1928–1929 after Holder left. A few months later, in preparation for a promising audition with Brunswick records and relying on the recommendation of his alto sax player, John Williams, Kirk hired John's wife, Mary Lou. In 1931 Kirk recorded on the RCA label with a white female vocalist named Calloway. After several tours in the southwest, he returned to Kansas City in 1934, where he performed for nearly two years before signing a contract with Decca.

The Clouds of Joy under Andy Kirk was, after the Bennie Moten Orchestra, the second "territorial band" to acquire a worldwide reputation that lasted until 1945. Through its ranks filed such important musicians as Dick Wilson, Don Byas, Ben Webster, Buddy Tate, Lester Young, Charlie Parker, Mary Lou Williams, Ken Kersey, Howard McGhee, Fats Navarro, and vocalist Pha Terrell.

48. Interview, National Endowment for the Arts, Jazz Oral History Project, Rutgers University, Institute of Jazz Studies, Newark, New Jersey. Born Mary Elfrieda Scruggs, Mary Lou Williams was also known by the names Mary Lou Winn and Mary Lou Burley.

49. Born in Chicago in 1900, Boyd Atkins did not get the recognition he deserved as a violinist and sax player. He played with Earl Hines, Louis Armstrong, and Eli Rice before heading his own group at the Sunset Cafe between 1929 and 1930. Starting in 1934, he directed a band in Minneapolis that included trumpeter Rook Ganz. After that he became the house musician at the Cotton Club.

50. Interview, National Endowment for the Arts, Jazz Oral History Project, Rutgers University, Institute of Jazz Studies, Newark, New Jersey.

51. "I began using the name Count the minute I thought it could help me. In any case, everyone called me that. But the very first one to do so was a disc jockey on radio station WHB. Don't ask me why; I have no idea" (Gretchen Weaver. "Up with the Count," *Band Leaders and Record Review,* February 1947).

52. Countess Johnson, who was considered by some to be the best

piano player in Kansas City, would occasionally sit in for Mary Lou Williams in the Andy Kirk Orchestra.

53. See note 3.

54. John Hammond, *down beat,* November 2, 1955.

55. Interview, National Endowment for the Arts, Jazz Oral History Project, Rutgers University, Institute of Jazz Studies, Newark, New Jersey.

56. Barefield interview.

57. John Hammond, *John Hammond on Record* (New York: Summit Books, 1977).

58. Ibid.

59. For a more thorough discussion of the "vertical" and "horizontal" concepts, see George Russell, *The Lydian Chromatic Concept of Tonal Organisation for Improvisation* (New York: Concept Publishing Co., 1959).

60. Gene Ramey interview by Bob Reisner, "A Biography in Interviews," *Jazz Review,* 9, no. 3, November 1960.

61. Informal discussion between Lester Young and some other musicians, reported by Alan Morrison in *The Jazz Record,* July 1946.

62. Miles Davis as interviewed by Francis Marmande, "De Plus en plus bluesy," *Le Monde,* July 25, 1984.

63. The producers, not the musicians, were the ones to propose a meeting of musicians for a recording session. Often the recording sessions were the only opportunity for musicians of long acquaintance to play together.

64. Interview, National Endowment for the Arts, Jazz Oral History Project, Rutgers University, Institute of Jazz Studies, Newark, New Jersey.

65. Earl Warren, "Basie's Beginnings," *Jazz Magazine,* no. 251, January 1977, 21.

66. One need only think of the Michael Jackson clothing mania, and of the break dancing that children five years of age and above have recently been practicing on pieces of cardboard laid out on the sidewalk.

67. Billie Holiday with William Dufty, *Lady Sings the Blues* (N.Y.: Avon, 1976) 50, 59.

Former Democratic governor of New York Franklin D. Roosevelt (1882–1945) became president in March 1933. To bring vitality and strength to the country, Roosevelt initiated his "New Deal" political campaign, which was much more of a vast social and humanistic program than it was an economic one. It gave fresh hope to hundreds of thousands of people by repeating to them, "Happiness does not lie in the simple possession of wealth, but rather in the satisfaction of the creative effort."

"When Roosevelt died, both the poor blacks and the poor whites of the South—mortal enemies for fifty years or more—sobbed together as they stood watching the train that was returning his body to Washington" (*The Atlantic,* Vol. 254, no. 1 [July 1, 1984] 41).

68. Refer to the extensive discography in appendix.

69. Interview, National Endowment for the Arts, Jazz Oral History Project, Rutgers University, Institute of Jazz Studies, Newark, New Jersey.

70. Jack McDaniels, "Buster Smith," *down beat,* July 11, 1956, 13.

71. Ross Russell, *Jazz Style in Kansas City and the Southwest* (Berkeley: University of California Press, 1971) 136.

72. Interview, National Endowment for the Arts, Jazz Oral History Project, Rutgers University, Institute of Jazz Studies, Newark, New Jersey.

73. Billy Taylor, *Jazz Piano: History and Development* (Dubuque: William C. Brown Co., 1982) 120.

74. *Lady Sings the Blues,* 48.

75. Interview, National Endowment for the Arts, Jazz Oral History Project, Rutgers University, Institute of Jazz Studies, Newark, New Jersey.

76. *Lady Sings the Blues,* 48–49.

77. Touring was always done either by car, by bus, or by train. A few musicians like Cab Calloway rented whole pullman cars which they outfitted according to their needs.

78. Interview, National Endowment for the Arts, Jazz Oral History Project, Rutgers University, Institute of Jazz Studies, Newark, New Jersey.

79. While rehearsals for "From Spiritual to Swing" were underway, Barney Josephson opened the first interracial nightclub, the Café Society, on Sheridan Square in Manhattan. John Hammond was in charge of the programming.

80. *Hot Record Society Rag,* January 1940.

81. On the record cut February 2, 1939, Lester and the band played "Jive at Five" and the solo by him which is now being most copied and imitated. See note 103.

82. Chapter 10 elaborates on this.

83. Interview, National Endowment for the Arts, Jazz Oral History Project, Rutgers University, Institute of Jazz Studies, Newark, New Jersey.

84. In several interviews, Count Basie refused to clarify this departure but denied having dismissed Lester because of his refusal to record on a Friday the thirteenth.

85. Interview, National Endowment for the Arts, Jazz Oral History Project, Rutgers University, Institute of Jazz Studies, Newark, New Jersey.

86. Ibid.

87. Ibid.

88. Ibid.

89. Ibid.

90. Ibid.

91. Leonard Feather quoting Budd Johnson in *Playboy*. Back in New York, Lester hurriedly collected his money from Sears and quit the band.

92. Interview, National Endowment for the Arts, Jazz Oral History Project, Rutgers University, Institute of Jazz Studies, Newark, New Jersey.

93. Barefield interview.

94. Interview, National Endowment for the Arts, Jazz Oral History Project, Rutgers University, Institute of Jazz Studies, Newark, New Jersey.

95. Dickie Wells, with Stanley Dance, *The Night People: Reminiscences of a Jazzman* (Boston: Crescendo Publishing, 1971) 62.

96. Interview, National Endowment for the Arts, Jazz Oral History Project, Rutgers University, Institute of Jazz Studies, Newark, New Jersey.

97. To my knowledge, there are no police files to substantiate Lester Young's arrest. There is the incident mentioned at the time of his passage through Kansas City when, in company of Ben Webster, he enjoyed disrupting traffic in the city streets. That had at most earned him a couple of warnings from the police.

Billie Holiday, on the other hand, had been repeatedly investigated for possession of marijuana. Lester never made a secret of his use of marijuana at the time, and when the American public became the target of an anti-Communist campaign—and the social stratum of jazz musicians was certainly not spared—a file was opened concerning the "suspect" tendencies of Lester Young.

98. It was apparently a case of benign syphilis. This subject was exploited to excess, based on certain joking references which alleged that Lester tended to visit houses of prostitution. All of this was entirely fabricated.

99. Jo Jones, who recalled this tragic episode in Lester's life, categorically refused to reveal the name of this young white trumpet player, although he did explain the circumstances that led to their meeting at Fort Ord, where Jo Jones was stationed.

> But this trumpet player—and it's on record—this same trumpet player was the one that they transferred and sent to Fayetteville. . . . North Carolina. . . . He was the same one that was on the bus when a black baby was crying and the white bus driver went back and choked the baby—the same M.P. blew his brains out and drove the bus into the station and turned himself in to the M.P.'s. . . . And when he came to Fort Ord he was supposed to ship out to go to fight. They just put him in prison and he stayed there for 6 weeks.

Interview, National Endowment for the Arts, Jazz Oral History Project, Rutgers University, Institute of Jazz Studies, Newark, New Jersey.

100. In musical terminology, a *tonic* refers to the primary tone of a diatonic scale.

101. Dizzie Gillespie, *To Be or Not to Bop* (New York: Doubleday, 1977) 407.

102. In 1947 (see beginning of this chapter). A few years later, Symphony Sid worked directly out of Birdland.

103. It was composed by Lester for the Basie orchestra and often cited for its skillful construction, says Martin Williams in *Jazz Tradition* (N.Y.: Oxford, 1970) 117.

104. *Hot Club Magazine,* March 1947.

105. Moe Gale was, together with Charlie Buchanan, the proprietor of the Savoy Ballroom, which opened in New York March 12, 1926, and closed in July of 1958.

106. Before this second, and final, marriage, Lester had to divorce his first wife, but the author has found it impossible to find any trace of the proceedings.

107. Whitney Balliett. *Ecstasy at the Onion* (Indianapolis: Bobbs-Merrill, 1971) 173–74.

108. Budd Johnson quoted in Gillespie, *To Be or Not to Bop,* 218.

109. Berendt, *Jazz* (Paris: Petite Bibliothéque Payot).

110. *Jazzletter,* 2.

111. Ibid.

112. *Jazzletter,* 4.

113. Bobby Scott, "The House in the Heart," *Jazzletter.* Vol 3, no. 2 (September 1983) 5.

114. "The House in the Heart," *Jazzletter,* 5, 8.

115. Today, Walter Schaap is owner of the West End Club in Manhattan.

116. Nat Hentoff, interview of "Pres," *down beat,* March 7, 1956 (that article not in that issue).

117. Armand Gordon, unpublished interview, 1984.

118. Bill Potts, "Liner Notes," *Pablo* 230 8219 (1980).

119. Interview, National Endowment for the Arts, Jazz Oral History Project, Rutgers University, Institute of Jazz Studies, Newark, New Jersey.

120. Reverend John Gensel, unpublished interview, New York, June 19, 1984.

121. Interview, National Endowment for the Arts, Jazz Oral History Project, Rutgers University, Institute of Jazz Studies, Newark, New Jersey.

122. Dan Morgenstern is currently [1987] director of the Rutgers Institute of Jazz Studies.

123. Dan Morgenstern, "Lester Leaps In," *down beat,* April 3, 1969, 19–20.

124. Barefield interview.

125. According to Jimmy Gourley, it is during this period the manager of the hotel where Lester was staying adamantly refused to give him permission to cook in his room. The hotel appears to have been situated near the Blue Note.

126. For the record, Bud Powell also stayed at this hotel, though at a different time.

127. On arriving in New York March 14, Lester confessed that he had coughed up blood during the flight and that the pain had been so great he had bitten deeply into his lips in an attempt to keep from yelling out loud.

Bibliography

Reviews

down beat.
—November 2, 1955, John Hammond.
—March 7, 1956, "Pres," Nat Hentoff.
—April 30, 1959, "The Last Sad Days of Lester Willis Young," Robert
     Reisner.
—March 1, 1962, "Early Prez," George Hoeffer.
Band Leaders and Records Review, February 1947.
Metronome, February 1937.
Jazz Discounter, vol. 2, no. 6, June 1949.
Jazzletter, vol. 3, no. 2, September 1983.
Jazz Review, November 1958; December 1959; January, February 1960.
The Black Perspective in Music, "Lester Leaps In: The Early Style of Lester
     Young," Lewis Porter, 1981.
Jazz Magazine (Paris).

Books

Blesh, Rudi. *Eight Lives in Jazz.* Hayden, New York, 1971.
Charters, Samuel B. *Jazz New Orleans 1855–1963.* Oak Publications,
     New York, 1963.
Charters, Samuel B., and Leonard Kunstadt. *Jazz, a History of the New
     York Scene.* Doubleday, New York, 1962.
Collier, J. L. *L'Aventure du jazz.* Albin Michel, Paris, 1981.
Ellison, Ralph. *Shadow and Act.* Random House, New York, 1964.
Goffin, Robert. *Aux frontières du jazz.* Editions du Sagittaire, Paris, 1932.
Green, Benny. *The Reluctant Art.* London, 1962.
Green, George F. *A Condensed History of the Kansas City Area.* Lowell
     Press, 1968.

Hammond, John. *John Hammond on Record.* Summit Books, New York, 1977.

Holiday, Billie. *Lady Sings the Blues.* Plon, Paris.

Horricks, Raymond. *Count Basie and His Orchestra.* Victor Gollancz, London, 1957.

Milligan, Maurice. *The Inside Story of the Pendergast Machine.* New York, 1948.

Newton, Francis. *Une sociologie du jazz.* Flammarion, Paris, 1966.

Ostransky, Leroy. *The Anatomy of Jazz.* University of Washington Press, Seattle, 1960.

Russell, Ross. *Jazz Style in Kansas City and the Southwest.* University of California Press, Berkeley, 1971.

Shaw, Arnold. *52nd Street. The Street of Jazz.* Da Capo Press, New York, 1977.

Simon, George T. *The Big Bands.* Macmillan Company, New York, 1967.

Stearns, Marshall. *The Story of Jazz.* Oxford, 1962.

Wells, Dicky. *The Night People.* Crescendo Publishing Company, Boston, 1971.

Wilson, John S. *Jazz, The Transition Years.* Appleton-Century-Crofts, New York, 1966.

Discography

Compiled by Daniel Richard

The reader will find below:

1. The list of 12" LPs emanating from commercial recordings grouped in chronological order and by label. Only those recordings have been included in which Lester Young appears as a soloist. For Each album and boxed set numbered from 1 to 38 (Excepting the J.A.T.P. concerts which appear under a single number) both the first 12" LP release and its equivalent(s) are indicated. These editions constitute the reference albums.

2. A selection of the best 12" LP editions emanating from non-commercial recordings, classified from A to Q.

* indicates that an album is unavailable.
Thanks go to Michel Ruppi, Jacques Lubin, and Marie-France Calas.

*1. THE LESTER YOUNG STORY VOLUME 1: JONES-SMITH & WILSON-HOLIDAY INC.
   BANDS: Jones-Smith Incorporated, Teddy Wilson and His Orchestra, Billie Holiday and Her Orchestra
   ORIGINAL LABEL: Vocalion-Brunswick-Columbia, 1936–1937
   REFERENCES: Columbia (U.S.) CG-33502 (double album)

*2. THE LESTER YOUNG STORY VOLUME 2: A MUSICAL ROMANCE
   BANDS: Billie Holiday and Her Orchestra, Teddy Wilson and His Orchestra, Benny Goodman Carnegie Hall Jam Session

ORIGINAL LABEL: Vocalion-Brunswick-Columbia, 1937–1938
REFERENCES: Columbia (U.S.) JG-34837 (double album)

*3. THE LESTER YOUNG STORY VOLUME 3: ENTER THE COUNT

BANDS: Teddy Wilson and His Orchestra, Basie's Bad Boys, Count Basie and His Orchestra, Glenn Hardman and His Hammond Five
ORIGINAL LABEL: Brunswick-Columbia-Vocalion, 1938–1939
REFERENCES: Columbia (U.S.) JG-34840 (double album)

*4. THE LESTER YOUNG STORY VOLUME 4: LESTER LEAPS IN

BANDS: Glenn Hardman and His Hammond Five, Count Basie and His Orchestra, Count Basie's Kansas City Seven, Billie Holiday and Her Orchestra
ORIGINAL LABEL: Columbia-Vocalion-Okeh, 1939–1940
REFERENCES: Columbia (U.S.) JG-34843 (double album)

*5. THE LESTER YOUNG STORY VOLUME 5: EVENING OF A BASIE-ITE

BANDS: Count Basie and His Orchestra, Billie Holiday and Her Orchestra
ORIGINAL LABEL: Columbia-Epic-Okeh, 1940–1941
REFERENCES: Columbia (U.S.) C2-34849 (double album)

The five volumes of the "Lester Young Story" make up the entirety of the recordings that Lester cut solo for what we know today as the Columbia label while a band member. Though this highly remarkable series is no longer available, the essential recordings under the headings Jones-Smith, Incorporated; Basie's Bad Boys; Count Basie and His Orchestra; Count Basie's Kansas City Seven are available in the excellent "Jazzothèque" series directed by Henri Renaud, soon to be available on compact discs.

Count Basie Vol. I, 1936 and 1939, The Count and the President, C.B.S. (H.) 88667 (double album) (C.B.S.)
Count Basie Vol. II, 1939/1940, Lester Leaps In, C.B.S. (H.) 88668 (double album) (C.B.S.)

Count Basie Vol. III, 1940/1941, Don for Prez, C.B.S. (H.) 88672
(double album) (C.B.S.)

In the absence of the entire "Lester Young Story," desirable substitute editions are by Teddy Wilson and Billie Holiday. Although the essential recordings under the names of Teddy Wilson and His Orchestra and Billie Holiday and Her Orchestra are available in older, non-chronological collections.

Billie Holiday: The Golden Years, Columbia (U.S.) C3L-21 (boxed set of three records)
Billie Holiday: The Golden Years, C.B.S. (F.) 66377 (boxed set of three records)
Billie Holiday: The Golden Years, Volume II, Columbia (U.S.) C3L-40 (boxed set of three records)
Billie Holiday: Lady Day, Columbia (U.S.) CL-637,
Billie Holiday: Lady Day, CD C.B.S. Sony (Japan) 32 DP-482

*6. COUNT BASIE: EARLY COUNT, COMPLETE RECORDED WORKS 1937–1939. 60 TITLES IN CHRONOLOGICAL ORDER
BANDS: Count Basie and His Orchestra
ORIGINAL LABEL: Decca 1937–1938–1939
REFERENCES: M.C.A. (F.) 510167/70 (boxed set of four records)

or

* COUNT BASIE: THE COMPLETE COLLECTION OF COUNT BASIE ORCHESTRA ON DECCA (1937–1939)
BANDS: Count Basie and His Orchestra
ORIGINAL LABEL: Decca 1937–1938–1939
REFERENCES: M.C.A. (J.) VIM-5501/4 (boxed set of four records)

In the two missing versions, Lester does not perform solo. The two boxed sets are no longer available; however, the complete Decca Count Basie and His Orchestra recordings are available in two non-chronological releases. (Lacking three choruses and one title song; Lester performs no solos.)

Count Basie: Best, M.C.A. (U.S.) 2-4050 (double album)
Count Basie: Good Morning Blues, M.C.A. (U.S.) 2-4108
(double album)

or (Lacking three choruses and one title song; Lester performs no solos.)

Jimmy Rushing: Good Mornin' Blues, Affinity (G.B.) AFS-1002
(Media 7)
Count Basie: Swingin' the Blues! Affinity (G.B.) AFS-1010 (Media 7)
Count Basie: Swingin' at the Daisy Chain, Affinity (G.B.) AFS-1019
(Media 7)

*7. JAZZ V.S.O.P.: M.C.A. JAZZ MASTERPIECE SERIES 5
BANDS: Sam Price and His Texas Blusicians
ORIGINAL LABEL: Decca 1941
REFERENCES: M.C.A. (J.) 3080

8. THE COMPLETE BENNY GOODMAN, VOLUME V
1937–1938
BANDS: Benny Goodman and His Orchestra
ORIGINAL LABEL: Victor 1938
REFERENCES: Bluebird (U.S.) AXM2-5557 (double album)

or

THE INDISPENSABLE BENNY GOODMAN VOLUME 5/6
(1938–1939)
Jazz Tribute no. 65
Double Black & White
BANDS: Benny Goodman and His Orchestra
ORIGINAL LABEL: Victor 1938
REFERENCES: R.C.A. (R.F.A.) NL-89587 (2) (double album)
(R.C.A./Ariola)

In the two missing renditions, Lester performs no solo.

*9. SWING VOL. 1: VINTAGE SERIES, ORIGINAL 1936–1946
RECORDINGS
BANDS: Una Mae Carlisle with Orchestra
ORIGINAL LABEL: Bluebird 1941
REFERENCES: R.C.A. (U.S.) LPV-578

or

THE COMPLETE UNA MAE CARLISLE (1940–1942) AND
JOHN KIRBY (1941–1942)

> Jazz Tribute no. 64
> Double Black & White

BANDS: Una Mae Carlisle with Orchestra
ORIGINAL LABEL: Bluebird 1941
REFERENCES: R.C.A. (R.F.A.) NL-89484 (2) (double album)
(R.C.A./Ariola)

*10. FROM SPIRITUALS TO SWING: CARNEGIE HALL
CONCERTS 1938/39

BANDS: Members of Basie Band (recording studio)/Count Basie
and His Orchestra/Kansas City Six/Jam Session: Benny
Goodman Sextet, Count Basie Band, Meade Lux Lewis, Pete
Johnson and Albert Ammons
ORIGINAL LABEL: Vanguard 1938–1939
REFERENCES: Vanguard (U.S.) VRS-8523/4 (double album)

FROM SPIRITUALS TO SWING: CARNEGIE HALL
CONCERTS 1938/39

BANDS: Members of Basie Band (recording studio)/Count Basie
and His Orchestra/Kansas City Six/Jam Session: Benny
Goodman Sextet, Count Basie Band, Meade Lux Lewis, Pete
Johnson and Albert Ammons
ORIGINAL LABEL: Vanguard 1938–1939
REFERENCES: Vanguard (U.S.) VSD-47/48 (double album)

FROM SPIRITUALS TO SWING: CARNEGIE HALL
CONCERTS 1938/39

BANDS: Members of Basie Band (recording studio)/Count Basie
and His Orchestra/Kansas City Six/Jam Session: Benny
Goodman Sextet, Count Basie Band, Meade Lux Lewis, Pete
Johnson and Albert Ammons
ORIGINAL LABEL: Vanguard 1938–1939
REFERENCES: CD Vanguard (J.) K26Y-0698/7 (double C.D.)

Two additional titles (members of Basie Band) on: *Lester-Amadeus!*,
Phontastic/Nostalgia (S. Nost-7639) (Schott), see B.

11. KANSAS CITY SIX AND FIVE: COMMODORE CLASSICS IN JAZZ
BANDS: Kansas City Six
ORIGINAL LABEL: Commodore 1938
REFERENCES: Commodore (U.S.) XFL-14937

KANSAS CITY SIX AND FIVE: COMMODORE CLASSICS IN JAZZ
BANDS: Kansas City Six
ORIGINAL LABEL: Commodore 1938
REFERENCES: Commodore (R.F.A.) 6-24057 AG (Special import Pathé)

12. THE KANSAS CITY SIX WITH LESTER YOUNG
A Complete Session
Commodore Classics in Jazz
BANDS: Kansas City Six
ORIGINAL LABEL: Commodore 1944
REFERENCES: Commodore (U.S.) XFL-15352

or

PREZ AND FRIENDS
A Complete Session
Commodore Classics in Jazz
BANDS: Kansas City Six
ORIGINAL LABEL: Commodore 1944
REFERENCES: Commodore (R.F.A.) 6-24292 AG (Special import Pathé)

*13. NAT "KING" COLE WITH YOUNG AND CALLENDER
BANDS: LESTER YOUNG-King Trio
ORIGINAL LABEL: Philo 1942
REFERENCES: Score (U.S.) LP-4019

or

NAT "KING" COLE MEETS THE MASTER SAXES
BANDS: LESTER YOUNG-King Trio

ORIGINAL LABEL: Philo 1942
REFERENCES: Spotlite (G.B.) SPJ-136 (Media 7)

14. HELEN HUMES: BE-BABA-LEBA 1944–1952
BANDS: Helen Humes and Her All Stars
ORIGINAL LABEL: Philo/Aladdin 1945/46
REFERENCES: Whiskey, Women, and . . . (Sweden) KM-701
(Media 7)

In the two missing titles, Lester performs no solo.

*15. THE COMPLETE ALADDIN SESSIONS VOL. 1
BANDS: Lester Young and His Band
ORIGINAL LABEL: Philo/Aladdin-Aladdin 1945–1946
REFERENCES: Liberty (J.) K 18 P-9256

or

LESTER YOUNG SERIES AND HIS TENOR SAX VOL. 1
BANDS: Lester Young and His Band
ORIGINAL LABEL: Philo/Aladdin-Aladdin (G.B.) 1945–1946
REFERENCES: Aladdin (F.) 801 (Pathé)

*16. THE COMPLETE ALADDIN SESSIONS VOL. 2
BANDS: Lester Young and His Band
ORIGINAL LABEL: Aladdin-Vogue (G.B.) 1947–1948
REFERENCES: Liberty (J.) K 18 P-9257

or

LESTER YOUNG SERIES AND HIS TENOR SAX VOL. 2
BANDS: Lester Young and His Band
ORIGINAL LABEL: Aladdin-Vogue (G.B.) 1947–1948
REFERENCES: Aladdin (F.) 802 (Pathé)

One missing rendition on *Tenor Triumvirate*, Queen, Disc (I.) Q-051
(Special import Harmonia Mundi) see 25.

17. SAXOPHONE GIANTS
BANDS: Dickie Wells and His Orchestra
ORIGINAL LABEL: Signature-Jazz Selection 1943

REFERENCES: R.C.A. (F.) FXM 3-7324 (box of three records)
(R.C.A./Ariola)

18. THE COMPLETE KEYNOTE COLLECTION: 334
IMMORTAL JAZZ PERFORMANCES OF THE 40'S
INCLUDING 115 NEWLY DISCOVERED GEMS
BANDS: Lester Young Quartet/Kansas City Seven
ORIGINAL LABEL: Keynote-Metronome (S.) 1943–1944
REFERENCES: Keynote (J.) 18 PJ-1051/71 (box of 21 records)
(special import PolyGram)

or

THE COMPLETE LESTER YOUNG: THE ESSENTIAL
KEYNOTE COLLECTION 1
BANDS: Lester Young Quartet/Kansas City Seven
ORIGINAL LABEL: Keynote-Metronome (S.) 1943–1944
REFERENCES: CD Keynote (J.) 32 JD-10002 (special import
PolyGram)

19. PRES: THE COMPLETE SAVOY RECORDINGS
BANDS: Johnny Guarnieri Swing Men, Earl Warren and His
Orchestra, Lester Young Quintet, His Band
ORIGINAL LABEL: Savoy 1944–1949
REFERENCES: Savoy (U.S.) SJL-2202 (double album)

PRES: THE COMPLETE SAVOY RECORDINGS
BANDS: Johnny Guarnieri Swing Men, Earl Warren and His
Orchestra, Lester Young Quintet, His Band
ORIGINAL LABEL: Savoy 1944–1949
REFERENCES: Savoy (R.F.A.) WL-70505 (double album)
(R.C.A./Ariola)

One missing title, session: Earl Warren and His Orchestra
The essentials (fifteen titles) on: *The Savoy Recordings*, CD Savoy (Fed.
Rep. of Germany) ZD-70819 (R.C.A./Ariola)

Because the J.A.T.P. and Norman Granz Jazz Concerts have never readily,
completely, or chronologically been reedited, we propose the following:
A. The list of the early 12" LP releases plus recent editions that
comprise unpublished versions.

B. The current incomplete and non-chronological release which, however, contains most of the titles featuring Lester.

*20A. NORMAN GRANZ' JAZZ AT THE PHILHARMONIC NEW VOLUME 2
BANDS: J.A.T.P.
ORIGINAL LABEL: Disc 1946
REFERENCES: Clef (U.S.) MG-New Volume 2

*JAZZ AT THE PHILHARMONIC ALL STARS: HOW HIGH THE MOON
BANDS: J.A.T.P.
ORIGINAL LABEL: Disc 1946
REFERENCES: Mercury (U.S.) MCG-608

*NORMAN GRANZ' JAZZ AT THE PHILHARMONIC NEW VOLUME 5
BANDS: J.A.T.P.
ORIGINAL LABEL: Mercury 1946
REFERENCES: Clef (U.S.) MG-New Volume 5

*NORMAN GRANZ' JAZZ AT THE PHILHARMONIC NEW VOLUME 4
BANDS: J.A.T.P.
ORIGINAL LABEL: Mercury 1946
REFERENCES: Clef (U.S.) MG-New Volume 4

*NORMAN GRANZ' JAZZ AT THE PHILHARMONIC NEW VOLUME 7
BANDS: J.A.T.P.
ORIGINAL LABEL: Mercury 1949
REFERENCES: Clef (U.S.) MG-New Volume 7

*NORMAN GRANZ' JAZZ CONCERT 1
BANDS: Norman Granz' Jazz Concert
ORIGINAL LABEL: Norgran 1950
REFERENCES: Norgran (U.S.) MG-JC-1 (box of two records)

*NORMAN GRANZ' JAZZ AT THE PHILHARMONIC VOLUME 15

BANDS: J.A.T.P.
ORIGINAL LABEL: Clef 1952
REFERENCES: Mercury/Clef (U.S.) MG-Vol. 15 (box of three records)

*NORMAN GRANZ' JAZZ AT THE PHILHARMONIC VOLUME 16

BANDS: J.A.T.P.
ORIGINAL LABEL: Clef 1953
REFERENCES: Clef (U.S.) MG-Vol. 16 (box of four records)

*NORMAN GRANZ' JAZZ AT THE PHILHARMONIC VOLUME 18

BANDS: J.A.T.P.
ORIGINAL LABEL: Clef 1955
REFERENCES: Clef (U.S.) MG-Vol. 18 (box of two records)

*THE J.A.T.P. ALL-STARS AT THE OPERA HOUSE

BANDS: J.A.T.P.
ORIGINAL LABEL: Verve 1957
REFERENCES: Verve (U.S.) MGV-8267/MGVS-6029

JAZZ AT THE PHILHARMONIC: THE RAREST CONCERTS

BANDS: J.A.T.P.
ORIGINAL LABEL: Verve 1946
REFERENCES: Verve (U.S.) 815149-1

JAZZ AT THE PHILHARMONIC: THE RAREST CONCERTS

BANDS: J.A.T.P.
ORIGINAL LABEL: Verve 1946–1957
REFERENCES: Verve (U.S.) 825101-1

20B. JAZZ AT THE PHILHARMONIC: BIRD & PRES THE 46 CONCERTS

BANDS: J.A.T.P.

ORIGINAL LABEL: Disc-Mercury 1946
REFERENCES: Verve (U.S.) VE-2-2518 (double album)

JAZZ AT THE PHILHARMONIC: THE RAREST CONCERTS
BANDS: J.A.T.P.
ORIGINAL LABEL: Verve 1946
REFERENCES: Verve (U.S.) 815149-1

JAZZ AT THE PHILHARMONIC: LESTER YOUNG CARNEGIE BLUES
BANDS: J.A.T.P.
ORIGINAL LABEL: Verve-Clef 1946–1953–1957
REFERENCES: Verve (U.S.) 825101-1

JAZZ AT THE PHILHARMONIC: BIRD & PRES, CARNEGIE HALL 1949
BANDS: J.A.T.P.
ORIGINAL LABEL: Mercury 1949
REFERENCES: Verve (U.S.) 815150-1

JAZZ AT THE PHILHARMONIC: BIRD & PRES, CARNEGIE HALL 1949
BANDS: J.A.T.P.
ORIGINAL LABEL: Mercury 1949
REFERENCES: Verve (F.) 815150-1 (PolyGram)

JAZZ AT THE PHILHARMONIC: NORGRAN BLUES 1950
BANDS: Norman Granz Jazz Concert
ORIGINAL LABEL: Norgran 1950
REFERENCES: Verve (U.S.) 815151-1

JAZZ AT THE PHILHARMONIC: THE TRUMPET BATTLE 1952
BANDS: J.A.T.P.
ORIGINAL LABEL: Clef 1952
REFERENCES: Verve (U.S.) 815152-1

JAZZ AT THE PHILHARMONIC: GENE KRUPA & BUDDY RICH, THE DRUM BATTLE

BANDS: J.A.T.P.
ORIGINAL LABEL: Clef 1952
REFERENCES: Verve (U.S.) 815146-1

JAZZ AT THE PHILHARMONIC: ONE O'CLOCK JUMP 1953

BANDS: J.A.T.P.
ORIGINAL LABEL: Clef 1953
REFERENCES: Verve (U.S.) 815153-1

JAZZ AT THE PHILHARMONIC: BLUES IN CHICAGO

BANDS: J.A.T.P.
ORIGINAL LABEL: Clef 1955
REFERENCES: Verve (U.S.) 815155-1

*21. BILLY ECKSTEIN: THE GREAT MR. B. WITH A BEAT

BANDS: Metronome All Stars
ORIGINAL LABEL: M.G.M. 1953
REFERENCES: M.G.M. (U.S.) E-3176

or

EVERYTHING I HAVE IS YOURS: THE M.G.M. YEARS

BANDS: Metronome All Stars
ORIGINAL LABEL: M.G.M. 1953
REFERENCES: Verve (U.S.) 819442-1 (double album)

*22. THE BIRDLAND ALL STARS AT CARNEGIE HALL

BANDS: Lester Young with Count Basie and His Orchestra
ORIGINAL LABEL: Roulette 1954
REFERENCES: Roulette (U.S.) RE-127 (double album)

THE BIRDLAND ALL STARS AT CARNEGIE HALL

BANDS: Lester Young with Count Basie and His Orchestra
ORIGINAL LABEL: Roulette 1954
REFERENCES: Roulette (F.) SLVLXR-618 (double album) (Vogue)

THE BIRDLAND ALL STARS AT CARNEGIE HALL
BANDS: Lester Young with Count Basie and His Orchestra
ORIGINAL LABEL: Roulette 1954
REFERENCES: CD Roulette (F.) 600089 (Vogue)

23. THE SOUND OF JAZZ
BANDS: Count Basie All Stars, Billie Holiday with Mal Waldron's
All Stars
ORIGINAL LABEL: Columbia 1957
REFERENCES: Columbia (U.S.) CL-1098/CS 8040

THE SOUND OF JAZZ: JAZZOTHÉQUE
BANDS: Count Basie All Stars, Billie Holiday with Mal Waldron's
All Stars
ORIGINAL LABEL: Columbia 1957
REFERENCES: C.B.S. (H.) 57036 (C.B.S.)

24. NEWPORT JAZZ FESTIVAL: LIVE (UNRELEASED HIGHLIGHTS FROM 1956, 1958, 1963), CONTEMPORARY MASTERS SERIES
BANDS: Newport All-Stars
ORIGINAL LABEL: Columbia 1958
REFERENCES: Columbia (U.S.) C2-38262 (double album)

*25. THE LESTER YOUNG-BUDDY RICH TRIO
BANDS: Lester Young Buddy Rich Trio
ORIGINAL LABEL: Mercury-Clef-Jazz Scene 1946
REFERENCES: Norgran (U.S.) MGN-1074

One rendition lacking on *Tenor Triumvirate*, Queen, Disc (I.) Q-051 (Special import Harmonia Mundi) see 16.

*26. PRES
BANDS: Lester Young Quartet
ORIGINAL LABEL: Clef 1950–1951
REFERENCES: Norgran (U.S.) MGN-1072

Four renditions lacking, two/four on: * *The Legendary Lester Young*, Verve (G.B.) VLP-9112.

*27. THE PRESIDENT (LESTER SWINGS AGAIN)
BANDS: Lester Young Quartet
ORIGINAL LABEL: Norgran-Clef 1950–1951–1952
REFERENCES: Norgran (U.S.) MGN-1005

*28. LESTER'S HERE
BANDS: Lester Young Quartet and His Band
ORIGINAL LABEL: Clef-Norgran 1951–1953
REFERENCES: Norgran (U.S.) MGN-1071

*29. THE PRESIDENT PLAYS WITH THE OSCAR PETERSON TRIO
BANDS: Lester Young with Oscar Peterson Trio
ORIGINAL LABEL: Norgran-Clef 1952
REFERENCES: Norgran (U.S.) MGN-1054

*30. LESTER YOUNG (IT DON'T MEAN A THING)
BANDS: Lester Young and His Band
ORIGINAL LABEL: Norgran 1954
REFERENCES: Norgran (U.S.) MGN-1022

*31. PRES & SWEETS
BANDS: Lester Young-Harry Edison All Stars
ORIGINAL LABEL: Norgran 1955
REFERENCES: Norgran (U.S.) MGN-1043

One title missing on: *The Greatest Names in Jazz, Verve (U.S.) PR (S)-2-3 (box of three records)

*32. THE JAZZ GIANTS' 56
BANDS: The Jazz Giants' 56
ORIGINAL LABEL: Norgran 1956
REFERENCES: Norgran (U.S.) MGN-1056

THE JAZZ GIANTS' 56
BANDS: The Jazz Giants' 56
ORIGINAL LABEL: Norgran 1956
REFERENCES: CD Verve (R.F.A.) 8256722 (PolyGram)

*33. PRES AND TEDDY
   BANDS: Lester Young-Teddy Wilson
   ORIGINAL LABEL: A.R.S. 1956
   REFERENCES: American Recording Society (U.S.) G-417

   PRES AND TEDDY
   BANDS: Lester Young-Teddy Wilson
   ORIGINAL LABEL: A.R.S. 1956
   REFERENCES: CD Verve (R.F.A.) 8312702 (PolyGram)

*34. COUNT BASIE AT NEWPORT
   BANDS: Count Basie and His Orchestra
   ORIGINAL LABEL: Verve 1957
   REFERENCES: Verve (U.S.) MGV 8243/MGVS 6024

   COUNT BASIE AT NEWPORT
   BANDS: Count Basie and His Orchestra
   ORIGINAL LABEL: Verve 1957
   REFERENCES: Verve (F.) 2304414 (PolyGram)

*35. GOING FOR MYSELF
   BANDS: Lester Young All Stars
   ORIGINAL LABEL: Verve 1957–1958
   REFERENCES: Verve (U.S.) MGV 8298

*36. LAUGHIN' TO KEEP FROM CRYIN'
   BANDS: Lester Young All Stars
   ORIGINAL LABEL: Verve 1958
   REFERENCES: Verve (U.S.) MGV 8316/MGVS 6054

*37. LE DERNIER MESSAGE DE LESTER YOUNG (LESTER
   YOUNG IN PARIS)
   BANDS: Lester Young Quintet
   ORIGINAL LABEL: Barclay (F.) 1959
   REFERENCES: Barclay (F.) 84069

38. THE PRESIDENT PLAYS WITH THE OSCAR PETERSON TRIO

BANDS: Lester Young with the Oscar Peterson Trio
ORIGINAL LABEL: CD Verve (W. Germany)
REFERENCES: (R.F.A.) 8316702 (PolyGram)

A. COUNT BASIE: THE COUNT AT THE CHATTERBOX

BANDS: Count Basie and His Orchestra
ORIGINAL LABEL: Radio 1937
REFERENCES: Jazz Archives (U.S.) JA-16

B. LESTER AMADEUS!

BANDS: Count Basie and His Orchestra
ORIGINAL LABEL: Radio 1937
REFERENCES: Phontastic/Nostalgia (Sweden) NOST-7639 (Schott)

See 10

C. COUNT BASIE: BASIC BASIE

BANDS: Count Basie and His Orchestra
ORIGINAL LABEL: Radio 1937–1938
REFERENCES: Phontastic/Nostalgia (S.) NOST-7640 (Schott)

D. COUNT BASIE: BASIC BASIE

BANDS: Count Basie and His Orchestra
ORIGINAL LABEL: Radio 1938–1939
REFERENCES: Jazz Archives (U.S.) JA-41

E. LESTER YOUNG & CHARLIE CHRISTIAN

BANDS: Count Basie and His Orchestra, Benny Goodman Octet
ORIGINAL LABEL: Private Radio (Studio Rehearsal) 1939–1940
REFERENCES: Jazz Archives (U.S.) JA-42

F. "1940" THE BANDS OF COUNT BASIE, LOUIS ARMSTRONG, ANDY KIRK, AND JIMMY LUNCEFORD

BANDS: Count Basie and His Orchestra
ORIGINAL LABEL: Radio 1940
REFERENCES: Everybodys (U.S.) EV-3006

G. HISTORICAL PREZ, 1940–1944

BANDS: Lester Young and His Orchestra, Lester and Lee Young's Orchestra, Count Basie and His Orchestra
ORIGINAL LABEL: Private Radio 1941–1944
REFERENCES: Everybodys (U.S.) EV-3002

H. COUNT BASIE AND HIS ORCHESTRA 1944

BANDS: Count Basie and His Orchestra
ORIGINAL LABEL: Lang-Worth Transcriptions (Studio) 1944
REFERENCES: Circle (U.S.) CLP 60

I. JAMMIN WITH LESTER

BANDS: Jammin the Blues, Jazz at the Philharmonic
ORIGINAL LABEL: (Studio) Sessions for the movie *Jammin the Blues*, Radio 1944–1946
REFERENCES: Jazz Archives (U.S.) JA-18

The version of "Jammin the Blues" heard in the film is different from that of JA-18. Compare with listings 20A and 20B. Verve 825101-1 and 815149-1.

J. COLEMAN HAWKINS-LESTER YOUNG

BANDS: Lester Young-Nat King Cole Quartet, Jazz at the Philharmonic All Stars
ORIGINAL LABEL: Armed Forces Radio Service Transcriptions 1946
REFERENCES: Spotlite (G.B.) SPJ-119 (Media 7)

K. PRES LIVES!

BANDS: Lester Young and His Orchestra
ORIGINAL LABEL: Private 1950
REFERENCES: Savoy (U.S.) SJL-1109

PRES LIVES!

BANDS: Lester Young and His Orchestra
ORIGINAL LABEL: Private 1950
REFERENCES: Savoy (R.F.A.) WL 70528 (R.C.A./Ariola)

L. MASTERS OF JAZZ VOL. 7
   BANDS: Lester Young Quintet with The Bill Potts Trio, with Idress
   Sulieman and The Bill Potts Trio
   ORIGINAL LABEL: Radio 1951–1953–1956
   REFERENCES: Storyville (Denmark) SLP-4107 (Media 7)

M. LESTER YOUNG AT OLIVIA DAVIS' PATIO LOUNGE: PRES
   BANDS: Lester Young with The Bill Potts Trio
   ORIGINAL LABEL: Private 1956
   REFERENCES: Pablo Live (U.S.) 2308219

N. LESTER YOUNG IN WASHINGTON, D.C.: PREZ VOL. II
   BANDS: Lester Young with The Bill Potts Trio
   ORIGINAL LABEL: Private 1956
   REFERENCES: Pablo Live (U.S.) 2308225

O. LESTER YOUNG IN WASHINGTON, D.C.: PREZ VOL. III
   BANDS: Lester Young with The Bill Potts Trio
   ORIGINAL LABEL: Private 1956
   REFERENCES: Pablo Live (U.S.) 2308228

P. LESTER YOUNG IN WASHINGTON, D.C.: PREZ VOL. IV
   BANDS: Lester Young with The Bill Potts Trio
   ORIGINAL LABEL: Private 1956
   REFERENCES: Pablo Live (U.S.) 2308230

Q. THE REAL SOUND OF JAZZ
   BANDS: Billie Holiday with Mal Waldron's All Stars
   ORIGINAL LABEL: Soundtrack of the television film "The Sound
   of Jazz" 1957
   REFERENCES: Pumpkin (U.S.) 116

Index

"After Theater Jump," 131
"After You've Gone," 65
Aladdin (Philco) Studios, 122, 150
Albany, Joe, 149, 150
Aldrich, 43
Alexander, Irving, 118
Alexander, Willard, 66, 68, 69, 78, 81, 83, 110
Allen, Henry "Red," 3, 190
Allen, Jap, 40, 44, 51
Alvin Hotel, 1, 2, 117, 124, 195
American Record Company, 80, 98
Ammons, Albert, 101, 109, 124
Andy Kirk Orchestra, 55–56
Andy Kirk's Clouds of Joy, 45
Apex, 21
Apollo Theater, 78, 81, 83, 128
Arcadia Ballroom, 19
Armstrong, Louis, 8, 22, 211, 216
Ashby, Irving, 150, 155
Atkins, Boyd, 27, 56–57, 216
Atlas, Jim, 190
Auld, George, 118, 196

Balliett, Whitney, 190
Barclay, 209
Barefield, Eddie, 22–23, 26, 35, 119, 199, 212
Barker, Danny, 190
Bar le Duc, 56
Basie, William "Count," 2, 11, 46, 51, 61, 64–65, 65–66, 70, 71, 79, 81, 85, 91, 96–97, 101, 110, 131, 185, 190, 213, 219; forms the Buster Smith and Basie Barons of

Rhythm, 60; joins the Blue Devils, 31; joins Bennie Moten's band, 32, 40; recordings, 78–79, 106; tour of the East Coast, 68
Bechet, Sidney, 8, 101
Beiderbecke, Bix, 13, 19, 20, 108
Belafonte, Harry, 161
Bell, Aaron, 158
"Bell Telephone Hour," 117
Benjamin, Ben, 201
Bennie Moten Orchestra, 51, 52, 59, 66, 213–14, 216
Benny Goodman Sextet, 109
Berendt, Joachim E., 165
Berg, Billy, 122, 154
Berry, Chu, 74, 88, 104, 105, 116, 118
Berry, Emmet, 85
Bess, Druie, 32
Bigard, Barney, 8
Billie Holiday Orchestra, 81
Billy Berg's Club, 120, 121
Billy King Orchestra, 31
Birdland, 1, 159, 162, 167, 168, 170, 174, 177, 183, 186, 193, 195, 198, 202, 220
Birdland Allstars, 185
Birdland Show, 186
Black Cat, 79
Black Pearl Club, 198
Blakey, Art, 178
Blesh, Rudy, 3
"Blue and Sentimental," 96
Blue Devils, 14, 30–39, 47, 57, 64, 78, 97, 213
Blue Note, 201, 209, 221

Blue Serenaders, 214
Blue Syncopaters, 14
"Body and Soul," 35, 116, 122
"Boogie Woogie," 70
Booker T. Washington Hotel, 43, 59, 105
Bostonians, 25–26, 28–29
Brecker, Leo, 78
Bridges, Henry, 44
Brisoe, Tex, 160
Bronson, Art, 14, 25, 28–29, 78, 213
Brooklyn Academy of Music, 199
Brooks, Dudley, 120
Broonzy, Big Bill, 101
Brown, Ray, 161, 169, 178, 189
Brunswick, 78, 84, 94, 216
Bryant, Marie, 133
Buchanan, Charlie, 220
Burley, Mary Lou. See Williams, Mary Lou
Burroughs, Alvin, 31
Bus, Ira, 58
Buster Smith and Basie Barons of Rhythm, 60–64
Byas, Don, 67, 116, 129, 216

Café Bohemia, 188
Cafe Society, 124, 125, 218
California Ramblers, 21
Callender, Red, 122, 124, 130, 133, 150
Calloway, Cab, 14, 215, 218
Campbell, Paul, 124
Carlisle, Una Mae, 118, 119
Carnegie Hall, 101, 109, 155, 161, 168, 174, 178, 182
Carpenter, Charlie, 152, 157, 159, 163, 168, 183, 189
Carter, Benny, 88, 212
Castle (Castaldo), Lee, 107
Catlett, Sid, 133, 165
Cecil Hotel, 112
Cedric, Gene, 3

Cheatham, Adolphus "Doc," 190
Cheathamm, Jimmy, 135
Cherry Blossom, 47, 48
Chicago Opera House, 182
Chocolate Dandies, 215
Christian, Charlie, 28, 32–33, 39, 43, 61, 72, 109, 116, 117, 125, 164
"Clap Hands, Here Comes Charlie," 164
Clarence Love and the Southern Serenaders, 14
Clarence Love Orchestra, 41
Clarke, Frank, 79
Clarke, Kenny "Klook," 79, 112, 115, 119, 178, 202
Clayton, Buck, 74, 77, 78, 81, 85, 100, 101, 155, 167, 183, 196; joins the Count Basie Orchestra, 65; recordings, 80, 98, 106, 108, 130
Cloud, Dr. Luther, 195, 199, 200
Clouds of Joy, 14, 34, 56, 216
Club Apex, 27
Club 331, 154
Cohn, Al, 178
Cole, Cozy, 165
Cole, Nat King, 122, 130, 150
Coleman, Bill, 34–35, 129
Collins, John, 118
Collins, Shad, 106, 109, 118, 119, 120
Coltrane, John, 191
Columbia, 84, 106, 191
Commodore, 98, 131
Cork 'n' Bib, 193
Cotton Club, 57, 58, 216
Cotton Pickers, 215
Count Basie Kansas City Killers, 96
Count Basie Orchestra, 47, 58, 71, 76, 111–12, 120, 131, 170, 186, 189; recordings, 106, 109; tours of the East Coast, 68–69, 128
Count Basie's Kansas City Seven, 108, 111, 130

"Countless Blues," 98
Cox, Ida, 60, 211
Creath, Charlie, 14

Davis, Miles, 73, 166, 186, 200
"D.B. Blues," 189, 203
Decca, 65–66, 70, 78, 84, 97, 120, 216
Delaunay, Charles, 202
Deluxe Melody Boys, 14
Dempsey, Reverend O. D., 2
"Destination K.C.," 131
Dickenson, Vic, 46, 109, 149, 150, 185, 190
Dickie Wells Orchestra, 129
"Dickie's Dream," 108
Dixie Ramblers, 14
"Doggin' Around," 96
Donahue, Sam, 118
Doo Dads from Ditty Wah Ditty, 26
Dorsey, Jimmy, 21, 22, 212
Dot Records, 200
Douglas, Tommy, 40, 214
down beat, 77, 112, 121, 125, 135, 153, 191, 200
Down Beat Club, 135
Drakes, Jessie, 158, 160, 167, 176, 177, 186
Dree, Lee, 25
Dree, Walt, 25
Duke Ellington Orchestra, 68
Durham, Eddie, 31, 32, 40, 51, 59, 81, 98
Duvivier, George, 193

Eager, Allen, 125, 166
Ebbins, Milt, 132, 134
Eckstine, Billy, 121
Eddie Barefield Orchestra, 67
Edison, Harry, 85, 106, 133, 183, 192–93, 200
Elbon Theater, 43
Eldridge, Roy, 74, 161, 178, 185, 189, 190, 192

Eleonora's, 43
Ellington, Duke, 77, 131, 211, 213, 215
Ellis, Herb, 178, 189, 193
El Paseo Ballroom, 43
Epstein, Sol, 63
Erika, 202, 203
Evans, Gil, 148
Evans, Herschel, 35, 39, 40, 44, 45, 46, 48, 49, 59, 76, 85, 87–88, 91, 100, 105, 120; death of, 103–04; friend-ship with Lester Young, 74; joins the Count Basie Orchestra, 66; recordings, 78, 81
"Evenin'," 70

Fairyland Park, 56
Famous Door, 97, 108
"Fast Bd Blues," 189
Feather, Leonard, 3, 57, 153
Fenton, Nick, 118
Field, Kansas, 203
"Fine and Mellow," 190, 191
Fitzgerald, Ella, 1, 94, 174, 178, 179, 189
Five Spot, 199
Fletcher Henderson Orchestra, 43, 51–55
Floyd, Troy, 14
"A Foggy Day," 189
Forest Park, 32
Frank Sebastian Garden, 67
Freeman, Lawrence "Bud," 20, 21
Freeman, Slim, 58
Friedman, Don, 185
"From Spiritual to Swing, an Evening of American Negro Music," 101, 109
Fuller, Curtis, 198

Gabler, Milt, 98
Gaillard, Slim, 122
Gale, Moe, 159, 220
Gale Music Agency, 161, 185, 186

Ganz, Rook, 27, 216
Garros, Christian, 186, 202
Gensel, Reverend John, 193
George Morrison Orchestra, 14, 216
Gershwin, George, 70, 71
Getz, Stan, 162, 166, 178, 189, 191, 200, 202
Gillespie, Dizzy, 3, 115, 154, 165, 168, 178, 179, 180
Gitler, Ira, 3
Giuffre, Jimmy, 166, 190
Gleen, Tyree, 3
Gonzales, Louis, 124
Goodall, Billy, 147
Goodman, Benny, 63, 64, 66, 76, 79, 80, 94, 96, 110, 117, 196
Gordon, Dexter, 125
Gourley, Jimmy, 201, 202, 203, 204, 209, 221
Grand Terrace, 68–69, 70
Granz, Norman, 3, 120, 122, 132, 134, 148, 152, 153, 154–55, 157, 167, 169, 179–80, 189, 192, 199
Gray, Wardell, 125, 166
Great Leaf Gardens, 56
Green, Freddie, 79, 85, 108, 149, 200; joins the Count Basie Orchestra, 81; recordings, 80, 98, 106, 108, 130, 150, 185
Greer, Sonny, 3
Guarnieri, Johnny, 130
Guillod, Eric, 155

H., Gunther, 3
Hadnott, Billy, 155
Hakim, Sadik. See Thornton, Argonne
Halley Richardson's Shoeshine, 32
Hamilton, Chico, 135, 149–50
Hammond, John, 3, 55, 63–64, 65, 66, 69–70, 72, 77, 78, 98, 101, 106, 107, 109, 119, 154, 170, 183, 218

Hampton, Lionel, 79, 109, 117
Handy, Willis. See Young, Willis Handy
Happy Black Aces, 14, 17
Hardmann, Gleen, 107, 108
Harlan Leonard's Rocket, 214
Harris, Wyonnie, 34
Hart, Clyde, 44, 118, 124, 125, 165, 215
Hawkins, Coleman "Bean," 43, 44, 45, 47, 48–49, 49–50, 51, 53, 71, 72, 74, 116, 118, 155, 161, 169, 189, 190, 191
Haymes, Dick, 1
Haynes, Roy, 150, 153, 158, 160, 165
"He Ain't Got Rhythm," 80
Helbock, Joe, 212
Henderson, Bobby, 88
Henderson, Fletcher, 13, 47, 51, 53, 54, 69, 73, 77, 211, 213
Hentoff, Nat, 184, 190, 198, 212
Herman, Woody, 76
Hibbler, Al, 1, 2
Hi Hat, 174
Hill, Teddy, 112
Hines, Earl "Fatha," 174, 216
Hines, Frank, 30
Hinton, Milt, 3
Hodeir, André, 72
Holder, Terence T., 14, 34, 216
Holiday, Billie, 1, 2–3, 76, 80, 81, 83, 90–91, 99, 119, 121, 122, 178, 190, 196; joins the Count Basie Orchestra, 78; leaves the Count Basie Orchestra, 95, 219; meets Lester Young, 55; recordings, 94, 182
"Honeysuckle Rose," 79
Hot Club, 170
Hot Club Magazine, 155
Howard, Paul, 67
Howard Theater, 128

Humes, Helen, 85, 96, 99, 101, 106
Hunt, George, 59, 66, 78, 81
Hunter, Lloyd, 163

"I Can't Get Started," 92, 99, 122, 178, 189, 203
"I Cover the Waterfront," 203
"I Didn't Know What Time It Was," 203
"I Got a Rhythm," 88
"I Must Have That Man," 80
"Indiana," 122, 203
"I Struck a Match in the Dark," 109
"It's Only a Paper Moon," 150
"It's Sad but True," 119
"I've Got a Date with a Dream," 99
"I Want a Little Girl," 98

Jacquet, Illinois, 3, 133, 178, 179, 189
James, Harry, 79
Jammin' the Blues, 133
Jazz at the Philharmonic (J.A.T.P.), 150, 152, 154, 161, 168, 174, 183, 189
The Jazz Giants of '56, 185
Jazz Hot, 169, 183, 211
Jean Goldkette Orchestra, 20
"Jeepers Creepers," 189
Jefferson, Freddy, 160
Jim Bell's, 34
Jimmy Dorsey Orchestra, 107
"Jive at Five," 177, 218
Joffe, Ken, 185
Johnson, Budd, 3, 46, 127
Johnson, Clarence, 22
Johnson, James P., 101
Johnson, J. J., 178, 189
Johnson, Lem, 32
Johnson, Margaret "Countess," 59, 99, 216–17
Johnson, Murl, 215
Johnson, Pete, 101, 109, 124, 215

Jones, Hank, 161, 169, 193
Jones, Jo, 3, 34, 39, 40, 49, 59, 66, 71, 73, 77, 81, 85, 91, 101, 106, 110, 132, 158, 165, 167, 178, 183, 189, 190, 196, 200; joins the Count Basie Orchestra, 64–65; military service of, 134, 135, 148, 220; recordings, 70, 79, 80, 98, 108, 130, 133, 185
Jones, Willie, 198
Jones-Smith Incorporated, 70
Josephson, Barney, 218
"Jumpin' at the Woodside," 79, 97
"Jumpin' with Symphony Sid," 152, 155

Kahn, Tiny, 150, 153
Kaminsky, Max, 161
Kansas City Five, 109, 130
Kansas City Six, 98, 101
Kapp, Dave, 65
Kay, Connie, 158, 160, 165, 176, 189
Keith, 211
Keith, Jimmy, 44
Kelley, Peck, 19
Kelly, Tel, 160
Kelly's Stable, 44, 118, 119, 124
Kersey, Kenny, 155, 216
Kessel, Barney, 133
Keyes, Joe, 66, 78, 81
Killian, Al, 154, 155
King Oliver Orchestra, 41–42, 43
Kinney, Mac, 215
Kirk, Andy, 56, 216
Konitz, Lee, 178

Lacey, Fred, 148
Lackman and Carson Show, 15
Lacy Blackburn Orchestra, 213
Ladnier, Tommy, 101
"Lady Be Good," 70, 71, 79, 203
Lady Day. See Holiday, Billie

Lee, George, 14, 31, 72
Lee Young Esquires of Rhythm, 120
Le Monde, 73
Le Ringside, 169
Les Rois du jazz (The Kings of Jazz),
    155
"Lester Blows Again," 150
"Lester Leaps Again," 130
"Lester Leaps In," 108
"Lester's Be-Bop Boogie," 150
Lester Young in Paris, 209
Levy, Morris, 198
Lewis, Ed, 3, 81, 81, 85, 106
Lewis, John, 109, 158, 167
Lewis, Meade Lux, 101
Lewis, Willie, 32
Lim, Harry, 130, 153
Lincoln Hotel, 128, 131
"A Little Bit North of South
    Carolina," 131
Lloyd Hunter's Serenaders, 14
Lone Star, 45
Louisiane Hotel, 202
"Lover Come Back to Me," 150
Lovett, Baby, 215
Lucht, Jim, 188
LuGrand, Jimmy, 31
Lynch, Reuben, 31

McGhee, Howard, 149, 150, 155, 216
McIntire, Clifford, 60
McPartland, Marian, 20
Madnott, Billy, 154
Mahones, Gildo, 176, 177
Mance, Junior, 158
Manning, Ted, 31
Mark, 161
Marmande, Francis, 73
Marmarosa, Dodo, 149, 150, 165
Mary, 93, 94, 108, 117, 120, 121, 126,
    149

Matthews, George, 85
Mern, Thorpe, 47
Mezzrow, Mezz, 20
Michelot, Pierre, 186, 202
"The Midnight Symphony," 133
Mingus, Charles, 178
Minor, Dan, 66, 78, 81, 101, 106
Minton, Henry, 112
Minton's Playhouse, 115
Missourians, 14
Modern Jazz Quartet, 176, 186
Moe Gale Concert Agency, 157
Monk, Thelonious, 46, 112, 115, 178
Monroe's Uptown House, 115
Moore, Bobby, 79, 81
Morgenstern, Dan, 3, 198, 221
Morris, Marlowe, 133
Morrison, Alan, 3
Morton, Benny, 85, 106
Morton, Jelly Roll, 8
Mosby, Curtis, 27
Moten, Bennie, 14, 31, 39, 40–41, 58,
    211, 213
Mound City Blue Blowers, 47
Mulligan, Gerry, 178, 190
Music Corporation of America, 66
Music Town Record Shop, 122, 154
Musso, Vido, 125
Myers, Bumps, 120, 124

Navarro, Fats, 216
Newark Kiosk, 199
Newport Jazz Festival, 195
Nichols, Red, 21, 22
Nick's, 115
Novelty, 47

Okeh, 20
Oliver, King, 8, 41–42, 211
Olivia Patio Lounge, 188
"One Hour," 47

"One O'Clock Jump," 86
"On the Avenue," 80
"On the Sunny Side of the Street," 133
Onyx, 212
Ore, John, 176
Orpheum Theater, 132, 211

Pablo, 189
Page, Hot Lips, 31, 32, 65, 101; with
    the Buster Smith and Basie Barons
    of Rhythm, 60; joins the Bennie
    Moten Orchestra, 51
Page, Walter, 30, 32, 33, 41, 61, 77, 81,
    85, 101, 196; with the Bennie
    Moten Orchestra, 40, 51; with the
    Buster Smith and Basie Barons of
    Rhythm, 60; forms the Blue Devils,
    31; leaves the Blue Devils, 34;
    recordings, 70, 79, 98, 106, 108;
    with the Teddy Wilson Orchestra,
    80
"Pagin' the Devil," 98
Palm, 133
Panassié, Hugues, 155
Pantages, 211
Parker, Charlie "Bird," 45, 61–62, 65,
    72, 116, 125, 149, 154, 155, 161,
    164, 165, 216; death of, 178
Parker, Charlie, Sr., 56
Parlophone, 215
Paseo Ballroom, 68
Pendergast, Tom, 9
Peps Musical Bar, 174
Perkins, Bill, 191
Peterson, Oscar, 177, 178, 189
Pettiford, Oscar, 28, 178, 213
Philco (Aladdin) Studios, 122
Philharmonic Auditorium, 154
Phillips, Flip, 161, 178, 189
Pierre, Nat, 198
Piney Brown's, 45

Pla-Mor Ballroom, 56
Plantation Cafe, 91, 134
Plantation Club, 121
Pleyel, 186
Pontelli Ballroom, 166
Pops Monroe's, 59
Porter, Lewis, 70, 135
Postif, François, 15, 55, 209, 211, 212
Potts, Bill, 188, 189
Powell, Bud, 185, 186, 199, 221
Powell, Jimmy, 85
Powell, Mel, 154
"Pres Returns," 185
Price, Jesse, 60, 61–62, 64, 65
Price, Sammy, 46, 91, 119–120
"Prince Charming," 130

Quinichette, Paul, 3, 163

Raft, George, 122
Rainey, Ma, 211
Ramey, Gene, 45, 68, 72, 117, 158–59,
    162, 165, 167, 185
Ranch 101, 8
Randall's Island Jazz Festival, 185
Ravel, Maurice, 21
R.C.A., 216
Redman, Donald, 215
Renaud, Henri, 171, 202
Reno, 46, 59, 60–61, 64, 65
Rice, Eli, 26–27, 216
Rich, Buddy, 155, 161, 178, 180
Richardson, Rodney, 130
Ritz Ballroom, 32
Ritz Roof, 82
R.K.O. Orpheum Theater
Roach, Max, 169
Roberts, Couchie, 66, 78, 81, 82
Robinson, Eli, 85
"Rock a Bye Basie," 106
Roddy, Reuben, 31

Rollins, Sonny, 191
Ronnie Scott Club, 171
Roos, Arnold, 155
Roseland Ballroom, 76, 77, 79, 81
Ross, Theodore, 36, 38, 40, 51
Rowles, Jimmy, 122, 124
Royal Roost, 157, 160, 161
Rushing, Jimmy, 3, 40, 85, 190; with
    the Buster Smith and Basie Barons
    of Rhythm, 60; joins the Bennie
    Moten Orchestra, 51; joins the
    Blue Devils, 31; leaves the Blue
    Devils, 32; recordings, 70, 79, 106
Russell, Curley, 150, 153
Russell, Pee Wee, 19, 190, 195
Russell, Ross, 49
Russin, Babe, 118

Salle Pleyel, 169
Salon du Jazz, 169
Satisfied Five, 31
Savoy Ballroom, 77, 78, 84, 94, 220
Schaap, Walter, 183, 221
Scott, Bobby, 178, 179, 180, 181–82
Scott, Bud, 27–28
Scott, Cecil, 116
Scott, Hazel, 124
Scott, Ronnie, 170
Scott, Toni, 3
Scruggs, Mary Elfrieda. See Williams,
    Mary Lou
Sears, Al, 127
Shaw, Artie, 91, 150
Shaw, William, 43
Sheen, Mickey, 193
Sheldon, Jack, 181
Sherman Hotel, 106, 107
"Shoe Shine Boy," 32, 70, 71, 79, 164
Shuffle Along Show, 31
Silver, Horace, 158, 178
Simmons, John, 133
Simmons, Lonnie, 79

Simpson, James, 31
Sims, Zoot, 166, 191
Sinatra, Frank, 1, 2, 131, 181, 200
Sioux City Six, 19
Sivire, Persy, 28
"Six Cats and a Prince," 131
Slaughter's, 32
Sleepy Lagoon Defense Fund, 154
Small's, 193
Smith, Bessie, 60, 211
Smith, Buster, 30, 33–34, 35, 36, 37,
    38–39, 44, 61, 62, 78, 212; with the
    Bennie Moten Orchestra, 40; with
    the Blue Devils, 31; forms the
    Buster Smith and Basie Barons of
    Rhythm, 60; joins the Bennie
    Moten Orchestra, 51; leaves the
    Bennie Moten Orchestra, 59;
    leaves the Buster Smith and Basie
    Barons of Rhythm, 66
Smith, Harry, 32
Smith, Mammie, 47
Smith, Tab, 111
Smith, Tatti, 66, 70, 78, 81
Smith, Willie, 154, 155
"Sounds of Jazz," 190
Spanier, Mugsy, 20
Stabile, Dick, 21
"Stampede," 47
"Stardust," 35
Stearns, Marshall, 193, 195, 198
Steward, Herb, 166
Stewart, Slam, 122, 165
Stitt, Sonny, 189, 190
Stone, Jesse, 31, 215
Storyville Club, 174
Strayhorn, Billy, 120
Subway, 46, 59
Sunset, 21, 44, 45, 46, 59, 61, 216
Swaine, Elaine, 1, 2, 3, 191, 192, 195,
    198, 199, 200, 210
"Swingin' the Blues," 79, 95

Tabou, 171, 201
Tate, Buddy, 3, 44, 54, 85, 105, 106, 196, 216
"Taxi War Dance," 106
Taylor, Billy, 3
"Tea for Two," 122, 189
Teagarden, Jack, 195
Teatro Manzoni, 186
Teddy Wilson Orchestra, 80
Terrell, Pha, 216
Terry, Sonny, 101
Teschemaker, Frank, 20
"Texas Shuffle," 97, 98
Tharpe, Sister Rosetta, 101
Theater Owner's Booking Association (TOBA) circuit, 61, 211
"These Foolish Things," 150
"This Year's Kisses," 80
Thomas, Turk, 31
Thompson, Charles, 34, 39, 125
Thornton, Argonne, 150, 152
"Three Little Words," 190, 203
Three Sams, 35
"Tickle Toe," 108
Torin, Symphony Sid, 152, 198, 220
Tormé, Mel, 120
Tough, Dave, 20
Towles, Nat, 163
Trent, Alphonso, 14, 33
Tristano, Lennie, 161, 166, 178
Trouville, 122, 154. See also Billy Berg's Club
Trumbauer, Frankie "Tram," 19, 20, 48, 108, 131, 166, 212
Turk, Tommy, 161
Turner, Joe, 45, 101
Tuxedo, 8

United Artists Record Company, 199
Urtreger, René, 186, 201, 203, 204, 209

Variety Fair Club, 56
Vaughan, Sarah, 1, 121
Ventura, Charlie, 154
"Very Thought of You," 99
Victor, 213
Village Vanguard, 109, 115
Vocalion, 84, 94, 99
Vocalion-Brunswick, 72

Walder, Herman, 44
Waldron, Mal, 190
Waller, Fats, 64, 118, 130, 213
Ware, Leonard, 101
Warren, Earl, 82, 85, 101, 106, 109
Washington, Charlie, 32
Washington, Jack, 60, 78, 81, 85, 106
Washington Hotel, 62
Watkins, Doug, 198
Watkins, Ralph, 118
"Way down Yonder in New Orleans," 98
Wayne, Chuck, 150, 153
Webb, Chick, 94
Webster, Ben, 17, 32, 44, 45–46, 48–49, 55, 59, 115, 190, 216, 219
Wein, George, 174, 189, 195
Wells, Dickie, 3, 49, 85, 106, 108, 130
West, Harold, 90, 118
West End Club, 221
WHB, 65
"When You're Smiling," 189
White, Leroy "Snake," 30
White, Zack, 37, 39
White Horse Club, 128
White House, 34
Whiteman, Paul, 21, 216
Whiteman, Wliberforce, 216
White Rose, 128
Whitman Sisters, 31
"Why Was I Born," 80
Wiedoft, Rudy, 212
William Morris Agency, 120, 131

William Penn Hotel, 81
Williams, Claude, 66, 79, 81
Williams, Cootie, 15, 16, 212
Williams, Ernest, 32, 34
Williams, John, 216
Williams, Mary Lou, 46, 48, 55–56, 59, 78, 216
Williams, Norman "Willie," 188
Wilson, Dick, 44, 45, 78, 216
Wilson, Teddy, 76, 80, 81, 94, 131, 185
Winn, Mary Lou. See Williams, Mary Lou
Woodside Hotel, 85, 94, 104, 108, 118
Wright, Florence, 161

Yellow Front Saloon, 59
Young, Austin "Boots," 13, 17–18
Young, Beatrice, 33, 57–58, 62–63
Young, Irma, 9, 17
Young, Isiah "Sport," 13
Young, Leonidas Raymond "Lee," 67, 100, 120, 124, 126, 127–28, 135, 154, 155; birth, 9
Young, Lester Willis, 43, 84; with the Andy Kirk Orchestra, 55–56; awards, 153; joins the Lee Young Esquires of Rhythm, 124; with Bennie Moten Orchestra, 40–41, 51–52; birth, 7; birth of daughter, 189; birth of son, 158; with the Blue Devils, 30–39; with Bostonians, 25–26, 28–29; with Boyd Atkins, 56–57; with Buster Smith and Basie Barons of Rhythm, 60–64; with the Clarence Love Orchestra, 41; death, 2; in family band, 11–13; with Fletcher Henderson Orchestra, 52–55; funeral of, 2–3; hospitalized, 183, 192; incarceration of, 147; joins the Count Basie Orchestra, 58–59; with the King Oliver Orchestra, 41–43; leaves the Count Basie Orchestra; leaves family band, 20, 24; marriages, 58, 158; military service of, 134–48; recording sessions of, 70, 78, 91, 96, 106, 108, 130, 150, 152, 182–83, 188–89; rejoins the Basie orchestra, 131; style of, 71–72, 167; tours in Europe, 169–70,170–74, 200, 201–10
Young, Lester, Jr., 158, 159, 184
Young, Lizetta, 7, 9
Young, Mary, 158, 183, 189, 192, 200
Young, Sarah, 9, 126
Young, Snooky, 85
Young, Willis Handy, 7, 9, 13, 15–16, 17, 20, 27, 66–67, 211; death, 126; forms family orchestra, 10–11
Youngblood, Jim, 34